DRAFTEE DIVISION

Padua

Venice

Genoa

Florence

Assisi

Rome

Anzio

Mount Cassino

Naples

Palermo

Messina

Salerno

Sicily

Calabria

Syracusa

DRAFTEE DIVISION

The 88th Infantry Division in World War II

JOHN SLOAN BROWN

★

PRESIDIO

Published by Presidio Press
505 B San Marin Drive, Suite 300
Novato, CA 94945-1340

This edition printed 1998

Library of Congress Cataloging-in-Publication Data

Brown, John Sloan, 1949–
  Draftee Division: the 88th Infantry Division in World War II
  Bibliography:p.213
  Includes index.
  1. United States. Army. Infantry Division, 88th—History. 2. World War, 1939–1945Regimental histories—United States. I. Title.
D769.31 88th.B76 1998 940.54'12'73
ISBN 0-89141-666-8

Printed in the United States of America

To my generation's parents and grandparents,
peaceable citizens who destroyed the most
threatening militarists of their time

Contents

Illustrations/Tables

Photographs follow page 100

Preface

Americans are an unmilitary people who have fought nine major wars and have been prepared for none. Peoples of a more martial temperament have defended their interests with large standing armies backed by even larger trained reserves. Americans create their armies after the crisis of war is already upon them. Of their military accomplishments, the most impressive has been the mobilization for World War II, an effort that included some fifty-five draftee divisions of all types.

Draftee divisions were the products of mass conscription; selective-service agencies turned over thousands of young men to tiny, professional cadres who organized and trained them, then led them into battle. These "new divisions" represented yet another chapter in a debate, older than the republic itself, concerning the proper constitution of America's military establishment. They carried forward public ventilation of such topics as the respective roles of professional and temporary soldiers and the right of a democratic state to require involuntary military service of its citizens. The draftee divisions of World War II also added a new twist to old arguments. As their name implies, the rank and file of these divisions consisted almost exclusively of conscripts. Although such divisions had been assembled during World War I, World War II provided the first effective test of their actual utility. Few of the World War I draftee divisions saw combat as divisions, and these were involved only briefly.

American draftees are the involuntary soldiery of an unmilitary people. If institutional means exist to make effective combat units out of such unlikely material in a reasonable time, our populace can rest somewhat easier in its general indifference to military affairs. America may not need to maintain large armies in times of peace in order to field enormous armies quickly and efficiently in times of war. Needless to say, the relative success of draftee divisions has tremendous implications for defense planning.

Surprisingly, draftee divisions as a genre have received relatively little scholarly attention. Indeed, most of the working details of World

War II mobilization have received little attention outside of discon-
nected and narrowly specialized studies. Serious historians of World
War II have, for the most part, focused on major battles or on issues,
decisions, developments, and personalities at the highest levels.[1]
Scholars in the behavioral sciences have addressed the psychological
and sociological aspects of combat without bridging the gap between
human behavior and mobilization planning.[2] Scholars in the more
technical fields are every bit as specialized as their military counterparts—no holistic picture there.[3] Finally, the popular literature concerning World War II, of which there is a great deal, concentrates on
grand tactics or individual adventures. The net result of the foregoing
is that the casual visitor to a library or bookstore can see a great deal of
World War II from the cabinet, command post, or foxhole, but not
much of it from the perspective of intermediate-level supervisors who
must make personnel, training, and logistics come together on the
field of battle.

This study is hardly the complete answer to the vacancy suggested
above, but it does follow a draftee division through the entire World
War II experience, relying upon sources drawn largely from the inter-
mediate levels of administration and command. The division was the
88th Infantry, the first into combat, the longest lived, and perhaps the
most respected of all World War II draftee divisions.[4] It was also the
division in which my father served and which my grandfather commanded. Elsewhere I have cited sources and acknowledged my particular indebtedness to the many "Blue Devils" who have been so
generous with their time and papers. Here it need only be said that this
is their story, measured against standards appropriate to scholarly
appraisal and heavily weighted with archival and external evidence. If
one were given to the penny-chasing descriptive titles popular in the
nineteenth century, this study might be subtitled "How We Created a
Division Out of Raw Draftees and Led Them on to Victory Over the
Most Highly Touted Army of Modern Times." There is much that is
instructive in their experience.

Acknowledgments

I am indebted to benefactors so numerous I risk failing to recognize them all. For my shortcomings in that regard, I apologize in advance. The veterans of the Blue Devils Association have been incredibly generous with respect to time, energy, sources, and advice. My notes and bibliographical essay detail the 88th's individual contributors; here I need say that this book would have been impossible without them. I take great pride in having been made an honorary member of the Blue Devils, truly an assembly of kindly and generous men.

Draftee Division began as a doctoral dissertation, written under the painstaking mentorship of Professor John E. Wilz of Indiana University, seconded by an able committee: Professors David Pletcher, George Juergens, and John Lovell. These men represent all that higher education is supposed to be; under their patient, six-year stewardship I grew as much as a person as *Draftee Division* did as a manuscript.

The staffs manning a number of archives—The Modern Military Records Branch of the National Archives; the U.S. Army Historical Research Center in Carlisle Barracks, Pennsylvania; the Combined Arms Research Library at Fort Leavenworth, Kansas; the U.S. Army Armor Center Library at Fort Knox, Kentucky; the U.S. Army Infantry School Library at Fort Benning, Georgia; the Library of the Center for Military History in Washington, D.C.; and the U.S. Military Academy Library at West Point, New York—proved very helpful and proficient. In all of my experiences with these several archives, I never posed an inquiry that was not cheerfully responded to in a timely manner. We are fortunate to be in receipt of such dedicated public service.

When one is writing a book, someone else inevitably takes up one's slack in other areas. This has been the lot of my wife, Mary Beth, who has sustained me through what she cheerfully refers to as an eight-year pregnancy. My children, Amy and Todd, have also cheerfully indulged me in *Draftee Division*. I do not believe they can remember the time when I was not yet working on this project. Others cheerful in adversity have been the numerous typists who, through my total of nine military postings, have in turn laid hands on the manuscript. I might particularly note Susie McCloy of Bloomington, Indiana, who started me out; Debbie Biddle of West Point, New York, who typed the final draft of the dissertation; and Darla Rutledge of Leavenworth, Kansas, who carried *Draftee Division* through its final submission.

My notes and bibliographical essay detail my intellectual indebtedness and suggest my personal indebtedness to the many individual contributors who became the basis of this manuscript. Here I might add that I had assistance with respect to maps and photographs as well. Col. Dixie Beggs, former 88th Infantry Division G-3, loaned me maps actually used when planning for Operation Diadem. These became the basis for the maps in this book. Insofar as photographs are concerned, I am indebted to the U.S. Army Signal Corps, the American Battle Monuments Commission, John P. Delaney's *The Blue Devils in Italy* (*Infantry Journal* and Association of U.S. Army), Colonel Beggs, and Messrs. Ovid U. Bay (captain, 337th FA Battalion, and author of the 337th's history, *We Left Home*), William E. Carnahan, and Edwin Gibreath, who reproduced them for the book.

My closest collaborator throughout the authorship of *Draftee Division* has been my father, Col. Horace M. Brown. He has encouraged me, secured sources for me, introduced me, advised me, edited me, and sustained me in adversity. Upon my assignment to Europe he took over the final stages of the project altogether. Truly he deserves to be listed as the coauthor, but in his own unassuming way he refused that recognition. My mother, Lucia ("Chick") Sloan Brown, indulged the both of us in this project, at some expense to the tranquility of her household. One's parents can number among one's best friends.

Finally, I acknowledge the inspiration of my maternal grandparents, Maj. Gen. John E. Sloan and his wife, Amy. They died before I began this project, yet even a casual reader may recognize their presence throughout it. I have strained every nerve to maintain scholarly objectivity, with what success others must judge. More than a few of the ancient historians believed the purpose of history was not just to instruct, but also to provide examples worthy of emulation. If so, one could do far worse than to emulate the Sloans.

1

Draftee Divisions: The Historical Roots

H hour was 2300, 11 May 1944. From Cassino to the Gulf of Gaeta, artillery barrages broke the stillness of the Italian night as fifteen Allied divisions hurled themselves against the Gustav Line, Hitler's string of defenses sealing southern Italy from Rome and points north. In the American sector infantrymen stormed into German positions seconds after carefully coordinated artillery barrages ceased. Mount Damiano, a critical point, fell in fifty-one minutes; the scarcely less important Mount Rotondo fell the following day. American time-on-target artillery fire annihilated a German battalion surprised in an assembly area, and in three days of savage fighting the Americans pushed tenacious German defenders out of Santa Maria Infante Village, another critical point.

The fall of Santa Maria, a subsequent push through the village of Spigno, and the progress of French *Goumiers* across the trackless Mount Majo area north of the American sector ripped open the vaunted Gustav Line. Within two weeks the attackers, at times moving so quickly that supporting artillery had difficulty keeping them in range, linked up with divisions attacking out of the Anzio beachhead fifty miles to the north. The Germans soon found themselves struggling to extricate their battered Tenth Army from a closing trap.

The identity of the assaulting units was at first held secret, but Americans soon knew that their newly mobilized all-draftee divisions had seen their first major combat. The army chief of staff, Gen. George C. Marshall, was delighted with the draftees' performance and called it "the first confirmation from the battlefield of the soundness of our division activation and training program." Many other Americans were scarcely less pleased. Headlines in *Stars and Stripes* read, "Something New Has Been Added," while the *Washington Post* exulted, "All-Draft Divisions Chase Nazis 30 Miles." The *Muskogee Daily Phoenix* noted "88th Division Spearheads Yank Smash in Rome Drive" and laid claim to a species of participation by referring to a nearby training camp in the sub-headline, "Gruber-Trained Units Make History in 14-Day Battle." In an article published a year after the war, the *Saturday Evening Post* concluded, "The Blue Devil's 88th Infantry Division Stumped the Experts," forcing a revision of thinking upon "regulars who once refused to believe that a draftee could ever be anything but a sad sack."[1]

Although they may not have been aware of it at the time, the soldiers of the 88th Infantry Division provided the nation's first effective test of conscripted divisions in the conduct of foreign wars. This test addressed a controversy as old as the United States itself: whether the professional soldier or the "citizen-soldier" is more properly the heart of America's military establishment.

A case study of a World War II draftee division sheds light on this important issue and speaks to the assertion of critics that all-draftee formations cannot measure up to standards of performance demonstrated by long-established units. Such a case study also contributes to the understanding of America's mobilization and subsequent conduct of ground operations in World War II. The 88th Infantry Division—the first into combat, the longest-lived, and perhaps the most highly regarded of the draftee divisions—seems an ideal subject for this study of the draftee divisions as a genre.[2]

Americans won their War for Independence because of the efforts of nonprofessional volunteers in state militias or the Continental Army. No major American leader and few American soldiers were professional military men. Anglo-Saxon practice had long held that all ablebodied male citizens had an obligation of military service. This tradition rested on the assumption that such service was intended for the defense of "home and hearth"—and in reasonable proximity thereto. Most post–Revolutionary War Americans opposed the expense of maintaining a professional army—the traditional instrument of monarchs or "men on horseback"—in the young republic. National leaders such as Thomas Jefferson, Patrick Henry, and George Mason were philosophically opposed to a professional army; Mason even went so far as to assert that "when once a standing army is established in any country, the people lose their liberty."[3]

Advocates of a strong national government, on the other hand, believed an army essential. Alexander Hamilton, a spokesman for strong central government, considered federal military forces necessary to suppress such insurrections as Shay's Rebellion in 1786 or the Whiskey Rebellion of 1794. George Washington was also dissatisfied with the militia system as it stood. He proposed that to guard arsenals and frontiers the country would be better served by a small professional army backed by an improved militia.[4]

The federal convention of 1787 compromised between these opposing points of view. Military clauses in the new Constitution balanced congressional prerogatives "to declare war" and "raise and support armies" against the president's role as commander in chief. Another balance was established between the right of the central government to call state militias into federal service and the guarantee that states would be liable to this federalization for limited purposes. Thus the military instruments in the hands of the commander in chief were subject to the largesse of the national legislature, and the states retained an independent military capability. In practice, Congress and the states assumed an even greater role in the direction of military affairs than the Constitution might have suggested.[5]

Legislative openhandedness proved less than the supporters of a strong national military establishment had desired. Nevertheless, the dismal militia failures of Josiah Harmar (1791) and Arthur St. Clair (1793), and subsequently the striking victory of Anthony Wayne's highly trained Legion of the United States at Fallen Timbers (10 August 1794) convinced even the skeptics that a standing army was necessary on the frontier.[6] Legislators found this army acceptable if it remained small, far away, and preoccupied with Indians rather than politics.

Whatever the lesson of Fallen Timbers, the government could not agree on how best to expand the military to a wartime footing. Washington had suggested that regulars—"professionals" by virtue of a three-year enlistment—could become the cadre of a larger military establishment. His critics viewed the regular army as a police force and preferred to expand military capability by mobilizing militias. These mobilizations would be under state control, whereas an enlarged regular army would be under federal control. This latter formula, with regulars and militia thrown together on the battlefield itself, proved adequate for the country's needs prior to 1812. A succession of defeats in the War of 1812, however, demonstrated the inadequacy of state militias in the face of sophisticated opponents. The British burned Washington, for example, after routing a militia force of forty-four hundred—stiffened by four hundred regulars and six hundred marines—at Bladensburg. The militia was so baffled by British fire and maneuver that it fled in terror after losing only eight killed and eleven wounded. Indignant Washingtonians faulted the secretary of war for the disaster. They drove him from their charred city even before he could resign and forced him to submit his resignation from Baltimore.[7]

Early in the 1820s Secretary of War John C. Calhoun sought to improve upon the discredited mobilization system. He proposed organizing the regular army as a leadership cadre that could be expanded with volunteers as necessary.[8] Under his plan the army would ordinarily consist of 6,316 officers and men and would be organized so that it could expand to 11,558 without adding a single officer or unit. His notion that an established unit could approximately double in size without losing efficiency would gain importance in later times. Calhoun was the first important American exponent of an expansible army.

Although Calhoun's Jacksonian contemporaries thought his plan rooted in a military elitism they found abhorrent, Calhoun did succeed in providing the army with a reservoir of leaders through increased professionalism of West Point under Superintendent Sylvanus Thayer. This leadership proved invaluable in the Mexican War. In 1846 Congress expanded the regular army as Calhoun had recommended, and it performed well throughout the war. The record of nonprofessional volunteer formations during the war was more uneven. Some, such as the 1st Missouri Regiment, did well, whereas others, such as the 2nd Indiana, did poorly. The concept of an expansible regular army supplemented, if necessary, by volunteer formations seemed vindicated during the Mexican War.[9]

The post–Mexican War expansible regular army probably would have proven adequate for the limited international needs of nineteenth-century America. Unfortunately, the contingency with which the regular army was next called upon to deal was neither limited nor international. The fratricidal warfare that followed the attack on Fort Sumter was on a scale far greater than that for which the regular army had been prepared. Regular formations were swamped early in the Civil War; the strength of the Federal army climbed from 16,000 in 1861, 637,000 in 1862, and 900,000 in 1863.[10]

In 1861 some military men suggested that the regulars might best be used if scattered as cadre among the numerous volunteer formations being raised by the states. General in Chief Winfield Scott rejected such proposals. The regular army expanded but remained small and intact while the states organized volunteers with their own resources. Except for a few veterans and West Pointers in civil life, the resources available to the northern states did not include many men with military experience. The southern states were only somewhat better off. The presence of the regular army itself was not much felt during the mobilization of volunteer forces on either side, although West Pointers did ultimately come to dominate the military leadership on both sides.[11]

The Civil War forced a change in recruitment philosophy. Prior to the Civil War military thinkers thought in terms of volunteers when they anticipated sustained or distant operations. Washington blandly asserted that there was a sufficient proportion of ablebodied young men between the ages of eighteen and twenty-five who had "a natural fondness for military parade (which passion is almost ever prevalent at that period of life)."[12] Young men with such a passion proved sufficient for military needs prior to 1861, but the manpower demands of the Civil War greatly exceeded this supply of enthusiasts. Faced with total war, first the Confederacy and then the United States resorted to conscription.[13]

European nations had frequently resorted to military drafts, and the mass warfare of the Napoleonic era brought conscription on an enormous scale. In the United States and the Confederacy, however, conscription proved a divisive issue, requiring as it did posing the rights of the individual against the rights of the state. Recognizing this implication, both the North and South avoided the universal application of the draft. Ever-increasing bounties were offered to encourage enlistment. In both the North and the South, a drafted man could hire a substitute. In the North a drafted man could purchase commutation with three hundred dollars. In the South one slaveholder or overseer was exempt for every twenty slaves owned or supervised. Individuals in "essential" occupations were also exempted.

Since conscription was conducted under the auspices of the individual states, inconsistencies inevitably invited abuse and evasion. One-third of the South's manpower under arms was the product of conscription, but this fraction comprised not so much newly drafted men as previous volunteers forced by new laws to extend terms of service. Similarly, only 6 percent of the two and one-half million who served the United States from 1861 to 1865 were conscripts. The extent to which the threat of conscription encouraged volunteering remains unknown. There were no separate conscript formations. Conscripts remained in or joined existing units or newly organized volunteer formations.[14]

The United States government never gained effective control of its military manpower, and it directly recruited relatively few units: the tiny Regular Army, the United States Colored Troops, two regiments of sharpshooters, the Invalid Corps, and six regiments of Confederate prisoners (the last used for Indian duty only). Each state was sovereign when raising its own units. Until 1863 all states save Wisconsin met new manpower quotas by organizing new units rather than by providing replacements to older ones. Postitions thus created may have contributed to political patronage, but the system did little to enhance military efficiency. Throughout the war new regiments went into action under inexperienced leadership, despite War Department efforts to standardize recruitment and training. Insofar as manpower mobilization and training were concerned, the Civil War was ambitiously, yet inefficiently, waged. This influenced the thinking of later military theorists.[15]

America's seminal military theorist, Emory Upton, wrote in the 1880s that the Civil War had been a bloodbath simply because "instead of expanding the Regular Army and making it the chief instrument in executing the national will . . . [Congress] violated the practice of every civilized nation by calling into existence an army of a million untrained officers and men." The failure to train troops properly was, in Upton's view, negligent homicide.[16]

Upton had commanded a division in the Civil War and had traveled widely after the war. During his travels he was much impressed by what he saw of the German army. In his great work, *The Military Policy of the United States* (published in 1904, long after his death but also long after his ideas had been publicized by others), he proposed a major reworking of America's military. He thought that the chaotic manpower mobilization employed in the Civil War should be replaced with a fully federalized draft. He further thought that the army should abandon the prewar militia system, professionalize leadership at all levels, develop a military educational system to improve and standardize training, and enlist troops for not less than three years. The army, he argued, should expand to wartime footing along the lines of "the expansive principle." Inductees, whether drafted or volunteer, should be assigned to established units.

Another former Union general took issue with Upton's somewhat elitist outlook. John A. Logan's *The Volunteer Soldier of America* (1887) was a testimonial to the citizen-soldier rather than the professional. Logan thought the "effect of the West Point system . . . had been to manacle and even to crush . . . the volunteer and his aspirations for recognition."[17] He did not propose to do away with the Regular Army altogether; he believed it necessary on the frontier and suitable as a repository of specialized skills (such as artillery ballistics). Logan's point was that in an emergency the Regular Army would—and should—be swamped in a mobilization so vast as to make the "expansive principle" meaningless. The idea of enlarging the Regular Army to anticipate such demands, an idea favored by Upton, was repugnant to Logan. In Logan's view, such a decision would mean enlarging, at considerable expense, an inbred elitist institution that would stifle the talents of volunteer citizen-soldiers.

Rumination concerning "Uptonian" ideas remained academic through the late nineteenth century. Congressional parsimony and the absence of a serious military threat from abroad—as well as the strength of the militia *cum* volunteer tradition and the states' preference for using "organized" militia (by then increasingly called "National

Guard") to suppress disturbances—all dictated against radical revisions.

Americans saw no particular reason to "tinker" with existing military arrangements prior to their embarrassingly disorderly mobilization for the Spanish-Amerian War in 1898. The Regular Army, even when expanded, proved too small to undertake the full burden of the war, yet volunteer and National Guard units were too poorly prepared initially to deploy overseas. Although of shorter duration, the mobilization effort in 1898 was as confused and inefficient as that of the Civil War. After the war, revelations and scandals, including the testimony of the commanding general of the army against his own commissary general, kept the memory of wartime confusion in the public mind. Among other miscarriages, the commissary general stood accused of serving the hastily mobilized troops "embalmed beef."[18] It may be the nature of armies to complain about their food.

The Spanish-American War experience was sufficiently sobering to give the new secretary of war, Elihu Root, support for thoroughgoing—if tactfully executed—reforms. Root borrowed heavily from Upton's *Military Policy of the United States* when he professionalized the schooling and staff structure of the Regular Army. Requirements overseas justified the enlargement of the Regular Army to about seventy thousand men in 1903,[19] thus assuring that growth along the lines of the expansive principle could generate a substantial force in a reasonable time. State "militias" reorganized and standardized under effective federal control as the National Guard. The Dick Act of 1903 identified the National Guard as a trained, equipped, and expansible supplement to the Regular Army.[20] When World War I broke out in Europe, the United States possessed an enlarged military establishment organized along Uptonian lines. Military writers foresaw that mobilization might require organizing additional units outside this existing structure, but they left little doubt that such "new" divisions would be accorded third-rate status.[21]

The Uptonian defense posture assumed with the adoption of Root's Reforms was not without its critics. Although these generally approved the changed staff structure, schooling, and the size of the Regular Army and the National Guard, they considered it unwise to depend entirely on established formations to sustain national defense. As World War I threatened to engulf the United States, some advocates of military preparedness combined the Uptonian notion of a federally supervised draft with an egalitarian notion of a *levee en masse*. Their proposals featured "new" divisions added on to those established by the Dick Act. Maj. Gen. Leonard Wood, a recent army chief of staff and a self-appointed spokesman for preparedness, advocated the "Plattsburg Idea" of summer training for college students, businessmen, politicians, and others to disseminate military knowledge. Wood repeatedly insisted that a small cadre of professionals could train recruits "from the ground up" within six months.[22] In truth, Wood found himself in an ambivalent position, defending Upton's proposals for conscription in the face of the passive Wilson administration while at the same time attacking such Uptonian notions as long terms of service, lengthy training cycles, and limitations on the use of new formations.

After prolonged controversy and considerable introspection, an effective decision on conscription emerged with the Selective Service Act of 18 May 1917. This act established that citizens would be drafted as necessary to meet military requirements. The availability of drafted manpower did not, however, resolve disagreements between Uptonians and egalitarians as to how drafted manpower might best be used. The War College Division of the General Staff, impressed by the manpower demands of the Western Front, recommended that the Regular Army and the National Guard be given over altogether to training an army of sufficient strength to decide the war in Europe quickly. This recommendation was anathema to the Uptonians, who continued to favor an orderly, amoebalike growth, whereby established formations would double in size and then train and go into battle, possibly doubling again at some later date when the recruits themselves had become "veterans." The War Department compromised. Faced with the deteriorating situation of the Western Allies, it hastily dispatched to France established regiments that were organized into divisions and fleshed out with recruits. Meanwhile, tiny cadres of regulars trained the conscripted "new" divisions of the "national army."[23]

By November 1918 the American Expeditionary Forces had received eight Regular Army, seventeen National Guard, and eighteen National Army divisions; the presence of the conscripted divisions did not necessarily represent a victory for their advocates, however. Gen. John J. Pershing, commander of the American Expeditionary Forces, was so Uptonian in his thinking that he sought lengthy in-theater training programs even for the Regular Army divisions, and more for the draftee divisions. He also favored the established divisions over these new ones. Of eighteen National Army divisions, he summarily broke up six before they experienced combat and sent their men into veteran units as individual replacements. Three other divisions served as replacement training centers rather than as combat units. Two divisions went to the front but never saw serious combat, and one was turned over piecemeal to the French in detached regiments. Of the remaining six divisions, the first into combat did not see action until 11

August 1918. Although the draftee divisions that did experience combat in World War I performed creditably, the treatment they received clearly accorded them third-rate status. They were, first, a source of replacements for veteran divisions, second, a stopgap for holding quiet sectors, and only third, combat divisions in their own right.[24]

World War I firmly established the principle of the federally supervised draft. The expansible principle had already been established. In an emergency the Regular Army and the National Guard were to provide the nucleus of forces approximately double their peacetime size. Expansions would be by virtue of draftees if sufficient numbers of volunteers were not available to meet a crisis. What was not yet clear was whether further growth should feature a host of draftee divisions or the more gradual development of units envisioned by the Uptonians.

In the aftermath of World War I, professional officers regarded the draftee more favorably than they had before. General Pershing, Chief of Staff Peyton C. March, and other leaders had been impressed by what they had seen of him as an individual soldier on the Western Front. Egalitarian theorists such as John McAuley Palmer advocated increased reliance on this "citizen-soldier." Palmer thought the expansive principle should be abandoned altogether; when war broke out the United States should raise new divisions to supplement those already deployed. In Palmer's view, the advantage of a regular army was not that it formed a nucleus (other than small training cadres) but rather that it was immediately available for deployment.[25]

Congress included some of Palmer's recommendations in the National Defense Act of 1920. This act authorized nine Regular Army divisions, nine "training corps" to absorb recruits and organize them into divisions, improvements in the National Guard, and the creation of the Army Reserve, a species of "organized militia" independent of the states. Interwar economic conditions and congressional frugality undermined the effectiveness of this act, however. The National Guard and the Army Reserve withered in numbers and effectiveness. The Regular Army dwindled to 134,957 in 1932, well below the size necessary to cope with a major overseas crisis. Palmer advocated reducing the number of divisions to a point where those on hand were combat-ready and thus could fight effectively until the training corps generated new divisions. Instead, the War Department liquidated the training corps, retained nine skeletal divisions, and made plans to expand in accord with the expansible principle.[26]

As World War II approached, disagreements between Uptonians and egalitarians continued to surface. The army chief of staff, Gen. George C. Marshall, sought unit reorganizations and a massive recruiting program that would have greatly increased the size of the expansible Regular Army. Secretary of War Henry L. Stimson, a longtime egalitarian in military matters and a member of the National Association for Universal Military Training, recognized and countered this Uptonian stratagem. The Selective Service Act of 1940, passed in peacetime, became the basis for military manpower procurement. The prewar expansible army reached its limits in the autumn of 1941. At that time, after a year of growth along Uptonian lines, the personnel composition of the Army stood at Regular Army, 503,000; Regular Army Reserve, 17,500; federalized National Guard, 256,000; and draftees, 712,000. The established formations had absorbed as many draftees as they could integrate at the time. If a need developed for further expansion in the next year or so, it would have to be accomplished by all-draftee divisions.[27]

As World War II dragged on, distinctions between the "new" draftee divisions and the "old"—Regular Army and National Guard—divisions faded. Combat replacements were almost exclusively draftees, particularly after the midwar suspension of voluntary enlistment.[28] A number of old divisions were virtually destroyed in order to provide individual replacements for divisions deploying overseas. When reconstructed, these divisions were draftee divisions in all but name. By 1944 the demography of all divisions was pretty much the same: a thin crust of regulars, supplemented by graduates of the Reserve Officers' Training Corps and officer candidate schools, leading formations manned by draftees.

In the early days of mobilization this fading of distinctions had not occurred, however. The "old" and "new" divisions had important differences in their genesis. Old divisions had organizational continuities stretching across years or decades; new divisions did not. The old divisions that deployed early in the war went overseas with much of their prewar cadre intact, whereas new divisions organized their cadre and activated at virtually the same time. War Department policies directed volunteers through replacement training centers into the old divisions, whereas the new divisions formed up with draftees alone in their enlisted ranks. The organizing principles of the old divisions were Uptonian: standing units, modest expansion to accept enlisted "fillers," and the consciously faced integration of replacements into the veterans. The new divisions were the antithesis of all this. Gen. George C. Marshall clearly understood that his draftee divisions represented an unproven concept.[29]

In the century and a half separating the federal convention from World War II, Americans crossed three thresholds in mobilization planning. First, they resolved the question of whether to have a standing professional army or to rely exclusively on militia formations for defense. They opted for a professional army, albeit a small one, as well as militias. Even the most committed idealists could not escape the rude facts of frontier warfare and international politics. Second, during the Civil War the United States decided to require involuntary military service of citizens in times of national crisis, thus abandoning volunteers as the sole source of military manpower. Popular acceptance of the draft developed over time; the public regarded it with some hostility during the Civil War, generally supported it during World War I, and strongly supported it during World War II. Third, Americans came to rely on the national government to direct a centrally managed mobilization in time of war. State-based recruiting and an easy fluidity between civil and military life gave way to federal mobilization firmly in the hands of military professionals.

A fourth threshold, not yet fully crossed in 1942, was a commitment to the rapid transformation of ordinary citizens into twentieth-century soldiers. If Uptonians were right, American draftees could be efficiently used in modern warfare only after extensive training in established units. Such a proposition suggested that war with the Axis nations would be a drawn-out enterprise. What was more, America might thenceforth, in the aftermath of the war, be saddled with a standing army whose numbers represented a major fraction of wartime needs. If, on the other hand, small cadres of professionals could quickly shape a mass of conscripts into combat-ready divisions, the time required for mobilization and war could be shortened. America could batter its Axis opponents into defeat, perhaps in a couple of years, then quickly return to its preoccupation with peaceful pursuits.

Crossing each of these thresholds had important implications for Americans. A national army, a draft, and a federally supervised mobilization all required individuals, local governments, and state governments to surrender some measure of their autonomy. If these sacrifices were to be minimized, Americans would have to convert draftees into combat-ready units quickly and efficiently. Otherwise, the war effort would needlessly squander human and material resources; if it went on too long it could dangerously disrupt the life and fabric of the American nation.

The experience of the 88th Infantry Division, the first of the draftee divisions into combat in World War II, illustrates the means whereby draftees could, in fact, be quickly and efficiently converted into combat-ready units. Uptonian and egalitarian notions would become reconciled as cadres of professionals made effective fighters from thousands of laymen without endangering the "amateur status" cherished by the nation that had produced them. The 88th Infantry Division would mobilize, organize, train, and fight without unduly militarizing the soldiers from which it was made—a genuinely American response to the crisis of war.

2

Personnel and Personnel Utilization: Bureaucratic Roulette

Of the ninety divisions with which the United States Army fought World War II, the 88th Infantry Division—the "Blue Devil Division"—was the forty-ninth activated. It was, however, the twenty-fourth into combat. In its training cycle it passed all previously activated draftee divisions, and three regular army and six National Guard divisions as well. The 88th Infantry Division went from activation to embarkation in sixteen months. This was a record in 1943 and, despite the subsequent shortening of division training cycles, only one division surpassed and three others equaled that record during World War II.[1]

Ideally, all divisions should have progressed from activation to embarkation as quickly as did the 88th. A report by Lt. Gen. Lesley J. McNair, the chief of staff of General Headquarters, to the War Department on 20 December 1941 identified seventeen divisions as combat-ready and seventeen others as to be ready by 1 April 1942. Divisions activated after Pearl Harbor were to undergo a fifty-two-week training cycle prior to embarkation. Allowing the wartime average of four months for administrative requirements, large-scale maneuvers, and travel time, the army should have had all its divisions available for embarkation within sixteen months of activation. Thus, divisions should have been prepared for combat at a rate corresponding to the solid line in Figure 1 rather than at the actual rate, shown by the dashed line.[2]

Army Ground Forces, the headquarters responsible for organizing and training ground combat troops, blamed the slow preparation of combat divisions on shortages of equipment, "fluctuation and depletions" of enlisted personnel, irregularities in cadre selection, scarcity and inexperience of officers, administrative burdens caused by nondivisional units, and initial deficiencies in its own (Army Ground

Figure 1. Division Overseas Deployments

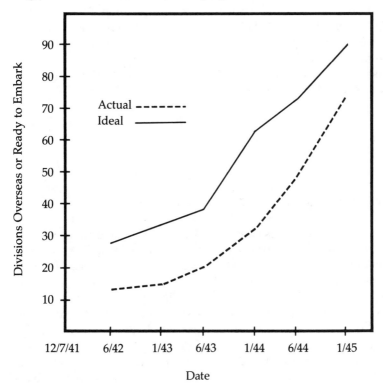

Forces) supervision. Of these six obstacles, three represented personnel problems. The 88th Infantry Division had the good fortune to avoid the worst effects of these personnel difficulties. Had the division been activated much before or much after its actual date of 15 July 1942, it might have fared worse than it did in a turbulent personnel situation as full of chance as a game of roulette.[3]

The army's most obvious wartime personnel problems were its fluctuations and depletions in numbers of enlisted personnel. Of these irregularities, the issue that most preoccupied Army Ground Forces seems to have been its competition with the Army Service Forces and the Army Air Forces, not to mention the navy and the marines, for its legitimate share of the nation's manpower.[4] The services vied for manpower, particularly for men who had achieved high scores on the Army General Classification Test (AGCT). The army rightly considered this test a measure of "usable" (rather than "raw") intelligence, thus giving the best indication then available of a recruit's "trainability."

The Army Air Forces and Army Service Forces received disproportionately large numbers of men who registered high AGCT scores
throughout 1942 and 1943. This was because of the emphasis the War
Department placed upon undertaking an early strategic air offensive in
Europe and because of the technical complexities the Army Service
Forces seemed to face. Percentile test distributions for the three major
commands in 1943 were as follows:[5]

	Classes I & II	Class III	Classes IV & V
Army Ground Forces	29.7	33.3	37.0
Army Air Forces	36.5	28.5	35.0
Army Service Forces	41.7	31.3	27.0

Officer candidates were drawn only from classes I and II. Army
Ground Forces planners believed that the preferred treatment of the air
forces and the service forces hampered their own efforts to train and provide officers for units—a formidable task in view of the War Department's
vision of deploying an army of 140 combat divisions by the end of 1943.[6]

The 88th Infantry Division reflected the test profiles of 1942 for
infantry personnel (5.3 percent Class I, 22.1 percent Class II, 29.0
percent Class III, and 43.6 percent Classes IV and V). The evidence
suggests that this somewhat asymmetric profile did not significantly
inhibit the 88th's training. Infantry divisions seem not to have needed
as many high-scoring men as did units from other services. Certainly
their tables of organization, dominated by infantry and artillery battalions, called for lower proportions of leaders or specialists. In truth,
the significant damage resulting from the use of the Army General
Classification Test was not that infantry divisions received too few
high-scorers. Rather, it resulted when AGCT scores became the basis
for diversions into special programs after divisional training cycles
were already in progress.[7]

When the army perceived a need to concentrate high-scoring men
into priority programs, it usually reassigned men from units that were
already partly trained. This represented a qualitative loss of talent
more damaging than quantities alone might suggest.[8] Within the new
units undergoing training, men in AGCT Classes I and II often rose
quickly to leadership or administrative positions. Although the
"raiding" of ground units for high-scoring personnel was a continuing
problem, there were two great surges of such raiding. The 88th Infantry Division escaped one of these because it was activated too late; it
missed the second because it completed its training so early.

One surge of AGCT raiding resulted from the runaway expansion
of officer candidate schools, which were intended to meet mobilization
demands for junior officers. Ultimately 300 thousand men left the

enlisted ranks and went through officer candidate school (OCS). To be eligible for OCS, an enlisted man needed an AGCT score of 110 or higher, a good record, and time in service of at least six months. The draftees of the 88th first became eligible for OCS in January 1943. In November 1942 the War Department reconsidered mobilization plans and eliminated fourteen divisions. Whereas commanders were relieved for failing to fill OCS quotas in 1942, in early 1943 the army found itself with a surplus of junior officers. Twelve additional divisions were cut in June 1943, resulting in a further increase of the officer surplus. Another ten thousand officers became redundant later in the war when the antiaircraft units for which they had been designated proved unnecessary. Units activated during the summer of 1942—such as the 88th—lost few men to OCS programs.[9]

The second great surge of AGCT raiding was associated with the Army Special Training Program (ASTP). The ASTP was, in fact, a college deferment within the army, whereby inductees were permitted civil schooling rather than immediate military service. The purpose of the program was, in the event of an extended war, to assure the steady flow of college-trained men into the armed forces. It was further hoped that the program, a benefit to the colleges and universities involved, might encourage a more positive attitude toward the War Department in the academic community. Commanders had few good things to say about diverting trained troops to a program whose "payoff," if any, would be so far in the future. They were even less pleased with the notion of courting academicians, whom they characteristically viewed as the most unstable of allies.[10]

The ASTP was to go into full operation in the spring of 1943. Commanders were to designate as eligible those enlisted men with AGCT scores greater than 115 who had completed high school, basic training, and, if over age twenty-one, one year of college. Unit commanders were so dilatory in designating men, however, that Gen. George C. Marshall, army chief of staff, issued a stinging memorandum on 1 April 1943, insisting that commanders support the program. Under such pressure, Army Ground Forces released 3,096 men for a cycle starting in May, 5,079 men for a cycle starting in June, and 12,626 for a cycle starting in July. By 1944 the ASTP involved 150 thousand men of military age.[11]

Recognizing the damage such personnel turbulence was causing units in training, in autumn of 1943 the War Department began drawing ASTP candidates exclusively from the ranks of inductees rather than from divisions. New divisions were under effective pressure to deliver up ASTP candidates only during the period May through October, 1943; units on major maneuvers or already alerted for overseas movement were exempted from the program. The 88th Infantry

Division departed for maneuvers in June 1943 and was alerted for overseas movement shortly thereafter, thus the division commander never came under serious pressure to provide ASTP candidates.[12]

Interestingly, in February 1944 General Marshall himself had second thoughts about the ASTP. Anticipating the invasion of France and lamenting "the number of non-commissioned officers who are below satisfactory standards of intelligence and qualities of leadership," Marshall reversed his position and cut the ASTP program by 80 percent in three months.[13]

Given the relative disadvantages with respect to AGCT scores and the dangers posed by AGCT raiding, Army Ground Forces nevertheless tried to deal equably with subordinate branches in the matter of distributing enlisted men of greater and lesser intelligence. Distribution of AGCT classes to each of the combat branches approximated that received by the Army Ground Forces as a whole. Exceptions were made for airborne divisions, which had attracted so many low-scoring personnel that they were allowed to clear out sufficient numbers of Class IV and Class V men to bring themselves up to the average intelligence profile.[14]

Within the 88th a policy of nonfavoritism continued to apply. If there were any special considerations, they were limited to the few men identified by the "playing of the needles" during induction.[15] This was a process whereby component units were allowed to request limited numbers of individuals with particular combinations of characteristics—if the units could justify their pressing need for the individuals thus requested. As inductees were processed in, each carried a card that was punched in different places to represent specific responses or items of information generated at the various interviews and stations. These cards were later laid over sets of needles arranged in such a manner that the cards of inductees with requested combinations adhered and other cards fell away. The information gained from these primitive computers went directly to the division adjutant general. Some units got what they ordered; others did not.

Fluctuations in the total number of enlisted personnel available to divisions at activation resulted from competing demands upon the Selective Service System. A division rarely received all of its draftees, or "enlisted fillers," at once; they tended to arrive a few hundred at a time over an extended period. The nature of the divisional training program prior to its seventeenth week was such that late arrivals could integrate into units without disturbing training progress overall. During the first seventeen weeks instruction focused on individual skills; latecomers could catch up on these when other troops were reviewing skills already learned or enjoying time off. After the seventeenth week the divisional programs moved on to much less flexible unit-training phases. The 88th received its final major increment of enlisted fillers in October, well within seventeen weeks of the beginning of its training on 3 August 1942. Some unfortunate later arrivals missed Christmas furloughs, but all caught up without delaying the progress of the division.[16]

In at least one respect the piecemeal reception of the fillers seems to have worked to the advantage of the division. The first increment of troops, drawn mainly from New England, New York, New Jersey, and Delaware, had an unusual concentration of technical and administrative talent. Generally these men filled out the enlisted ranks of the division's logistical superstructure, which thus stood intact from an early date. Later arrivals, including the second major increment of fillers, came from a wide area of the Midwest and Southwest. Loosely labeled "Okies," these personnel settled comfortably into less technical slots.[17]

Once divisions actually began training, the most damaging single source of personnel turbulence proved to be the "stripping off" of individuals for reassignment to divisions in combat or en route overseas. During World War I, draftee divisions often had been broken up to provide replacements for other divisions. Replacement training depots had existed in 1918, but these had failed to meet the demands of combat. Interwar planners hoped to avoid a repetition of this stripping, and by September 1941 a system had been developed of replacement training centers, which the War Department considered "eminently satisfactory."[18]

Unfortunately, the new replacement system was satisfactory only during the gradual growth of 1941, and it proved inadequate for the massive needs of 1942. Divisions activated so rapidly that their personnel requirements dwarfed the capacity of the replacement training centers to provide recruits. Rather than sanction further expansion of the centers, General Marshall routed draftees directly from reception centers to newly created units.[19] The "new" divisions conducted their own basic training while "old" divisions continued to receive replacements from the replacement training centers.

Unfortunately, the replacement centers still could not keep pace with mobilization demands and combat losses. Selected divisions underwent stripping in the autumn of 1942 to support the campaign in North Africa. Another cycle of almost continuous stripping from September 1943 through September 1944 hampered the training efforts of other divisions. One division suffered a cumulative stripping of 22,235 men. Two divisions, the 76th and 78th infantries, lost their active status altogether and served as replacement training centers from September

1942 until March 1943. Another twenty-one infantry divisions lost a total of 103,244 men to stripping between September 1944 and the end of the war.[20]

Again the 88th Infantry Division, its training sandwiched between the most hectic period of mobilization and the bloodiest period of combat, was fortunate. Its troops had not progressed far enough in their training to be considered for the stripping that preceded the North African landings. The victims were six National Guard divisions; the 88th subsequently passed five of these in its training cycle. In September 1943 the 88th was alerted for overseas movement and thus was no longer vulnerable to stripping. That was the very month in which the army began its longest and most damaging cycle of personnel stripping. Indeed, the 88th itself was filled out with trained replacements stripped from other units.

Another obstacle to the preparation of ground combat divisions originated with "abuses in cadre selection." Draftee divisions were organized with the hope that a small cadre of experienced officers and enlisted men could train and lead a much larger body of draftees. The World War II cadre system was highly structured (see Figure 2). Each cadreman had a specific and carefully considered role. A division could be as good, and only as good, as its cadre. Unfortunately, new divisions did not always receive good cadres. The bulk of a cadre's enlisted men usually came from a single parent division. No commander wants to give up good men; the commanders of the parent divisions had to balance concern for their own units against loyalty to the larger purposes of the army. Too often "the formation of a cadre meant a housecleaning." The commanders of several new divisions complained that their cadres consisted of rejects from the parent division.[21]

Insofar as cadre acquisition was concerned, the 88th Infantry Division again was fortunate. Maj. Gen. John E. Sloan, the new division commander, and Maj. Gen. Geoffrey Keyes, commanding general of the parent 9th Infantry Division, were longtime friends, and both had reputations as perfectionists. Keyes determined to deal fairly with Sloan in transferring cadre from his division. Brig. Gen. Stonewall Jackson, then the assistant division commander of the 88th, also influenced cadre selection. Jackson had served three tours as an instructor in the Infantry School and was personally acquainted with most of the officers who commanded in the 9th Infantry Division. The leaders of the 9th showed no inclination to shortchange their old friend, especially since Jackson traveled to the 9th's cantonment, observed the entire cadre selection process, and interviewed most of the candidates. An incompetent would have found it difficult to slip past him.[22]

When Sloan himself was called upon for a cadre in February 1943,

Figure 2. A World War II Infantry Division: Enlisted Cadre and Total Enlisted Strength

1,859
15,007
12.4%

INF REG	INF REG	INF REG	DIV ARTY (4 BN)
396	396	396	354
3,538	3,538	3,538	2,162
11.2%	11.2%	11.2%	16.4%

ENGR BN	MED BN	CAV RCN TRP	SIG CO
86	82	19	39
604	421	143	291
14.2%	19.5%	13.3%	13.4%

HQS SUPPORT

SPEC TRP	HQS CO	QM CO	ORD CO	MP PLT
4	20	26	28	13
19	212	176	140	169
21.0%	9.4%	14.8%	20.0%	7.7%

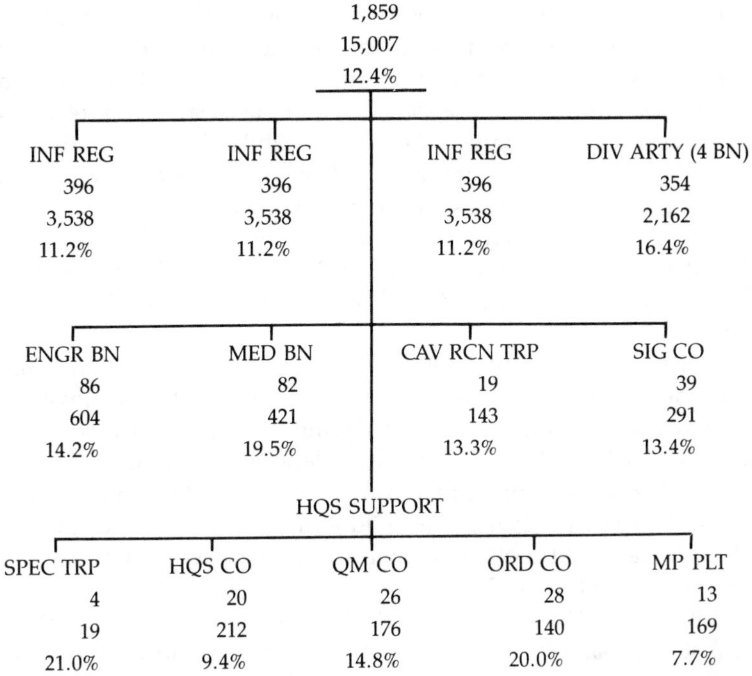

NOTE: In each cell, top number is cadre strength, middle number is total strength, and percentage represents cadre as percent of total personnel. Not shown, but included in division whole figures, is division band, total enlisted strength 56.

he gave up men who were as qualified as those he had received. This was both proper and wise, for units caught making a housecleaning often suffered further turbulence when called upon to replace the inadequate cadre they had provided. The commanding general of the 11th Airborne Division, the division cadred by the 88th, later wrote an appreciative letter citing his cadre's quality, which in effect protected the 88th from further cadre levies. The 11th Airborne subsequently achieved a creditable record of its own, and was the only division to surpass the sixteen-month activation-to-embarkation record set by the 88th.[23]

As he sorted through records reflecting his prospective cadre assets—197 cadre officers; 427 OCS officers; and 1,172 enlisted cadremen, of whom most were for "housekeeping" and including fewer than two hundred who had been in the army longer than three years—

in the months before the 88th activated, General Sloan may have reflected ruefully back on his own first army assignment. In the halcyon spring of 1911 he had reported to Battery Parrott, Fort Monroe, Virginia. The young lieutenant was immediately taken aside by the first sergeant, who told him in brogue what a delight it was to see him and what a wonderful professional experience Battery Parrott would be, provided Sloan observed things from a little distance and didn't get in the way of the noncommissioned officers. Lieutenants, said the sergeant, were apprentices whose battery-level experiences would be wonderful preparation for subsequent positions of high responsibility. The NCOs would groom him well and take great pride in his growth and achievement. He shouldn't, however, make the mistake of actually trying to run things.[24]

Thirty years later, Sloan enjoyed no real counterpart to the tightly knit, noncommissioned cadre that ran Battery Parrott. The tiny regular army was expanding so rapidly during 1942 that each of the new divisions got but a sprinkling of the fabled "leather-lunged" NCOs. At best, each company or battery would get one or two, not enough to mirror the role of NCOs in the "Old Army." There was no short-term solution that could replace the maturity, experience, savvy, and confidence of the older NCOs.

Most of the NCOs who would lead the draftees of the 88th into combat were simply promising young men who moved through the ranks a little more quickly than the rest. Many had come from the rank and file of the parent 9th Division, and others emerged from the 88th's own enlisted filler. There were schools outside the division to train technicians, but no formal programs existed for line NCOs. The unmarried NCOs lived, ate, and slept with the men in garrison and in the field. They experienced the same training, were about the same age, and shared comparable views of their world. They became leaders among the men without ever quite being the leadership one step above the men. This made them ideal for monitoring health and welfare and interceding on behalf of their erstwhile peers, but it could create problems with respect to enforcing discipline and pursuing commander's objectives.[25]

Somewhat too much has been made of the fact that draftees, on the average, had more education and intellectual "flexibility" than prewar-vintage NCOs. The old NCOs may have been uneducated, but they commanded a specialized body of knowledge that gained them enormous respect given the job at hand. What was more, the asymmetry in education may have been true for the army as a whole, but in rifle companies the profiles were more nearly equal. At most, a rifle company contained two or three draftees from AGCT Class I, and first sergeants almost invariably snatched them up as company clerks,

supply specialists, and the like. These men were protected from ha-
rassment and, in return, they kept company paperwork in order while
appeasing higher headquarters with morning reports, inventories,
and other documents. An AGCT Class II was a smart man in an
infantry platoon, and far more likely than his peers to be considered for
promotion to corporal or other positions of responsibility. An AGQT
score proved as good an indicator as any of leadership potential, but
other factors also caught the eye of senior cadremen: age, social maturity, physical size, energy, and apparent dedication.[26]

It took time and experimentation to identify the best leadership
selections within a unit. The rude fact is that one cannot accurately
forecast how an individual will do in a position of responsibility; one
has to try him out.[27] The 88th was not subject to gross losses of
personnel, particularly not of high-AGCT personnel, so it was able to
experiment until it got the best fits possible. Company commanders
could "bust" any man up to and including their first sergeants, and
they did so until they got the chain of command they wanted. This led
to the infamous "blood stripes," rank acquired because some other
individual had been demoted. It also led to chains of command generally considered competent.

The problem remained, nevertheless, that most of the 88th's NCOs
were engaged in peer leadership. This suggested the need to amend
traditional officer-NCO relationships. Sloan decided that his officers
would be more directly involved in matters of discipline and detailed
guidance than had been the case in the prewar army. He drove himself
and his subordinates hard, taking an interest in details and conducting
inspections so closely they were labeled "chicken." On several occasions when he discovered a soldier with field jacket unbuttoned or
some other minor violation, he called every officer in the offender's
chain of command—including colonels or brigadier generals—into his
office. He personally apprehended Pvt. Richard C. Prassel for attempting to return a library book at an unauthorized time, and again he
summoned the chain of command. Fortunately for the terrified private, as the plot unraveled it turned out that Prassel had been dispatched to the library by his own battery commander—who in turn
took the heat. Sloan's point was that no detail was too minor for an
officer's attention, and that matters formerly left to NCOs were the
exclusive province of NCOs no longer. His disciplinary techniques
were tough, centralized, immediate, and straightforward. He once
stood an entire battalion at attention in the heat of the day until it came
up with recompense for watermelons stolen from a farmer's fields.
There would be no "looting" of civilian property by his division.[28]

Sloan viewed the muddying of distinctions between officer and
NCO roles as a necessity, not a virtue. Officers, however inex-

perienced, were more distant from the men and thus in a better position to enforce discipline. He continued to consider the old division of labor—officers responsible for general supervision and tactical direction, NCOs responsible for detailed supervision, discipline, health, and welfare—as an ideal. As time passed, the division would come closer to the old model. In Italy, NCOs who were combat veterans would enjoy a certain prestige over officer and enlisted replacements alike. In practice, each company-grade officer worked out his own relationship with his NCOs, approximating the ideal insofar as personalities would allow. It took time, and personnel stability, to work all this out. It also took considerable attention to officer development.

One striking aspect of the U.S. Army's World War II growth to a strength in excess of eight million was that it was shepherded by a mere 14,000 professional officers. These eventually were outnumbered forty to one by officers drawn from civilian sources: 19,000 from the National Guard; 180,000 from the Officers' Reserve Corps and Reserve Officers' Training Corps; 100,000 commissioned directly as doctors, dentists, chaplains, technicians, and administrators; and 300,000 graduates of officer candidate or aviation cadet schools. Most of the National Guardsmen and about half of the reserves received a modicum of military experience in the limited mobilization preceding Pearl Harbor. The rest were as new to the army as the privates they were called upon to lead.[29]

The 88th's complement of officers reflected these profiles. Of 197 cadre officers, about 60 were experienced soldiers. Shortly before activation, 427 OCS graduates joined the division. This latter number grew by approximately half over the next six months when the War Department cut back its proposed total of divisions and found it had an excess of junior officers on hand. Some of the young officers proved unfit, but most were bright, consumed with a sense of mission, and quick to learn. In 1942 the army had the largest and most qualified slice of America's junior executive talent that it had ever had. This phenomenon did not go unnoticed by the senior officers, who nevertheless approached the task of training a body of apprentices twelve times their number as serious business.[30] The senior officers proved to be relentless pedagogues, a characteristic captured in a ditty popular among the younger officers: "Swing and sway with Sammy Kaye, / Moan and groan with General Sloan."

Here an examination of General Sloan's background is in order, both because of his role in the division and because of the extent to which he epitomized soldiers of his vintage.[31] John Emmitt Sloan was born into a prosperous Greenville, South Carolina, family in 1887. He was a direct descendant of Capt. David Sloan of the American Revolution. His grandfather, Lt. John B. Sloan, CSA, was killed in 1862 in the

Peninsular Campaign. John E. attended public schools and Furman University, and graduated from the United States Naval Academy in 1910. Sea duty was not as much to his liking as gunnery, so he transferred into the Coast Artillery in 1911. He served in Coast Artillery assignments, including Panama, until July 1917, when the demands of World War I suggested the conversion of coast artillerymen to field artillerymen. During World War I he attended Fort Sill's Field Artillery School as a student, taught in it as an instructor, and activated and commanded the 30th Field Artillery of the 10th Division. This unit did not get overseas before the war ended.

Between the wars Sloan served in the Chesapeake Bay Coast Defenses; commanded the 17th Field Artillery at Fort Bragg, North Carolina; served as executive officer of the 13th Field Artillery and 11th Field Artillery Brigade in Hawaii; commanded the 76th Field Artillery in Monterey, California; and, as prewar mobilization progressed, successively organized and trained the division artilleries of the 7th and 8th Infantry Divisions. He attended the field artillery advanced course in 1924, was a distinguished graduate of the Command and General Staff School in 1926, and graduated from the Army War College in 1932. He also served a tour as professor of military science and tactics at Texas A & M College; a tour as instructor in the Command and General Staff School at Fort Leavenworth, Kansas; and a tour as professor of military science and tactics at Oregon State College. In addition, he organized and commanded a Civilian Conservation Corps (CCC) camp. If he had a professional "break," it may have been the recognition he received organizing and conducting the umpire school for a major army field tactical exercise in the summer of 1939.[32]

Patterns that emerge in Sloan's biography include appreciable troop duty, twelve years as an instructor in army schools or ROTC, and the number of occasions in which he created new organizations where none had existed. Troop duty, particularly command, is the most important experience in any army. Sloan had been among the troops at each rank from lieutenant through brigadier general for a total of fourteen years. Instructor duty also sharpened professional skills: it is almost a tautology that teachers learn more than their students. The opportunity military instructors have to reflect on military topics provides invaluable professional development, and for Sloan, instructor duty paid off in other ways. When teaching in the command and general staff school from 1932 to 1936, he had the opportunity to meet, teach, and size up many of his future subordinates and peers. Duties with ROTC exposed him when in his forties to the very generation that would make up his OCS contingents. He understood these young men and what it took to develop them. He knew the difference between training, which is appropriate for units, and education, which is appropriate for one's eventual successors; words like patronage and mentorship fall under the province of the latter heading.

Sloan had created an organization out of thin air on five occasions: the 30th Field Artillery in World War I, the CCC camp, the Fourth Army Umpire School, and the 7th and 8th Infantry Division Artilleries. He had never activated and trained an entire division before, but he certainly knew something about the process.

Generals Marshall and McNair considered the selection of cadre for new divisions one of their most important missions.[33] Together these chiefs of staff picked the division commanders and ruled on nominations for regimental commanders and primary staffs. A further forty-six officers in each division were chosen by the heads of branches and services for such key positions as battalion command. The remaining cadre officers, generally majors or company grade, were less-experienced men nominated by the parent division or its army headquarters. The resulting sixty officers formed the true nucleus of the 88th's cadre.

Sloan was fortunate in his immediate subordinates.[34] Brig. Gen. Stonewall Jackson had served three tours in the Infantry School and had provided invaluable personal insights during the organization of the cadre. When Jackson was selected to command the 84th Infantry Division, the equally dynamic Paul W. Kendall, "Bull," took his place as assistant division commander. Brigadier General Kendall proved an ideal alter ego for Sloan. Sloan was a career artilleryman, with all of the technical and logistical orientation that implied. Kendall was a veteran infantryman who had earned the Distinguished Service Cross while a member of the Siberian expedition of 1918-1919. Kendall characterized himself as not as smart as Sloan, but he had keen tactical instincts that carried him into the thick of the fighting. He would engage in such heroism as crossing the Rapido River under fire to extricate 36th Infantry Division troops he was supposed to be observing, and he characteristically accompanied the flying columns Sloan detached from the division.

At the regimental level one found younger men of a similar stamp. The 349th's Col. James A. Landreth, an experienced infantryman, was noted for hs systematic, no-nonsense approach and utterly unflappable nature. Col. Charles P. Lynch took command of the 350th Infantry Regiment, the same unit with which he had served in World War I. (The World War I 88th Infantry Division, also draftee, had been assigned to a quiet sector but had managed to harry the Germans through appreciable combat patrolling.) Colonel Lynch's son would die commanding a company of the 350th in Italy. The 351st's Col. Arthur S. Champeny had won the Distinguished Service Cross leading infantry in France during World War I; he would win another leading his regiment in Italy and yet another commanding a regiment in Korea. Winning a Distinguished Service Cross in each of three wars is an unusual achievement. Colonel Champeny replaced Col. William W. Eagles, who commanded the 351st briefly before being promoted out of the job. Eagles rose to command of the distinguished 45th Infantry Division, a testimony of his caliber. The division artillery commander, Brig. Gen. Guy O. Kurtz, came to the 88th from service on high-level staffs. In particular, he had distinguished himself working for the chief of field artillery, and he was generally regarded as one of the most knowledgeable and current of his generation of artillery officers.

Chief of Staff Col. Weyland B. Augur, a masterful organizer, pulled together the division staff and its logistical establishment. When Augur, a cavalryman, left the division to organize a mechanized cavalry brigade, his G-3 (operations and training officer), Col. Robert J. McBride, moved up to replace him. McBride was quiet, competent, and diligent. He also proved to be an accomplished diplomat—or "flak absorber." When Sloan or Kendall flew into one of their occasional rages, McBride contrived to defer action until tempers cooled and reason prevailed. Conversely, when one of the subordinate commanders felt an impulse to share strong words with the generals, McBride preemptively corralled the individual in isolated conversation until he himself resolved the problem or at least until he was confident the pending exchange would take a moderate tone. In the day-to-day tasks of coordinating staff officers and logisticians, patience and firmness were McBride's trademarks. McBride was chief of staff from December 1942 through August 1946; thus, for four years he was an important source of stability and the renderer of an invaluable service—keeping the division's assertive personalities from bruising each other too badly.

Within the larger body of branch- and service-selected officers were even younger versions of the same professional caliber as the division's generals and colonels.[35] All of the sixty senior cadremen had seen appreciable troop duty, and all had attended the army school system insofar as was appropriate to their prewar rank. Most had also taught in ROTC and army schools. Thus they knew the generation that would provide company-grade officers of World War II, and they had polished their professional knowledge while in an academic setting. The sixty experienced cadre officers would educate a contingent of officers twelve times their number. These would in turn train the division. Given time, the senior officers were fully qualified to develop the junior officers, shuffle them around a bit, and get the right men in the right jobs. Americans may have been unprepared for World War II, but in their senior officers they quickly fielded an impressive combination of qualified mentors.

World War II U.S. Army personnel policies have been criticized as detrimental to the development of discipline, leadership, morale, and cohesion. Much of this criticism is misleading because it stems from inflated images of the German *Wehrmacht*, or from sociological and psychological analyses that have no foreign counterpart. We simply do not know how the attitude, motivation, and behavior of our soldiers compared with those of foreign troops. We do know that our divisions had differing personnel experiences, however, and little that has been written takes those differences into account. The Army Ground Forces divisional training program was a conscious effort at team building, designed to enhance morale, cohesion, discipline, and leadership. It envisioned a carefully chosen cadre, personnel stability, and about twelve months of unmolested training time. We have seen why personnel turbulence afflicted so many divisions and why the 88th escaped the worst of it. The 88th demonstrated the personnel system as it was intended to work. So did the 1st, 3rd, 5th, 9th, 29th, 37th, 40th, 41st, 85th, 91st, and 98th infantry divisions—all highly regarded units. Recognizing that too few divisions enjoyed stateside personnel stability, it should be noted that one that did was able to develop discipline, leadership, morale, and cohesion.[36]

Morale is a slippery word that defies precise definition. One authoritative study suggests it comes in several guises: sense of well-being, sense of obligation, job satisfaction, and approval or criticism of the unit. Insofar as sense of well-being was concerned, the draftees of the 88th, summarily off-loaded from trains into Camp Gruber, Oklahoma, were no better off than other conscripts. They didn't want to be in the army, didn't want to fight overseas, didn't want to risk death or injury, didn't want to suffer physical hardship, and didn't want someone always telling them what to do—in short, they were true to American tradition. What was more, they disliked the food, despised the living accommodations, and were lonely and homesick. Fortunately, none of this mattered much because there was a war on and neither they nor anybody else expected them to be thoroughly happy.[37]

Another aspect of morale, sense of obligation, proved more important in the 88th. American public support for the war effort was unquestioned. However much they might have preferred that someone else carry the burden, the draftees thought they were doing the right thing. To quote one Pvt. William S. Frederick, "I would like to be back home, but the country seems to have a job to do and I guess I might as well help as anybody."[38] This sense of purpose was generally vague; less than one in seven of the draftees could name three of the "Four Freedoms," and few could give a coherent discussion of the genesis of the war. Orientation classes and "Why We Fight" films were supposed to redress this lack of information, but troops absorbed such formal presentation in bits and pieces, at best. For example, the orientation program gave considerable attention to Brazil's entry into the war; Brazil demonstrated the unanimity of the civilized world in opposing Axis aggression. Nevertheless, when the 88th Infantry Division first fought alongside the Brazilian Expeditionary Force more than a few befuddled GIs wondered who these strange people were, what language they were speaking, and why they were drawing on American supplies.[39]

General Sloan's cadre could not reverse the draftee's general indifference to formal orientation programs, but over time it could subtly reinforce a sense of righteousness. Sloan was straightforward in enlisting the assistance of army chaplains and civilian clergy. He had long considered the pulpit an appropriate platform for mobilizing support in just causes. In the circumstances of World War II, many clergymen agreed with him.[40] Senior officers of the division also diligently promoted the war effort through speaking engagements in front of such organizations as local chapters of the American Legion, the Kiwanis Club, and the Shriners. They then enlisted these patriotic citizens to do such things as have a few soldiers over for dinner. It was a soldier's dream come true: a few hours relief from the regimen of camp life, a home-cooked meal—generally turkey—and the opportunity to chat with the father of the house about how depraved the Axis powers were and how badly they were going to be whipped. It didn't hurt at all if a few admiring youngsters sat in on the conversation. Army regulation insisted that soldiers wear their uniforms off post. In the nearest town, Muskogee, Oklahoma, they encountered a supportive atmosphere on the streets. This is not to mention the letters, gifts, and boxes of cookies from home. Everything the soldiers read, the *Saturday Evening Post* in the dayroom, for example, supported the war effort.[41] Movies, news clips, radio broadcasts, and commercial advertising all carried supportive themes. However vague their understanding of World War II might have been, the draftees of the 88th had no doubt who was fighting for freedom and justice against tyranny and oppression.

The sense of purpose that developed in the 88th took time in maturing. The drumfire of signals reinforcing attitudes soldiers were already disposed to believe influenced different men at different rates. Ultimately, veterans of a year at Camp Gruber accepted that they had obligations as members of an organization mobilized for a worthy purpose. Their sense of virtue could be reinforced by chance. In May 1943 catastrophic floods inundated the Muskogee area. The 88th's 313th Engineer Battalion, with attached pontoon companies and boats, snatched twelve hundred civilians from the torrent. Other units housed, fed, and provided medical support to seventeen hundred others.[42] It was morale-enhancing to do good in the world—and to find an ever more supportive atmosphere among local civilians.

Then, too, many of the draftees were at a very impressionable age, not quite adult. A single encounter could have an enormous effect. Private Sam Lepofsky, a medic, was quietly sorting through personal gear one day when General Sloan himself walked into his room. Lepofsky and everyone else assumed the posture, part attention and part petrification, customary when someone of unusual rank invades a soldier's space. Sloan looked around a little, walked up very closely to Lepofsky, and said, "You know, son, we're counting on you. Someday you'll make the difference between men living or dying." To this day Lepofsky remembers the brief encounter as a significant emotional event, the first time he had ever thought of himself as doing something important.[43] Lepofsky went on to become a medical platoon sergeant highly regarded for his energy—and occasional fisticuffs—in getting the job done.

Sloan depended heavily upon his officers to provide examples of commitment. He was a firm believer in that portion of War Department Field Manual 21-50 (*Military Courtesy and Discipline*, 1942) that read:

> There is a tendency on the part of a few officers to think too much of the personal benefits which they may derive from their status as an officer. In the interests of good discipline officers are required to wear distinctive uniforms, to live apart from their men in garrison, and to confine their social contacts to other officers. But do not make the mistake of thinking yourself as a superior individual; rather, regard yourself as one who has been accorded certain aids in order that he might best carry out the responsibilities of his office. In your relations with your men in the field never demand any bodily comforts for yourself which are denied to them. Think of yourself only after your men have been cared for.

This ideal was not always easily achieved. Soldiers were disposed to believe officers took advantage of their positions,[44] so it was important not only to be fair in fact, but also to be fair in appearance. All other things being equal, for example, officers are likely to get more mileage out of time off than privates. They have more money, are in better position to foresee opportunities, have the rank and administrative savvy to assure that the necessary paperwork stays straight, and may be in the habit of making more elaborate plans. This is not to mention hidden advantages rank brings when pursuing women or making financial arrangements. Sloan rode herd on his junior officers to see that their behavior was fair both in fact and in appearance.

A case in point seems to have been the Christmas season of 1942.

Plans for parties perked and bubbled along among the officers and their wives, yet an increment of soldiers that had training to make up was to get no furlough, and many draftees bleakly faced their first Christmas away from home. Sloan saw to it that local women's organizations had the names of all personnel remaining at Gruber. The women made sure that every soldier got a Christmas dinner invitation and boxes with gifts, cookies, and candy. Meanwhile, Sloan circulated a letter noting that frivolity was customary during the holidays and that if officers wanted to participate, they could. However, since there was a war on and so many of his comrades were already overseas—some having already made "the final sacrifice"—he himself would not feel comfortable indulging; he was going to stay home, so don't invite him, it said. In a rippling effect, many of his subordinates discovered they also would be uncomfortable if partying too heavily, and the officers' more elaborate plans fizzled. The net result was that the enlisted and the commissioned Christmas seasons were equivalently modest experiences—and that a number of junior officers considered Sloan a killjoy. The point was, no matter how innocent an officer's intentions, he must measure his every act against how it will appear to his troops.[45]

Another factor affecting the morale of the 88th Infantry Division was job satisfaction. Given that few of the draftees would have chosen to be in the army, it nevertheless proved possible to move many into jobs wherein their talents could be used. One must remember that the 88th's table of organization did call for over eight thousand infantrymen, and those jobs would be filled—with luck, by men who were satisfied with them. Many fared well as riflemen, a role that had the advantage of some machismo. The division structure also contained 60 technical sergeants, 173 staff sergeants, and 3,912 rated specialists.[46] Upon induction the draftees had encountered a somewhat hasty physical, the Army General Classification Test, and an elaborate effort to identify usable skills.[47] These initial records provided receiving units with information of considerable value when making initial assignments. The 788th Ordnance Light Maintenance Company was, for example, the direct product of induction efforts to identify mechanics and mechanical aptitude.

The most valuable commodity in getting the right man into the right job was time. Given personnel stability, the cadre of the 88th had time to try men out in various positions, to shuffle them around, and to see who worked out best where. Most jobs were modest in their technical demands, and few draftees had much of an initial idea what any of them were like. Experimentation led to the best fit possible among talent, temperament, and task. This settling-in process would have been impossible had the 88th experienced the personnel turbulence of other divisions.

Insofar as approval or criticism of the 88th was concerned, at first the draftees did not take the division itself seriously. Rumor had it that "this outfit is just a replacement division—it'll never leave Gruber."[48] This was a recognition of the fate of so many World War I draftee divisions. General Sloan tried to set aside these doubts and conjured up an exciting nickname, "Ranger Division." The draftees did not like that one—perhaps it sounded too enthusiastic—and the whole "ranger" promotional scheme fizzled. Not until the fighting in Italy would the division gain a nickname everybody liked, "Blue Devils."

Confidence that the 88th was truly a combat outfit grew slowly. As the division progressed steadily from individual training through squad, platoon, company, battalion, regimental combat team, and division maneuvers, the men became increasingly convinced that they were actually going to fight as a unit. Because few people left, the division got high marks on proficiency tests, and events seemed to be moving steadily in the direction of deployment as a unit, soldiers had less and less reason to doubt that they would be fighting alongside the men with whom they were training.[49] The growing conviction that the 88th would actually fight seems to have reached a climax when President Franklin D. Roosevelt, en route to Mexico, stopped by Camp Gruber for a visit. Characteristically, he gave considerable attention to being among the troops. He ate supper with 208 enlisted men, artfully chosen for their esprit and breadth of geographical origin, and four officers. If the president himself spoke of them as a fighting outfit, why shouldn't they consider themselves one?[50]

As was the case with morale, unit cohesion, too, took time to develop. As with any other unit, cohesion in the 88th built up from the bottom. Men felt their strongest loyalties to the handfuls of men nearest them, and the intensity of their commitment diminished with vertical and lateral organizational distance. For most, the day-to-day significance of being in the 88th was that it distinguished one from members of other organizations that were increasingly regarded as "riffraff." The truly strong bonds were to the immediate, or primary, group.[51]

One of the 88th's policies took advantage of the social mechanics involved in developing cohesion.[52] When the division was first organizing, the temptation existed to have the few cadremen who knew a specific topic teach it on a mass scale, or to rotate groups of soldiers past such individuals organized as teaching committees. This would be efficient and would provide time to further train OCS graduates and prospective junior NCOs. Sloan would have none of it; he insisted that instruction and leadership be in the hands of the chain of command at all levels from the first day of training. His formula was to have the knowledgeable men teach night classes for the apprentice leadership in whatever they were next going to need to know, then to have these junior leaders teach their own troops the same subjects the following day. Fortunately, the technical subjects proceeded from simple to complex, and the junior leaders could stay a little ahead of their men. There are hazards involved in training through minimally qualified instructors, but the chain of command was visibly present and in control from the beginning. The policy seems to have worked. When Lt. Gen. Lesley J. McNair visited Gruber, he cited morale indicators as "exceptionally good" and commented approvingly that "when spoken to, individuals were prompt in their replies. Junior officers were conducting instruction enthusiastically and with assurance."[53]

The American army has come under some criticism for scrambling men of diverse geographical origins together.[54] This mixing is alleged to have interfered with the development of cohesion. It seems, however, that region of origin was not much of a deterrent in forming strong friendships and close primary group ties. People from the same state can hate each other, and regional origin seems to have less to do with personal identity in twentieth-century America than does such considerations as social class, educational level, or vocation. No veteran I have interviewed considered the geographical origins of his comrades a problem—unless there was a language barrier as well. An endearing example of the opposite being true occurred in Italy when the 88th had to quickly conjure up mule-pack liaison teams for logistical support in the tortuous terrain. This effort threw together Missouri farm boys, who knew mules, with Italian-Americans, who knew the local language. The unlikely comrades took to each other, and the urbanite Italian-Americans took great pleasure in acquainting the Missourians with "the ways of the world," as embodied in lyrics attributed to Pfc. Sam Petralia:[55]

> Hey, Paesano! Have you gotta the vino?
> I gotta the chocolate, cigarette, caramele;
> Signorina, tu sei molta bella,
> I gotta the chocolate, cigarette, caramele.

In 1942, however, Italy was months down the road and yet to be imagined by the men of Camp Gruber. Given the stability of its personnel situation and the qualities of its cadre, the 88th Infantry Division was in a good position to sort through difficulties and train itself. It needed time to shape amalgams of men into combat units, and time it got. Alas, the 88th was one of relatively few divisions for which this held true. Largely through luck, it avoided the crippling personnel traumas experienced by other army units. Activated too late to be stripped in support of OCS or North Africa, the division embarked too early to be stripped for ASTP or in support of the battles in Europe. It received its fair share of talented cadre and enlisted filler, and its senior officers were uniquely qualified to train junior officers and cadremen. All factors considered, in personnel matters the 88th represented an ideal case for a World War II draftee division.

Why did so few other divisions enjoy such good fortune in personnel matters? One answer has been that American manpower arrangements suffered a period of chaos before they stabilized and mobilization "matured." That was not the case; American manpower arrangements remained in chaos throughout the war.[56] Indeed, the situation got worse, not better, and Army Ground Forces ultimately would consider the last division embarked to have been, through no fault of its own, the least prepared of all.[57] It is impossible to exaggerate the effect of personnel turbulence upon the efficient use of military manpower. All other personnel considerations fade in significance when compared to this single factor. Despite the War Department's failure to adequately forecast requirements for individual replacements, it remains difficult to understand the extent of the personnel turbulence that afflicted so many divisions while they were in the United States. Perhaps too many cooks were stirring the wartime broth.

3

Training: Honing the Edge

In a retrospective report on Army Ground Forces activities during World War II, Gen. Jacob L. Devers, the postwar commander of Army Ground Forces, expressed satisfaction with the training programs the draft divisions had undergone. His report acknowledged that personnel turbulence had impaired the training of these divisions, but it nevertheless held that the programs had been eminently satisfactory overall and had required few changes, except in matters of detail, throughout the war. The wartime army chief of staff, Gen. George C. Marshall, agreed and in particular cited the battlefield performances of the 85th and 88th Infantry Divisions.[1]

Marshall's own policies had made it essential that the training of the new divisions be comprehensive and thorough.[2] In January 1942 he decided not to expand the capacity of replacement training centers, although at that time these could barely provide sufficient personnel to those established divisions that already had a priority on replacements. Another of Marshall's policies directed that any voluntary enlistee be sent to the replacement training center appropriate to his chosen branch of service. The effect of these two policies during 1942 was that established divisions received, for the most part, voluntary enlistees who were basic training graduates from replacement training centers, while the new divisions received draftees who had had no training at all.[3] The training programs of the new divisions necessarily worked, as the expression went, "from the ground up."

On balance, the assessments of Devers and Marshall concerning the successes of the divisional training program were accurate. Tiny cadres of professionals had in fact used these programs to shape masses of untrained draftees into units whose combat performance measured up to standards set by the older divisions. The training programs for the new divisions were not without shortcomings, however. Cadremen were better prepared for some responsibilities than for others; some blocks of instruction were poorly taught or inappropriate; and serious omissions existed in the program as a whole. The 88th

Infantry Division itself would demonstrate the strengths and weaknesses of the training program it had undergone.

A striking characteristic of American training programs during World War II was the extent to which they were run from the center. The concept of geographically dispersed units supervised in their training by a single headquarters was hardly new,[4] but in the United States of 1942-1945 a combination of affluence and technology made possible a training program far more centralized than any before.

In former wars, commanders and senior staff representatives could visit dispersed training camps only after tedious journeys. In World War II the general use of the airplane allowed quick access to units in training. Liaison planes were available down to the division level—the higher the level of command, of course, the more extensive the aviation assets. Ever-present automobiles and command vehicles sped visitors from airfields to training sites. In 1942, Army Ground Forces teams could adequately inspect a training camp per day of travel; they became so sophisticated that they filled two large planes for a single major inspection. One planeload of senior officers attended ceremonies and gathered general impressions, while junior officers from a second plane conducted detailed inspections within their staff areas of responsibility. During its first four months the 88th Infantry Division was inspected by the commanding generals of its corps, army, and service command, as well as by the commanding general of Army Ground Forces, Lt. Gen. Leslie J. McNair. Another facet, of course, was the frequent presence of senior staff officers in the divisional training area, Camp Gruber, Oklahoma.[5]

One might have expected the division's leadership to resent so much attention. Apparently it did not.[6] The prewar army had been so small that the officers who made up the "visiting brass" and those who made up the "local brass" usually knew each other personally. If not, the inspecting teams—known as "feather merchants"—visited often enough to develop acquaintances in short order. The inspection teams did provide a genuine service; they were designed not merely to insure compliance with regulations and guidance, but also to identify problem areas with respect to logistics, personnel, and training. The 88th received valuable logistical assistance as a result of these inspections.[7] Inspections became a means whereby units could communicate both their needs and their accomplishments. Commanders wanted their superiors to see what they were doing well and to understand their problems firsthand.[8] The magnitude of the tasks facing headquarters at all levels tended to preclude pettiness in relations among them.

Improved transportation further influenced training by allowing the shuttling of personnel to and from special schools. The initial training of the cadre was the most important case in point, but selected personnel also traveled to attend courses in such subjects as land fortifications (taught at Fort Belvoir, Virginia) and antitank warfare (taught at Fort Hood, Texas). Instructors also shuttled into Camp Gruber—veterans of the North African fighting, for example—to share their experiences with the trainees.

Efficient transportation facilitated the supervision of training within the division. The table of organization for 1941 allowed 212 light command vehicles, more than enough to provide a vehicle to every commander and field grade officer. Division and regimental staffs could observe dispersed training activities daily and still fulfill administrative responsibilities at their several headquarters. Commanders covered ground quickly and were apt to turn up anywhere. Junior officers seldom found themselves isolated from several echelons of training supervision.[9]

The division's table of organization called for 1,622 vehicles in addition to the command vehicles. Because more than half of these were cargo trucks suitable for transporting troops, the 88th could readily truck troops, and thus save time, when traveling to outlying training facilities. Army Ground Forces found it could economize by locating special training facilities in such a manner that they could be reached by truck from several divisional cantonments. An example of such a facility was a mock European village in Camp Bullis, Texas. Troops trucked in to experience realistic training for urban warfare: movements through narrow streets, breaking into buildings, live-fire engagements with pop-up targets, and overhead machine-gun fire amidst TNT artillery simulators.[10]

Improvements in communications paralleled improvements in transportation. At the higher levels of command, telephone conferences allowed geographically scattered officers to participate in decisions without leaving their own headquarters. As was the case with inspections, telephone conversations deepened the personal and professional relationships of the officers involved. Within the division camp improved communications had similar effects. Camp Gruber had telephones installed in all offices down to and including company headquarters. Information could be communicated through telephone calls or, in unusual circumstances, through radio messages. Alterations in training schedules, unanticipated changes in the status of facilities, newly approved subject matter, and weather reports quickly reached the lowest echelons of command.[11]

Training films were another innovation that lent themselves to a centralized training program. In 1942, Army Ground Forces set out to produce training films that would "hold the interest of trainees long accustomed to viewing the finest Hollywood productions."[12] It is doubtful that the draftees appreciated the moving parts of the M-1 Garand rifle as much as the moving parts of Betty Grable, but the films did prove an asset in assuring uniform instruction at a time when qualified instructors were spread so thinly. Films also gave troops vicarious exposure to equipment too valuable or too scarce for allocation to training camps. To show these films Camp Gruber had five military theaters, and the 88th Infantry Division had an additional movie facility in each of its regimental areas.[13]

The Army Ground Forces training program also depended upon printed materials for dissemination. Since the nineteenth century the War Department had published training guides of one sort or another. During World War II the stock titles of field manuals and similar publications tripled. Changes in these materials were not merely quantitative; Army Ground Forces developed a genre of training literature tailored to the perceived requirements and interests of the draftees. This new literature was considered innovative by the virtue of its "comprehensible" writing and its extensive use of photographs, illustrations, and drawings. If Army Ground Forces planners expected the draftees themselves to do much reading in their new field manuals, however, they must have been disappointed. Still, officers and NCOs training the troops read the new manuals and incorporated them into training activities. The general availability of this literature did much to standardize training across the country.[14]

All the developments discussed above enhanced the ability of Army Ground Forces to supervise training, but no development was more important in this regard than the detailed, highly structured, and unit-specific Army Training Program (ATP), initially called the Mobilization Training Program (MTP). Developed on the premise that similar units should be trained in accordance with a common plan against common standards, the ATP epitomized the determination of Army Ground Forces to run its war from the center. For infantry divisions, the ATP provided four major blocks of instruction: basic and individual training (seventeen weeks), unit training (thirteen weeks), combined arms training (fourteen weeks), and maneuvers (eight weeks).[15]

Each of these blocks allocated a week to standardized proficiency tests administered by a higher headquarters. Divisions could not advance from one block into the next without having passed these tests. Units that failed usually had to repeat the entire block of instruction, sometimes under a new commander. In the 88th Infantry Division, basic and individual training concluded with tests administered by X Corps and the Third Army. Unit training concluded with a physical training test administered by X Corps, a platoon combat firing test administered by the division commander, and artillery battery and battalion firing tests administered by X Corps and the Third Army. Combined arms training concluded with battalion field exercises and combat firing tests administered by X Corps and Third Army. The division's final maneuvers were observed by the Army Ground Forces itself. Tests were rigorous, demanding, and instructive. In all of them the 88th did well.[16]

Ostensibly, the training publications of the Army Ground Forces were aids to division commanders, not absolute directives. The rigor of the proficiency tests and the consequences to a commander's career should his unit fail them discouraged straying from approved programs. However, these programs did in fact prepare a unit to pass its proficiency tests. Insofar as the skills necessary to pass the proficiency tests were those needed in combat, they prepared a unit for combat as well.[17]

In an earlier era this elaborate program of proficiency testing would have been physically impossible. In World War II proficiency testing combined with improved transportation, frequent inspections, continual staff visits, improved communications, audiovisual aids, and a massive publishing effort to create military training that was at once more extensive and more centralized than ever before. It greatly increased the ability of a few experienced men to direct the training of a much larger mass.

Given the extent to which General Marshall and his immediate subordinates intended to supervise the training of the new divisions, it is not surprising that a division's program started even before the first draftee set foot in its cantonment. Preactivation training prepared officers and enlisted cadre in accordance with detailed Army Ground Forces guidelines. The idea of building a unit around a trained nucleus of cadremen was not new, but systematic preactivation training for cadremen appeared for the first time in the War Department's activation plans of January 1942. Preactivation training fell under three headings: the training of cadre officers, the training of noncadre officers, and the training of the enlisted cadre.[18]

The cadre officers, of whom the 88th Infantry Division received 197, attended special courses appropriate to the positions they were to fill.[19] General Sloan and twelve officers of his senior staff attended a month of instruction at Command and General Staff School (Fort Leavenworth, Kansas). The assistant division commander and ninety-one infantry officers attended a month of instruction at Infantry School (Fort Benning, Georgia). The division artillery commander joined thirty-one artillery officers for a month of instruction at Field Artillery School (Fort Sill, Oklahoma). Smaller contingents of officers scattered to one-month courses at the engineer school (Fort Belvoir, Virginia), the quartermaster school (Fort Lee, Virginia), the medical field service school (Carlisle Barracks, Pennsylvania), the signal school (Fort Monmouth, New Jersey), and the cavalry school (Fort Riley, Kansas).

More significant than the wide geographic scope of this schooling was the centralizing purpose it served. Cadre officers of the 88th had already attended the military schools appropriate to their prewar ranks. This earlier schooling had provided a somewhat broad and general preparation.[20] In April 1942 the 88th's cadre officers attended courses designed to prepare them individually for their new positions. These officers knew the positions to which they were to be assigned and they learned exactly what Army Ground Forces expected of them in those positions.[21] Despite a certain lack of experience with respect to mechanized warfare and vehicular maintenance, the 88th's officer cadre was, all factors considered, as highly trained and proficient as the circumstances of the time allowed.[22] These officers had had a variety of assignments in a prewar army that, although small, had been highly professional. Many had been instructors in military schools. This pedagogical experience proved of considerable value when training the noncadre junior officers.

During the week of 19 June 1942, 427 officer candidate school graduates joined the 88th's cadre officers at Camp Gruber. Officer candidate schools experienced problems throughout the war, but their program of instruction seems to have prepared the candidates about as well as thirteen weeks would allow. As a group, the graduates proved intelligent and technically competent, although often deficient in their understanding of tactics and in their "feel" for leadership.[23]

Largely because of lack of time—less than three weeks separated the arrival of the OCS contingent from the arrival of the draftees—General Sloan's training program for junior officers did not immediately address either tactics or leadership. Instead, it first emphasized technical subjects and subjects due to appear early in the troop training program. This reinforced the technical background developed during OCS and anticipated a training strategy Sloan had found effective when activating earlier units. For several months after activation the division's junior officers taught the troops blocks of material they themselves had only recently learned. As training progressed, the junior officers attended night classes covering the subjects they would teach next. When tactics became pertinent—during the unit training block—tactics became part of the junior officer's extra-duty training program. It is no exaggeration to say that the junior officers of the 88th were part-time students who were just a step ahead of their troops throughout the training cycle.[24]

The training program for the junior officers served its purpose in that from the outset they served as both leaders and instructors. At each phase they knew as much as they needed to know at the time. This arrangement developed professional expertise and leadership experience simultaneously. Although it did not provide many opportunities for analysis or reflection, it did further centralize the entire program. No training could be more standardized than that in which fledglings received instruction mere days before they repeated it to their students.

Sloan's training program for his junior officers succeeded in part because enlisted cadremen carried most of the burdens of administration and logistics, thus freeing junior officers for training and supervision. The enlisted cadre included senior NCOs actively involved in the training of the draftees, but most enlisted cadremen were clerks, cooks, drivers, mechanics, and other types of administrative personnel. Indeed, of the 1,172 enlisted cadremen the division received, fewer than 200 were experienced line NCOs. This meant that there were far more "ninety-day wonders" (that is, OCS graduates) training troops than there were "leather-lunged NCOs," popular literature to the contrary notwithstanding.[25]

As has been discussed, most enlisted cadremen of the 88th came from the 9th Infantry Division, which had been designated as the 88th's "parent" division. Approximately two months before the activation of the 88th, the commander of the 9th selected enlisted men from its own ranks to fill cadre positions designated by Army Ground Forces. The 9th then undertook on-the-job training for these men to prepare them for their new responsibilities. Because this training occurred within an active division, the enlisted cadremen received practical experience that complemented the somewhat more theoretical preparation of officers in the army school system. The enlisted cadre joined the officer cadre at Camp Gruber during June 1942. They assumed ranks appropriate to the positions they were to fill and, after a week of further training, took over administrative and logistical responsibilities.[26]

When the 88th Infantry Division activated on 15 July 1942, it was led by men who had spent months preparing for that event. Each cadreman had recently trained for the specific job he was about to undertake. There were areas of weakness in the leadership of the new division, but it seems to have been as well prepared as time and circumstances would allow.

The arrival of the enlisted filler initiated the next phase in the division's training cycle. In the two weeks following 15 July 1942, troop trains delivered approximately twelve thousand draftees onto Camp Gruber's Bragg Railroad Siding. These were not necessarily a sight likely to inspire confidence. Hustled through induction centers, many wore ill-fitting khaki uniforms. Here a man had rolled up trouser legs and shirt sleeves in order to have the use of feet and hands; there a man exposed inches of forearm and ankle beyond the full reach of his clothes. Cloth garrison caps stood on disparately groomed heads at every conceivable angle; those too big came down to the ears like grocery bags while those too small perched precariously and tumbled off with every quick head movement. The first trains, in from Massachusetts and New York, delivered perspiring Northeasterners into the blazing Oklahoma sun. Those a little chubby and a little Nordic were true spectacles, with their lather of sweat and their flushed red faces. As the draftees muscled bulging barracks bags off the trains, they stumbled, collided, cursed, and swore—mostly in English, but in a variety of immigrant tongues as well. Twenty-nine of the draftees were not yet Americans; they would be sworn in as citizens as training progressed. In these early days of the mobilization, the appearance of new draftees varied not only because of ethnicity and physique, but also because of age. Along the dusty road to Camp Gruber, forty-four-year-old Pvt. William S. Frederick, Sr., encountered his own son, twenty-year-old Pvt. William S. Frederick, Jr. Both were taxicab drivers from Olean, New York; neither had dependents; and both had been snapped up by their local draft board. The cadremen of the 88th looked out over the disorderly swarms of draftees and saw their mission. The training of the cadre ended as the training of the division began.[27]

Formal basic training began on 3 August 1942. Prior to this the cadre broke the draftees in to the "Army way" of doing things, assuming that if they could be made to look and act like soldiers, they would begin to think of themselves as soldiers.[28] Looking and acting like soldiers meant a number of things. It started with neatness. Off went the ill-fitting uniforms and on came others of a more appropriate size. Personal preferences with respect to the garrison cap disappeared; every soldier wore his the same way atop an appropriate GI haircut. Shoe polish and brass polish became important features of daily routines. Each draftee was shown the proper way to sweep and mop a floor, then was expected to use his new skill regularly. Men were to be out of bed at 0545 and were to go from reveille formation to the latrine for a shave—whether they needed it or not. Each bed was to be tight enough that a quarter tossed upon it bounced; socks were rolled up in a certain way; personal equipment was stored in designated places; and the uniform was worn properly at all times. This standardization of the smallest details had a purpose: to subordinate the soldier's individuality to the unit of which he was becoming a part.[29]

Close-order drill was another means of subordinating the individual to the unit. The training schedule included twenty hours of formal instruction in close-order drill. During this men progressed from executing maneuvers alone—"about face," "forward march," "right oblique, march"—through executing the same maneuvers in massed formations of battalion size. Formal training represented only a part of the draftee's exposure to close-order drill; from the day they arrived, troops found that groups of men ordinarily moved about in accordance with drill procedures. Drill provided a means for efficiently moving large numbers of men and, it was thought, for conditioning them psychologically as well. On duty the draftees marched as part of a team; off duty they were to carry themselves with the erect posture and measured cadence appropriate to soldiers.[30]

Fatigue details provided another means to promote cooperation among the troops. The most famous of these details was the much-maligned KP—kitchen police—an assignment to do whatever the mess sergeant thought needed doing. The popular image of KP is peeling potatoes, a frequently assigned task given the army's wartime dependence upon that potent and versatile vegetable. KPs also loaded and unloaded delivery trucks, prepared food for the cook's use, washed dishes, and mopped out mess halls. Other fatigue details included exterior guard duty, interior guard duty, and a host of miscellaneous details best described as janitorial. Sharing these unpleasant, yet necessary, tasks was considered good for developing a spirit of cooperation and teamwork in the soldiers.

Physical conditioning was a pervasive aspect of basic and individual training. Mobilization training programs prescribed a minimum of thirty-six hours of physical training and twenty of conditioning marches for all of the division's units. Infantry regiments, understandably enough, were expected to do more of both. Physical training progressed from light calisthenics and short runs, done in uniform cadence, through difficult calisthenics and long runs. It included on-duty athletics stressing team sports and off-duty athletics stressing team sports and the combatives. Athletic activity was encouraged not merely for its own sake but was subordinated to a general training program stressing conditioning and teamwork.[31]

Obstacle courses resembled the battlefield rather than the gymnasium. The culmination of physical training was the requirement that the soldier, with rifle and thirty-pound pack, negotiate a 1,500-foot obstacle course in three and one-half minutes. Specific requirements were that he[32]

> Take off with a yell, [yelling or singing frequently accompanied physical activity], mount an eight-foot wall, slide down a 10-foot pole, leap a flaming trench, weave through a series of pickets, crawl through a water main, climb a 10-foot rope, clamber over a five-foot fence, swing by a rope across a seven-foot ditch, mount a 12-foot ladder and descend to the other

side, charge over a four-foot breastwork, walk a 20-foot catwalk some 12 inches wide and seven feet over the ground, swing hand-over-hand along a 15-foot horizontal ladder, slither under a fence, climb another and cross the finish line at a sprint.

Conditioning marches also developed physical attributes the draftees would eventually need. During the first weeks draftees undertook short marches in light gear. Distances and weight of gear steadily increased. Marches were conducted in accordance with long-standing War Department guidance, found in field manuals already familiar to the senior officers.[33] Within the 88th, marches were earnest and competitive. Rates of march provided a tangible measure of unit progress—probably more tangible than any measurement other than collective marksmanship scores. Ultimately the division's 351st Infantry Regiment received recognition from General Marshall himself when it conducted a record sixty-two-mile march in full gear in twenty-nine hours without a man falling out.[34]

In the third week of basic training the infantrymen of the 88th began firing the M-1 Garand rifle and artillerymen began firing live ammunition from their guns. Every soldier, regardless of branch, was required to "qualify" with his assigned weapon through a cumulative training process allotted more than one-hundred hours in the training schedule. Individuals and crews progressed from lectures through demonstrations, called "tables," to a qualification table fired for record. Individual soldiers repeated as much of this process as was necessary until they achieved qualifying scores.

Infantrymen qualified with the M-1; they also fired and "familiarized" themselves with the automatic rifle, the light machine gun, and the 60-millimeter mortar. Artillerymen familiarized themselves with the 37-millimeter antitank gun and the .50-caliber machine gun; all soldiers familiarized themselves with the M-1 rifle, regardless of branch. Familiarization was a systematic process akin to qualification, but it required less time and no particular score on the final firing table.

During basic and individual training, infantrymen received more than one hundred hours of instruction in individual, squad, and platoon tactics. Training progressed from lectures through demonstrations, "walk-throughs," and practical exercises. During this period emphasis was not so much on the performance of squads and platoons as on the individual roles of soldiers within squads and platoons. Soldiers learned to do such things as use cover and concealment, maintain spacing, and provide covering fire for a maneuvering element.

In addition to out-of-doors training, the 88th also gave formal classroom instruction. The training schedule devoted the following classroom time to this instruction:[35]

Military courtesy and discipline, articles of war	6 hours
Orientation ("Why We Fight," etc.)	7 hours
Military sanitation, first aid, and sex hygiene	10 hours
Defense against chemical attack	12 hours
Equipment, clothing, and shelter tent pitching	7 hours
Hasty field fortifications and camouflage	4 hours
Elementary map and aerial photograph reading	8 hours
Protection of military information	3 hours
Organization of the army	1 hour

Classroom instruction had advantages in that it could be conducted in inclement weather—in training time that otherwise might have been totally lost—and it could make use of films to compensate for instructor deficiencies. Nevertheless, it seems to have been the most unpopular of the division's training efforts, largely because it lacked immediate application.[36] Military courtesy, discipline, and the articles of war seem to have become familiar by virtue of daily contacts with the chain of command rather than through classroom instruction. Equipment, clothing, and shelter tent pitching proved to be learned on bivouacs more readily than in the classroom. Sex hygiene was more often an occasion for ribaldry than for serious instruction.[37]

The troops seem to have been unimpressed with the classroom training they received. The new divisions simply were not suited to this type of instruction. In the press of mobilization it proved impossible to provide uniformly qualified instructors, coherent cumulative curricula, or assigned readings. Army Ground Forces eventually reduced the time allotted to such instruction. Fewer than sixty of the division's training hours were lost to this classroom activity.[38]

The most pressing problem the cadre of the 88th faced during basic and individual training was in the delays the division experienced before receiving its full enlisted complement. As was the case with most other new divisions, the 88th did not build up to full strength until several months after activation. Unlike many other divisions, however, the 88th received its full enlisted complement before the end of basic and individual training. Instruction for basic and individual training could be flexibly scheduled, in contrast to later unit training blocks. A number of expedients, including overtime training and deferring some make-up instruction into the Christmas furlough period, allowed the 88th to rush latecomers through and catch them up to the training cycle. The division's unit training block began on 1 December 1942, on schedule.[39]

The unit training block of the 88th Infantry Division lasted until 28

February 1943; its combined arms training block spanned from 1 March
to 22 May 1943. Taken together, these formed continuous-process
training units of steadily increasing size, from squad to platoon, to
company, to battalion, to regiment. During unit training the instruction of the several branches was, for the most part, conducted separately. Combined arms training integrated the activities of several
branches.

The infantrymen and cavalrymen were already familiar with such
Unit training stressed instruction in the field and included little on-
duty garrison activity. The men spent increasing amounts of time
living under conditions they were likely to encounter in combat. There
was no sharp break with previous training. Squad and platoon tactics
continued; during unit training commanders emphasized the performance of units as a whole rather than the skills of individual soldiers.

The infantrymen and cavalrymen were already familiar with such
individual skills as covering by fire or advancing by bounds. During
the first weeks of the unit training block, they practiced these tactics as
units, one squad covering while another advanced by bounds. When
squads were proficient, platoons began to practice similar tactics on a
larger scale, integrating the greater firepower available in their heavy
weapons squads. In addition to infantry tactics, the cavalrymen also
practiced special techniques of scouting and screening. This phase of
unit training culminated with the Army Ground Forces Platoon Combat Firing Proficiency Test.

Artillery exercises also expanded in scale as batteries and then
battalions fired for record. This expansion was more of a change for
chains of command and fire direction centers than for gun crews, who
continued to execute the crew duties they had learned earlier. During
unit training artillery officers added variations in service practice,
cross-training with alternate weapons, motor marches, vehicle recov-
ery, and difficult traction expedients to the gun drills that had dominated basic and individual training.

The training of support troops also increased in complexity. Medical technicians advanced from practicing simple first aid to administer-
ing enemas and blood transfusions; ordnance personnel undertook
increasingly complex maintenance tasks; and signalmen attended divisional schools in their specialties. Support troops also trained as units.
The medical battalion practiced evacuating casualties over long distances through difficult terrain and simulated the movement of casualties through several levels of collecting and clearing stations.
Ordnance and quartermaster companies conducted motor marches
and bivouacs. The engineers constructed and removed field fortifications, built fixed and floating bridges, laid and breached mine fields,
built roadblocks, and constructed roads. By the time the 88th began its
combined arms training, its infantry regiments, artillery battalions,

cavalry reconnaissance troop, and engineer battalion had all trained as units in their respective combat roles.

Combined arms training welded these several components into teams capable of acting in concert as a whole. The most easily executed of the combined arms exercises involved command post training. In these, commanders and staffs worked through tactical problems while simulating the presence of personnel and equipment. Command post exercises progressed from simple terrain walk-throughs to complex division problems in which officers moved extended distances as if their units were with them. These exercises gave the officers of the several branches the experience of working together, improved tactical communications systems, and resolved problems with respect to command and staffing. Some command post exercises were rehearsals for specific regimental or divisional maneuvers.[40]

Regimental combat team exercises were the next step in the division's progression through combined arms training. In these, a regiment maneuvered with an artillery battalion and cavalry and engineer elements attached. Commanders coordinated infantry movements and artillery fires during attacks, night movements, defenses of prepared positions, and river crossings. Regimental combat teams developed particular proficiency with respect to the coordination of artillery and infantry.[41]

Division maneuvers brought together the entire division and climaxed the combined arms training block. In six separate exercises the division operated against simulated opponents or against one of its regimental combat teams while practicing attacks, defenses, and phased withdrawals. In May 1943 these rigorous, full-scale exercises concluded and X Corps observers designated the 88th as prepared for maneuvers on an even larger scale.[42]

When the 88th Infantry Division departed for its Louisiana maneuvers on 13 June 1943, it had achieved a high state of training. It also had a full complement of personnel and equipment. These advantages were not unusual for a maneuver-bound division in 1943. The 88th enjoyed another advantage as well; it had a rival.

The 88th was scheduled to maneuver against the 31st National Guard Infantry Division—the "Dixie Division"—an old division characterized as experienced and maneuver-wise. The Louisiana maneuvers of the summer of 1943 involved three "green" draftee divisions: the 95th Infantry, the 11th Armored, and the 88th. Of these, the 88th most particularly "came to regard the 31st as its own personal enemy." It is not altogether surprising that the draftees envied the old division's status; apparently the 88th's cadremen inconspicuously encouraged this nascent rivalry.[43]

Rivalry between the 88th and the 31st manifested itself in a number of ways. The draftees attempted to perform better than the guardsmen even when the two units were not maneuvering against each other. When they were, the draftees were usually reluctant to withdraw on the umpire's orders if they thought the guardsmen had not demonstrated the necessary tactical advantages. On occasion, soldiers ignored umpires altogether and fought on their own terms until officers restored order. Usually these informal battles went no further than an exchange of insults, but sometimes fistfights broke out on the line of contact.

The rivalry between the "green" draftees and the "maneuver-wise" guardsmen probably enhanced the performance of both. For the draftees, the very novelty of the maneuvers proved worthwhile. Accounts written by draftees during this period boast of poison ivy, mosquitoes, chiggers, ticks, snakes, hogs, mud, and dust.[44] Mosquitoes were big enough to drag a man out of his tent. Ticks were so numerous that soldiers spent days picking them off of each other. Chiggers and snakes stood formation with the troops. Armed guards were posted to keep hogs out of the mess areas. All this embellished unpleasantness seems to have raised morale; the draftees were proud of themselves for having graduated into the "real thing." The toughness of the environment was a psychological asset to units that had conducted training in conditions ever closer to those expected in combat. The steady advance from parade-ground drills through sweeping maneuvers across challenging terrain lent the draftees a sense of purpose and progress.

The Louisiana maneuvers began with operations on the level at which combined arms training had concluded. Divisions spent the first week conducting unopposed attacks, night movements, defenses of fortified positions, and river crossings. These exercises were followed by flag exercises in which umpires simulated the presence of opponents with flags of different sizes and descriptions. After the divisions negotiated problems without opponents, they maneuvered against each other, first in scripted problems and then in free maneuvers, or war games. Throughout the exercises umpires observed performances and teamwork.[45]

During the first river crossing of the war games, the 88th's performance received particularly favorable comment from umpires and observers. The 88th had been ordered to withdraw into Texas and defend a river line against the 31st, 95th, and 11th Armored. As it withdrew, it left a reconnaissance radio team deep within enemy territory. This tactic was unconventional at the time, as was the ad hoc radio relay net that enabled the team to report regularly to the division's G-2 (intelligence officers). The team demonstrated considerable initiative identifying troop movements and evading detection. Given ideal intelligence, the 88th easily forestalled every enemy initiative. The operation continued to be one-sided until the umpires extended the problem—and the radio team ran out of food and water. The men of the division, and most maneuver observers, regarded this defense as a triumph for the 88th.[46]

Few people had more experience than General Sloan in the subtleties of looking good on maneuvers. His reputation as an accomplished military pedagogue had in part resulted from his organization and direction of the Fourth Army Umpire School for a major command post exercise conducted during the summer of 1939. This exercise became something of a model when the War Department increased the resources allocated to major maneuvers; the experiences of 1939 and 1940 were drawn upon extensively in planning the maneuver programs of the new divisions. Maneuver umpires followed standard procedures and checklists in a complex rating system with which Sloan, formerly the trainer of umpires, was familiar. Sloan was not a man to take unfair advantage of his special knowledge, but he could legitimately lay stress on things likely to influence the appraisal of the umpires.[47]

As the summer wore on, the 88th continued to perform well and look good in the maneuvers and exercises. In particular, observers cited the division for the "marching power" of its infantry, the proficiency of its artillery, and the teamwork demonstrated by its component elements. In fact, the division so impressed umpires and observers that Army Ground Forces changed the embarkation sequence of the participating divisions and selected the 88th to precede the 31st overseas. This particular adjustment, which moved a new division ahead of an old one, was the principal reason the 88th was the first of the draftee divisions overseas.[48]

It is worth noting that the four divisional participants in the Louisiana maneuvers of the summer of 1943 saw their first combat in widely separated theaters: the 88th entered combat in the mountains of Italy; the 31st, in the jungles of Mindanao; the 95th, on the plains of northern France; and the 11th Armored, in the rolling terrain of Southern France.[49] Although fighting in different environments, all had undergone similar training programs—with certain obvious exceptions in the case of the 11th Armored. This serves to illustrate the standardization that was at once a strength and a weakness of the Army Training Program.

The 88th Infantry Division, given its stable personnel situation and relatively minor logistical problems, provides an excellent case study of the training program Army Ground Forces envisioned for the new divisions. The 88th's performance on the Louisiana maneuvers validated that program insofar as it could be tested short of combat. Progress from induction through basic, individual, unit, combined arms, and maneuver training had been steady and purposeful. The draftees had practiced individual skills time and again, and their physical conditioning was superb. Units repeatedly conducted challenging field exercises under realistic conditions and commanders at all levels matured during a year of rigorous training. All factors considered, the 88th seemed likely to give a good account of itself anywhere in the world.

For all the strengths of the Army Training Program, there seem to have been weaknesses as well. The draftees themselves commented that training they received in the classroom proved to be of little value. The soldiers of the 88th practiced most combat skills thoroughly, but there were some skills—combined arms support for patrolling, tactical communications, integration of tanks and infantry, land mine warfare, and close air support—that were not stressed much during the division's training, but that proved particularly important in Italy. A program applicable everywhere in general is not necessarily the ideal program for somewhere in particular.

The test of combat would dramatically demonstrate both the strengths and the weaknesses of the training program the 88th had undergone. The creators of the highly structured and rigidly centralized Army Training Program had anticipated most of the division's training needs. Unfortunately for the draftees and for the draftee divisions, they had not anticipated them all.

4

Logistics: The Strongest Card

Of all the arguments that advocates of an incremental expansion of the army made against a *levee en masse*, the most persuasive were logistical. Even if masses of men could be summarily levied and properly trained—which Uptonians by no means conceded—of what use would they be in modern warfare if ill-equipped? Also, how much would it cost to feed, house, uniform, and supply so many poorly equipped troops?[1]

More than any other military activity, logistics require planning and preparation. Americans have a poor record in preparing for war while still at peace. Until the tenure of Elihu Root as secretary of war (1899-1904), American mobilization planning had been superficial at best. Even after Root it was not entirely adequate; the American Expeditionary Force in World War I could not have taken the field without supplies and munitions from the British and the French. After World War I, American logistical planners assumed that in the event of another war they could break out stockpiled World War I inventories, reopen World War I cantonments, and thereby accommodate whatever personnel the situation demanded. Within a decade, however, mobilization plans became more sophisticated and mobilization planners more attentive to logistical considerations. Gen. Douglas MacArthur and Gen. Malin Craig, the U.S. Army chiefs of staff from November 1930 to October 1935 and from October 1935 to August 1939, respectively, undertook extensive mobililization planning and stressed logistics as a critical consideration in that planning.[2]

MacArthur, Craig, and their principal subordinates believed that the American political process would not allow for much more than planning during peacetime; they further believed that the logistical assets initially available in another war would be slender at best. They thought it would be wiser to concentrate assets on hand into established formations rather than to dissipate them uselessly among a host of new ones. Mobilization Plans 1933, 1938, and 1939 featured modest rates of military expansion along Uptonian lines and favored the use of established, rather than levied, divisions in operations overseas. Draftee divisions were never eliminated from mobilization plans, but they seemed destined to be second-rate combat units or administrative headquarters training and transporting replacements for established divisions.[3]

Pressed by events in Europe and East Asia, President Franklin D. Roosevelt initiated active preparedness measures as early as 1938. The army, augmented by the National Guard and the draft, underwent a relatively orderly expansion from 1939 through 1941. In the aftermath of Pearl Harbor such a modest rate of expansion could not, of course, continue. There was no alternative to general mobilization and the rapid rates of expansion draftee divisions represented. Nevertheless, the draftee divisions that went overseas were no worse fed, housed, uniformed, or equipped than the established divisions that preceded them. The American logistical achievement in World War II defied suppositions that mass mobilization would produce a rabble in arms. Not even the most ambitious of the prewar mobilization plans suggested that a year of involvement in a general war would end with an American army half as large as the one actually raised, equipped, and supplied during 1942.[4]

The magnitude of this achievement should not obscure the fact that the new divisions did encounter logistical difficulties, even if they never were without adequate food, clothing, fuel, ammunition, shelter, and equipment. The difficulties encountered were not the simple matters of quantity anticipated by the Uptonians nor, given the circumstances, were they inevitable.

When considering logistics, one often thinks first of supply—the tons of rations, clothing, personal equipment, petroleum products, repair parts, vehicles, ammunition, and miscellaneous materials necessary to support an army. It was with respect to this single logistical function of supply that the critics of the *levee en masse* had made their gloomiest predictions and, in the outcome, proved widest of the mark.[5]

Mobilization plans of the 1930s were dominated by the concept of M-day—Mobilization Day—a distinct division between peace and war. Contrary to War Department expectations, American political leaders undertook extensive preparations for war—quasi-mobilization, if you will—while America was technically still at peace. Indeed, after the fall of France in June 1940, congressional preparedness measures were in some respects more ambitious than those recommended by the War Department. War Department planners feared that enthusiasm and special interest would interfere with the orderly expansion they hoped to achieve.[6] Popular literature to the contrary notwithstanding, [7] December 1941 dawned on an American army well prepared for mobilization insofar as supply per se was concerned. Consider in turn each of the r..ajor classes of supply: rations, clothing and personal equipment, table-of-organization equipment, petroleum products, and ammunition.[7]

Rations never proved a serious problem for the fifteen million men America ultimately put under arms. The Subsistence Branch, the most firmly entrenched of all quartermaster sub-bureaucracies, had been a separate service until 1912 and had retained a tradition of autonomy through numerous administrative realignments, including the wholesale quartermaster reorganization of March 1942. Stable bureaucracy produced stable procedure. Cadremen of the 88th were familiar with Subsistence Branch's prewar rationing system and with its recommended diet. War brought few changes in procedures for divisional personnel, so the 88th's cadremen found themselves fully prepared for their responsibilities with respect to rations.[8]

There were some changes in rationing procedures at levels higher than that of the division, but these went smoothly because the related plans had existed for some time. Indeed, they had already been exercised in part to support the Civilian Conservation Corps. Upon mobilization, the prewar local crediting system called the garrison ration ceased, and the Subsistence Branch assumed direct responsibility for all purchases through a system of regional market centers. Centralization allowed the Subsistence Branch, in concert with other agencies, to reconcile competing demands, control prices, and limit profiteering. Because all the army had to do to procure an adequate supply of food in midcentury America was to buy it, it is hardly surprising that quantitative subsistence demands were easily met.[9]

Given the demands on the nation's transportation system during mobilization and the advantages of mass purchasing, the Subsistence Branch found it could best guarantee efficient rationing through stockpiling. Within the United States it stockpiled rations against a facility's anticipated forty-five-day demand. Thus requisitions were not against meals on the table but against stockpiled inventories. Indeed, rationing seems to have been, if anything, unduly lavish. One quartermaster study estimated the army threw away $117 million worth of food in one year.[10]

The 88th Infantry Division, like other new divisions, lacked neither food nor cooks to prepare it. Cadre cooks ranged in numbers from one-third to one-half of the total numbers required by tables of organization, and every company had an experienced cadre mess sergeant. With high percentages of experienced personnel, mess teams had little difficulty training their draftee cooks while at the same time supporting their assigned units.[11]

The experience of the 88th with respect to petroleum products also posed few problems. Quartermaster's Fuel and Heavy Equipment Branch was never as stable as the Subsistence Branch, and effective centralized administration of petroleum products disappeared altogether for a time. Nevertheless, the 88th was well enough served even by the uncoordinated systems that remained. General Sloan was on cordial personal terms with the commander of the Eighth Service Command, near the Texas and Oklahoma oil fields, and with representatives of the Missouri Pacific Railroad, which serviced Camp Gruber. This may have helped; the division never seems to have been short petroleum products.[12]

In December 1942 the War Department seemed to rediscover petroleum as a strategic commodity requiring centralized administration and procurement. This rediscovery, one might note, coincided with President Roosevelt's establishment of the Petroleum Administration for War to cope with nationwide disorganization in the petroleum market. By May 1943, War Department reorganizations led to the establishment of the Fuel and Lubricants Division, a thoroughly integrated commodity organization handling all aspects of army petroleum use. Although the 88th was not suffering prior to the reorganization, petroleum supplies were clearly more secure thereafter.[13]

Fuel handling posed as few problems as did fuel supply. Each of the separate services had developed its own equipment for transporting and pumping fuel. The many different types of such equipment caused some difficulties in obtaining spare parts, but these difficulties had minimal effect. The widely issued five-gallon can, variously called the "jerry can" or the "blitz can," provided an alternative means for dispensing fuel. Because fuel itself had been standardized in 1941, it could be readily transferred between vehicles, dispensing systems, and branches without contamination.[14]

Another class of supply that posed few problems was ammunition. Rounds in all calibers were sufficiently available to conduct the lavish firing exercises of the Army Ground Forces training schedules. The War Department had stocked small-arms ammunition in considerable quantity after World War I. Training demands and physical deterioration caused stocks to dwindle, but in early 1940 the army still possessed over one-half billion usable rounds. This situation improved further because of an enormous increase in American productive capacity during the eighteen months preceding Pearl Harbor, increases spurred by Roosevelt's decision to aid the British after Dunkerque. The notion of America as an "arsenal of democracy" did not altogether appeal to War Department planners, who preferred to hoard resources rather than divert them to the British. However, without these highly visible shipments overseas—and the resultant equally visible declines in ammunition stockpiles—it is doubtful that congressional leaders would have voted funds for plant expansion on the scale they did during 1940 and 1941.[15]

Given a blank check, the Ordnance Corps and its civilian contractors managed to exceed all realistic needs by the summer of 1942. In the words of the chief of Ordnance's Industrial Service, the army had small-arms ammunition "running out its ears." In June 1942, the month before the 88th activated, the Industrial Service recommended major cuts in production plans and reduced 1942 goals from the astronomical figure of fifty-nine billion rounds to the more realistic but still lavish figure of twenty-three billion rounds.[16]

Concerning small-arms ammunition, accountability presented more problems to the 88th than did supply. Far from worrying about too little ammunition, commanders worried about "surreptitious ammunition," ammunition that was not in its proper place and thus was available for misuse.[17] Camp Gruber's ordnance warehouse carefully doled out ammunition on the day it was to be used. When leaving ranges, troops shook out clothing and equipment to find rounds inadvertently lodged in cuffs, pockets, or folds, and cadremen inspected barracks and vehicles daily for lost rounds.

The supply of artillery ammunition proved somewhat more troublesome than did that of small-arms ammunition. There had been technological changes, in particular increased calibers, between the wars, so World War I stocks were of little value. Production, procurement, and distribution all involved unique complexities. The Ordnance Corps' sixty government-owned, contract-operated artillery ammunition plants were not able to exceed all reasonable demands until August 1943. Despite these problems, artillery production fulfilled the actual needs of the army even if it was tardy in fulfilling army desires. The 88th fired all required training missions with live ammunition and did not suffer significant shortages during the course of its training cycle. Despite some miscarriages with respect to forecasting during 1944, American artillery ammunition production sufficed to meet the actual needs of Allied forces fighting overseas and of new divisions training at home from the summer of 1942 until the conclusion of the war.[18]

The 88th Infantry Division also suffered little from shortages of clothing and personal equipment, other than in a few of the less-common sizes. The 88th did not, however, train with all the items of clothing and personal equipment it later was to use in combat. This was largely because of the lag between development and procurement; obsolescent clothing and personal equipment continued in production to meet mobilization needs even as replacement items were coming into production to modernize the inventory. Belated changes in headgear and uniforms were not particularly consequential—not even the dramatic change from khaki to olive drab. Belated developments in army footwear led to more serious problems. Until November 1943, footwear consisted of the basic service shoe and leggings. The combination was inadequate in cold, wet weather and was so difficult to put on and take off that it contributed to poor foot hygiene. The 88th suffered a high incidence of trench and immersion foot during cold, wet weather until early 1944, when the improved high-top combat boot with overshoes and shoepacs became generally available.[19]

Virtually all items of personal equipment—field packs, barracks bags, ammunition carriers, shelter halves, sleeping gear, entrenching tools, web gear, etc.—changed significantly during 1942 and 1943. Each individual change was, in itself, not particularly consequential, but the cumulative effect of changes and delayed deliveries was to render the draftees less familiar with their final issue than they otherwise would have been. This was especially true of new gear designed for cold, wet weather. Water-resistant "duck" material replaced cotton or wool. Shelter halves and barracks bags (later, duffel bags) increased in volume and closure. Sleeping bags replaced wool blankets as standard sleeping gear, and the waterproof poncho became an item of general issue. The draftees of the 88th had little opportunity to train with this new equipment prior to embarkation, and they suffered from this lack during the winter of 1943-1944.[20]

Insofar as the 88th Infantry Division was concerned, supply shortages predicted by critics of the *levee en masse* failed to materialize with respect to four of the five major classes of supply. Food, petroleum products, and ammunition were available in abundance. Clothing and personal equipment were adequately available insofar as quantity was concerned, and initial qualitative shortcomings were not particularly related to the numbers of draftees being inducted. Of all the classes of supply, only table-of-organization equipment involved the 88th in quantitative shortcomings.

Table-of-organization equipment, hereafter referred to as T.O. equipment, consists of items neither expendable nor uniformly available for personal use: vehicles, weapons, tools, auxiliary-powered equipment, communications equipment, etc. Extracts from the table of organization of June 1941 appear in Tables 1 and 2. As was true with other classes of supply, T.O. equipment benefited from massive increases in congressional funding beginning in May 1940. T.O. equipment was more complex and required more production lead time than did other classes of supply; it was not yet available in sufficient quantities to meet the requirements of 1942. Production of most items peaked in 1943, before the draftee divisions went overseas but well after most of them had activated.[21]

Table 1. Table-of-Organization Weapons Specified for
Infantry Divisions, June 1941

	Div HQ and MP Co	Recon Troop	Sig Co	Inf Reg (3)	Div Arty	Eng Bn	QM Bn	TOTAL
Machine gun, cal. 50	—	—	—	36	—	—	—	36
Machine gun, cal. 30, heavy	—	32	—	72	—	18	—	122
Machine gun, cal. 50, heavy barrel	—	17	—	—	60	—	—	77
Machine gun, cal. 30, light	—	3	—	54	—	—	—	57
Submachine gun, cal. 45	—	35	—	—	—	—	—	35
Antitank gun, 37 mm	—	—	—	36	24	—	—	60
Gun, 75 mm	—	—	—	—	8	—	—	8
Howitzer, 105 mm	—	—	—	—	36	—	—	36
Howitzer, 155 mm	—	—	—	—	12	—	—	12
Mortar, 60 mm	—	—	—	81	—	—	—	81
Mortar, 81 mm	—	—	—	36	—	—	—	36
Pistol, automatic, cal. 30	183	147	261	3,543	2,685	118	262	7,199
Rifle, automatic, cal. 30	—	—	—	375	—	—	—	375
Rifle, cal. 30	47	32	—	6,297	516	—	50	6,942

SOURCE: *Tables of Organization of Infantry Units* (Washington, D.C.: Infantry Journal, 1941), T.O.70.

Insofar as T.O. equipment was concerned, the War Department gave units in training a priority behind units embarking and lend-lease shipments to Allies. Until July 1943 new divisions were programmed to receive only 50 percent of the T.O. In fact, they received somewhat less (see Table 3). This equipment did not arrive prior to activation, as planned; instead, it trickled into division cantonments over a period of months.[22]

Just how consequential were these temporary shortages of T.O. equipment? The issue became a matter of heated dispute between the Army Ground Forces and the Services of Supply. Insofar as the 88th is concerned, the evidence indicates the shortages were of little consequence. The division's training schedule developed in such a manner that actual requirements for T.O. equipment were minimal at first and increasing with time. The division was seldom short of equipment it needed to train or support itself. Unlike some earlier divisions, it never had to simulate the presence of vehicles, weapons, or equipment.[23]

Vehicles were available in sufficient numbers even if those numbers fell short of T.O. authorization; the table of organization provided

Table 2. Table-of-Organization Vehicles and Special Equipment
Specified for Infantry Divisions, June 1941

	Div HQ and MP Co	Recon Troop	Sig Co	Inf Reg (3)	Div Arty	Eng Bn	Med Bn/ Surg	QM Bn	TOTAL
Air compressor	—	—	—	—	—	3	—	—	3
Assault boat	—	—	—	—	—	10	—	—	10
Lighting set	—	—	—	—	—	1	—	—	1
Earth auger	—	—	—	—	—	1	—	—	1
Water purification unit	—	—	—	—	—	4	—	—	4
Scout car	—	16	—	—	—	—	—	—	16
Bulldozer	—	—	—	—	—	3	—	—	3
Ambulance, ½ ton	—	—	—	—	—	—	36	—	36
Sedan	—	—	—	3	1	—	1	5	10
Motorcycle, solo	—	12	—	—	—	10	3	—	25
Motorcycle with side car	8	—	2	78	43	4	—	5	140
Trailer, 1 ton	2	—	10	45	123	23	4	53	260
Trailer, 250 gal	—	—	—	—	—	—	7	—	7
Motor tricycle	—	7	—	—	—	—	—	—	7
Truck, ½ ton, carryall	—	—	6	—	—	—	—	—	6
Truck, ½ ton, command	2	1	3	99	69	5	8	13	200
Truck, ½ ton pickup	—	1	15	—	—	10	6	6	38
Truck, ½ ton, radio	—	—	6	6	10	—	—	—	22
Truck, ½ ton, weapon carrier	3	—	—	321	46	—	—	—	370
Truck, ½ ton, cargo	6	—	30	129	—	—	21	—	186
Truck, 1½ ton, dump	—	—	—	—	—	53	—	—	53
Truck, 2½ ton, cargo	—	4	1	—	276	1	15	63	360
Truck, 1½ ton, cargo with winch	—	—	—	—	—	—	3	—	3
Truck, 2½ ton, wrecker	—	—	—	—	—	—	—	2	2
Truck, 4 ton cargo	—	—	—	—	16	3	—	—	19
Truck, 4 ton wrecker	—	—	—	—	—	—	—	2	2

SOURCE: *Tables of Organization of Infantry Units* (Washington, D.C.: Infantry Journal, 1941), T.O.70.

lavishly. Some observers, Winston Churchill among them, thought the table allotted more trucks than any division could possibly need. It certainly provided for more trucks than were necessary to support a division training at a fixed installation. At full T.O. strength, the 88th

Table 3. Table-of-Organization Equipment on Hand for New Divisions, April 1943

Item	Percentage of allowance on hand
Flame thrower, M-1	15.4
Binoculars, M-3	52.2
Light armored car, M-8	6.8
Submachine gun, cal. 45	67.2
Howitzer, 105 mm	71.5
Mortar, 60 mm, M-2	54.9
Mortar, 81 mm, M-1	52.9
Rifles and carbines, all types	46.7
Rifle, BAR	30.1
Truck, 2½ ton, 6 x 6	48.3
Radio set, SCR-510	35.1
Switchboard, BD-71	48.2
Vehicle medical kit	100.0

NOTE: These figures represent totals across Army Ground Forces. Figures varied from division to division depending upon the point reached in the training cycle and the priority for embarkation.

SOURCE: Army Ground Forces letter (subject: equipment for Army Ground Forces) to commanding general, Army Service Forces, 6 April 1943, AGF 401-1, MMRB, National Archives.

would have had 707 vehicles with a cargo capacity of one ton or more, and a net cargo capacity of 1,514.5 tons, this to support approximately 14,000 men.[24]

During basic training the only transportation requirements within the division involved hauling supplies several miles from Camp Gruber's railroad sidings to division facilities, or hauling ammunition somewhat greater distances to firing ranges. The vehicles on hand proved more than adequate for such modest requirements. By the time major field problems increased demands upon transportation assets, the numbers of vehicles available had also increased. When the 88th left Camp Gruber to participate in its Louisiana maneuvers, it had all the vehicles specified in the table of organization. Thus, although the 88th did not receive its full allowance of vehicles until eleven months after activation, the division always had sufficient vehicles to meet transportation requirements. Indeed, the 88th had enough transportation to support not only its own needs but also nondivisional activities and facilities at Camp Gruber.[25]

Shortages of weapons proved only a little more troublesome than shortages of vehicles. Every rifleman in the 88th had his own weapon.

One out of every two crew-served weapons was available from the beginning, so crews rotated in such a manner that each crew trained upon an actual weapon. Troops trained as individual crews first; by the time mass fire was called for by the training schedule, more weapons were available to support the training.[26]

Shortages of communications equipment did not adversely affect the division's conduct of the Army Ground Forces training program, although inexperience with certain aspects of tactical communications later proved a handicap.[27] Units did well on proficiency tests using communications arrangements—such as runners and mounted messengers—that later would prove inadequate in combat. In addition, communications equipment the 88th used when training was obsolescent by the time the division moved overseas.

At first, auxiliary-powered equipment was in short supply—for example, kitchen ranges, generators, specialized engineer equipment, pumps, and mobile maintenance shops. Fortunately this equipment, designed for field use, was duplicated by fixed facilities at Camp Gruber, so training did not suffer. The division used garrison equipment during its first several months. By the time the division had to support itself in the field, adequate auxiliary-powered equipment was available and had been issued.

In summary, shortages of T.O. equipment did not much affect the progress of the 88th Infantry Division through its training cycle. It was true that equipment arrived later than mobilization planners had hoped, that equipment shortages complicated scheduling, and that there was no real substitute for the experience of operating at 100 percent of T.O. Nevertheless, equipment on hand sufficed to meet actual needs, and equipment shortages never forced major adjustments in the training program.

If T.O. equipment shortages posed no serious problems, the maintenance of T.O. equipment, especially vehicles, did. None of the armies that fought World War II seems to have been fully prepared for the technological demands of modern warfare.[28] The U.S. Army did as well or better than any in keeping up its equipment—and that of a number of allies as well—but proper maintenance did not come easily to the fledgling draftee divisions.

The 88th Infantry Division was no exception. Within a month of activation, 5.1 percent of the division's vehicles had been "on deadline" (inoperable) for more than three days—they were so unserviceable reasonably expedient repairs could not make them available for use. After another month the rate of three-day deadlines climbed to 9.3 percent. Much larger numbers of vehicles were deadlined for briefer periods. An inspector general's report entitled the "Automotive Disability Report of the 88th Division" was sufficiently alarming to receive attention at the highest levels of the War Department.[29]

The body of correspondence—smoke and thunder—generated by this report causes one to believe neither the Services of Supply nor the Army Ground Forces fully comprehended the maintenance problems the new divisions faced. Indeed, an officer familiar with the army's present vehicular maintenance apparatus is apt to marvel that the 88th's deadline rate was not even higher.[30] The new divisions faced critical problems: an uneven distribution of organizational mechanics, an utter lack of effective support maintenance within divisions, and repair part shortages.

Organizational mechanics are the men who first address maintenance problems that go beyond the driver's capability. While the driver can carry out most checks and services and many simple repairs and diagnostics, he generally consults a mechanic for complex checks, services, repairs, and diagnosis. Mechanics are ordinarily assigned to units in proportion to the vehicles in the T.O. The ratio presently used in the army, after decades of experience, is about one mechanic for every eight wheeled vehicles.[31]

In 1942 experience in wheeled vehicle maintenance was still slight. Each branch and service had its own notions concerning the numbers of mechanics necessary to support its vehicles, ranging from one mechanic for twenty vehicles in the case of Signal Corps to one mechanic for three vehicles in the case of Mechanized Cavalry. Even more erratic than these perceived needs were the actual distributions of experienced mechanics assigned to the various branches and services. Mechanized Cavalry, Artillery, and the Medical Corps had adequate automotive maintenance expertise available. Signal, Quartermaster, and Infantry had ridiculously few experienced mechanics. The Corps of Engineers naively assumed that the general mechanical aptitude of their NCOs qualified them to be motor sergeants without any immediate need for trained mechanics. Table 4 shows how many mechanics were involved, both cadre and draftee, in the division's maintenance establishments and the numbers of vehicles they were expected to maintain. As it suggests, the mechanics of the 88th represented an amalgam of branch and service solutions that bore little relationship to actual maintenance needs.[32]

Support maintenance within the new divisions was in even greater disarray than was organizational maintenance. Support maintenance performs repairs beyond the capabilities of organizational mechanics. Within the newly activated 88th, vehicular support maintenance was virtually nonexistent. Prewar bickering had equivocally settled such

Table 4. Automotive Maintenance Personnel, New Divisions, July 1942

Unit	NCOS	Cadre EM	Draftees	Draftees to cadre	Vehicles
Div HQ	1	1	1	1:2	11
Sig Co	0	0	3	3:0	61
Recon Troop	1	2	6	2:1	22
QM Bn	1	0	48	48:1	91
Eng Bn	6	0	12	2:1	74
Inf Reg	3	0	63	21:1	558
Div Arty	29	21	62	6:5	417
Med Bn	5	1	9	3:2	90
Overall	46	25	204	3:1	1,324

SOURCE: *Tables of Organization of Infantry Units* (Washington, D.C.: Infantry Journal, 1941).

responsibilities upon two branches—quartermaster for vehicles of essentially civilian design (for example, trucks) and ordnance for equipment without civilian counterparts (for example, tanks). This compromise represented extensions of quartermaster's traditional role as a procurement service and ordnance's traditional superintendency of military technology. All but sixteen of the division's T.O. vehicles were trucks, ambulances, or sedans, and thus they were quartermaster's support maintenance responsibility. The 88th Quartermaster Battalion Maintenance Platoon consisted of one NCO and forty-four raw draftees. It was hardly prepared to provide adequate support maintenance to hundreds of vehicles.[33]

Even if it had had an adequate maintenance establishment, the 88th still would have suffered from armywide shortages of repair parts. During 1941 and 1942, quartermaster procurement emphasized purchasing vehicles, which filled out organizational tables of organization, rather than spare parts, which did not. At a time when the battle-wise British characteristically purchased spare parts worth 35 percent of the value of new vehicles ordered, the Quartermaster Corps doled out 5 percent. An initial lack of standardization in the army's vehicle fleet complicated inadequate spare parts stockage. Prewar standardization efforts had run afoul of congressional suspicion and vested interest. Not until the summer of 1941 could the army negotiate contracts specifying design; before then it had to purchase vehicles "off the street." During 1942 the newly mobilizing divisions coped with 330 makes of vehicles requiring a total of 260,000 different repair parts. Civilian jobbers who had supported prewar vehicle fleets were overwhelmed by the mobilization, and civilian spare parts stockages proved inadequate for military use.[34]

Table 5. Changes in Cadre Automotive Maintenance
Personnel, July 1941 to November 1942

Component unit	Raw change	Percent change
Div HQ	+1	+33
Sig Co	+2	+ Infinity
Recon Troop	−1	−33
QM Bn	0	0
Eng Bn	0	0
Inf Reg	+24	+800
Div Arty	−5	−10
Med Bn	0	0
Ord Lt Maint Co	New Unit	+Infinity

The maintenance situation of the 88th would have been even worse than it was had it not been for several factors. Virtually all of the division's vehicles were new. The 88th did not immediately receive its full T.O. authorization, so its ratio of mechanics to vehicles was always higher than that provided for in the table. Transportation requirements and, thus, vehicular wear were moderate during the first several months of training. The chain of command at all levels carried on preventative maintenance—"motor stables"—with a persistence that in part compensated for lack of expertise. Finally, most operators had sufficient mechanical know-how to assist the harried mechanics.[35]

The 88th could not have muddled through indefinitely. The ultimate resolution of underlying maintenance problems required the direct intervention of the War Department. Recognizing the uneven distribution of organizational mechanics, that department cut across branch and service lines and redistributed cadre automotive maintenance personnel.[36] By November 1942, the changes reflected in Table 5 were complete; that is, branches and services short of mechanics received more and those with excesses were trimmed.

The War Department's answer to the absence of support maintenance was equally heavy-handed and equally effective. Brushing quartermaster prerogatives aside, Lt. Gen. Brehon B. Somervell, commanding general of the Services of Supply, designated ordnance as the service into which support maintenance was to be concentrated. The Ordnance Corps was already well along in a program for training maintenance companies to support major headquarters. It found itself able to graft similar units—Ordnance Light Maintenance Companies—onto the new divisions as well. The new divisions simply had not been an appropriate environment in which to train teams of maintenance specialists. Ordnance absorbed the Motor Transport Service of the

Quartermaster Corps, trained new maintenance companies separately, then transferred these companies intact into the new divisions. Support maintenance that had not existed suddenly appeared in the 88th.[37]

The Services of Supply handled spare parts shortages with another simple expedient: more money. Purchases leaped from $50 million in 1941 to $730 million in 1942 and $1.36 billion in 1943.[38] This last figure equaled 27 percent of the value of new vehicles purchased. By late 1942 massive purchasing yielded salutary results—adequate spare parts stockages—in the new divisions.

The effects of changes with respect to maintenance cadres, support maintenance, and spare parts were soon apparent in the 88th Infantry Division. By January 1943 the three-day deadline rate dwindled to 2.5 percent, even though training schedules by then placed increasingly severe demands upon the division's vehicles.[39] Except during certain peculiarly demanding combat situations, vehicle maintenance never again became as severe a problem as it was during the division's first six months.

Of all the logistical problems faced by the new divisions, inadequate automotive maintenance was the most dangerous and required the most time, energy, and adjustment to resolve. The 88th fared relatively well, for all its deficiencies. In other divisions maintenance deficiencies proved even more severe.[40]

One should note that the conditions that weakened automotive maintenance within the new divisions did not affect the maintenance of weapons, communications equipment, or auxiliary equipment to the same degree. In part this was because of the nature of the equipment itself. Vehicles have more moving parts that undergo more vibration, wear, and tear. One estimate holds that three mechanic man-hours went to automotive maintenance during World War II for every mechanic man-hour spent on the maintenance of other equipment.[41]

In the case of communications equipment, a single separate service, the Signal Corps, supervised procurement, maintenance, and use. While the Signal Corps encountered problems during mobilization, it did succeed in providing sufficient numbers of trained maintenance personnel to the new divisions. Indeed, it had undertaken to train all communications personnel for the new divisions, including radio and telephone operators. In the press of mobilization this proved too ambitious, but the corps managed to provide a cadre of forty-three out of the ninety-seven communications maintenance personnel the division required.[42]

Weapons also proved to be more easily maintained than automotive equipment. The Ordnance Corps was responsible for procurement and support maintenance. The corps provided two NCOs and six mechanics to each of the new infantry divisions. Although each infantry company designated a promising draftee as "armorer-artificer," in actual practice NCOs in the tactical chain of command provided the organizational maintenance of small arms. There had been an ample supply of machine guns and rifles in the interwar army, and newer models represented no important technological changes. Cadre NCOs proved sufficient to assure the maintenance of small arms, with only occasional reliance on armorer-artificers or ordnance support maintenance mechanics. Heavier weapons were a more difficult proposition, so Artillery provided one cadre artillery mechanic to each of its firing batteries, one mechanic to every four guns. Initially, the mortars and antitank guns of the infantry regiments were maintained without specialists. This posed fewer problems than one might have expected, since mortars virtually defied the need for maintenance and antitank guns were not at first available for issue.[43]

Weapons maintenance demands within an infantry division had not changed much since World War I. It was true that there had been technological innovations, but these did not require a reorganization of maintenance arrangements. The same mechanics had to learn to do some slightly different things. In the cases of some weapons, maintenance techniques and records of repair parts stockages dating as far back as the Civil War continued to be useful.[44] In 1942 the army was prepared to maintain the weapons it had on hand.

Auxiliary-powered equipment also seems to have been readily maintained, although hauling this equipment around placed increased automotive maintenance demands on the carriers. Original designs, prototypes, and models of auxiliary equipment generally called for aluminum and stainless steel. During the first years of the war, these metals were designated as critical, so manufacturers substituted heavier metals. The weight of the M1937 field range, for example, increased from 138 to 178 pounds. Changes in auxiliary equipment thus increased demands upon carriers at a time when automotive maintenance was already the division's greatest single problem.[45]

One might conclude a discussion of the maintenance problems of the draftee divisions by reflecting on the maxim that armies prepare for the last war rather than for the next one. Weapons and auxiliary equipment had not changed much between the wars, so the army of 1942 was prepared to maintain them. Of the communications equipment, the wired was old and the wireless, new. The wired presented relatively few maintenance problems and, unfortunately, the wireless did not reveal the full extent of its vulnerabilities until the division was actually in combat. Radically increased numbers of vehicles posed maintenance problems with which the army was not prepared to cope. Quantitative changes were so great that they became qualitative; divi-

Table 6. Changes in Divisional Logistical Personnel, June 1941 to
November 1942

	1941 Cadre	1941 Draftee	1941 "Student-teacher" ratio	1942 Cadre	Cadre percent change
Automotive maintenance	71	204	3:1	92	+30
Administrative & clerical					
Ammunition	6	23	4:1	4	−33
Finance	14	0		12	−14
General	128	97	4:5	158	+23
Postal	0	13	13:0	4	+ Infinity
Supply	99	78	4:5	115	+16
Food services	282	277	1:1	275	−2
Legal services	4	0		4	0
Chemical	4	0		4	0
Police	2	65	32:1	2	0
Religious	18	4		14	−22
Communications	65	939	14:1	62	−5
Medical					
Specialist	111	124	1:1	93	−16
Nonspecialist	5	365	77:1	20	+300

sions, new and old alike, were forced to rebuild automotive maintenance establishments after demolishing the ramshackle provisions
they had inherited from the past.

Maintenance was not the only logistical service within the 88th
plagued by shortages of trained personnel or inequities in their distribution. Few of the logistical services escaped a period of change and
adjustment with respect to cadres and personnel allocations before the
composition of both stabilized late in 1942. Table 6 summarizes the
changes that proved necessary between June 1941 and November 1942.
As it indicates, only cadre provisions for military police, legal assistance, and chemical services remained unchanged in 1942.

Logistical services showed a high interchange between civilian and
military skills. The War Department attempted to utilize technical
skills the draftees brought with them, and the new divisions seem to
have been better able than the old to find useful vocational experience
within their ranks. For certain services, such as those of meteorologist,
draftsman, carpenter, welder, musician, gymnasium manager, recrea-

tion specialist, or instrument specialist, there were no cadremen, and the draftees themselves were the only source of talent. The potential richness of the draftees' experience is exemplified in the division's response to its rabbi's request: he wanted, as an enlisted assistant, a Jew who could drive, service a jeep, type, sing, and play a portable organ. The New York contingent of the enlisted filler contained ten men who possessed this unlikely combination of characteristics.[46]

Logistical personnel also often received support from local civilian agencies and businesses. This proved particularly important during the initial months, when the division was not yet prepared to support itself. The Muskogee Veterans Administration Hospital treated a total of 2,314 personnel while the Camp Gruber Hospital was being organized. Victory Bus Lines, expanded from two to fourteen vehicles by enterprising businessmen, provided transportation between Muskogee and Camp Gruber. Civilian contractors installed and initially operated the telephone system servicing Camp Gruber. Local realtors housed married service members; local jobbers maintained and serviced auxiliary equipment; local clergymen provided religious services; local policemen detained the errant and rescued the lost; and, of course, local businessmen supplemented the division's recreational program with facilities and diversions of their own. Camp Gruber was never entirely dependent upon military resources for its own logistical support.[47]

Army Ground Forces found it necessary to augment cadre provisions for that collection of logistical functions best described as administrative and clerical. Even those increases proved insufficient to meet the administrative and clerical demands of 1942. Ultimately it proved necessary to establish special schools within the division to train administrative and clerical personnel. Given the increased material demands of World War II, schooling for supply sergeants proved particularly necessary.[48]

One should note that administrative and clerical cadremen, responsible for training subordinates, were usually inexperienced themselves. Often they were merely promising young men who had been in the service a brief period before being selected for the 88th. Fortunately, the personnel chosen to be clerks, often designated AGCT Class I, were exceptions to the general rule that soldiers do not learn much about their jobs by reading. All of these men were literate, and many were well educated.[49] Clerks, whether cadre or draftee, did much to train themselves. Army regulations provided them detailed administrative guidance: technical manuals with examples of correspondence and administrative actions, standard forms outlining administrative actions, and electrical messages dictating the format of specific reports. Grizzled first sergeants and harried sergeant majors may not have fully understood the paperwork involved, but they valued their clerks' contribution—in particular, the appeasement of higher headquarters—enough to provide them that special genre of patronage traditionally associated with orderly rooms.[50]

Finance and postal services were exceptions to this policy of self-instruction because they required more standardization than did the other clerical tasks. The 88th's postal clerks received considerable training and follow-on attention from the Post Office Department. The division's entire finance contingent trained *en bloc* at the Army Finance Center (Fort Benjamin Harrison, Indiana), then transferred bodily into the new division. These functions were too important to be left to the good intentions of the 88th's partially trained cadremen or to their capability to teach themselves over time.[51]

Clerics of another type, the chaplains, proved readily available in the new division. Each division received fourteen chaplains, for the most part officers drawn directly from civilian life. This could cause problems. General Sloan himself once stormed into a group of officers in whom he detected a lack of military bearing—they wore their uniforms poorly, were milling around purposelessly during the duty day, and, worst of all, none of them called the group to attention to salute him. Outraged, Sloan collared the group as a body, "raising hell" with them for their slovenly behavior. Shortly, to his surprise and embarrassment, he learned that the objects of his tirade were a contingent of chaplains new to the army and recently arrived at Gruber. He resolved to put such direct commissions into a special training program before they exposed themselves to the division.[52] The chaplains' personal assistants came from the enlisted filler and experienced somewhat less culture shock.

Chaplains had a military as well as a religious role in the draftee divisions. The public statements of General Sloan, his principal subordinates, and the chaplains themselves indicate that they considered crusading zeal and evangelical fervor important components of the American will to fight.[53] Commanders and chaplains worked in concert within the division and in promoting the war effort in communities surrounding Camp Gruber.[54] The division's head chaplain acknowledged that his role was to enhance the draftees' motivation and morale as well as their spiritual health.

The draftee's physical health was cared for by a medical establishment that initially was uneven in quality. The individual medical skills of physicians and technicians, for the most part drawn directly from civilian practice, was of a high order.[55] These men proved more than competent to train the additional medical technicians specified in the table of organization. The division's total medical establishment, however, required considerable nonspecialist activity as well. Nearly four hundred ward attendants, litter bearers, drivers, cooks, and clerks in the medical units also had to be organized and trained. Medical officers were not altogether suited for this task, largely because of the more properly medical demands on their time, their relative lack of military experience, and, in some cases, their nonmilitary tastes and temperaments.

The division surgeon recalls an incident wherein four veteran army wives observed an officer with his felt hat on backwards, accoutrements scrambled, pants pressed sideways, and trousers three inches too high. They correctly assumed that he was medical. On another occasion General Sloan had his jeep jerked to a halt because it had just passed a captain who failed to salute. Confronted by the bantam Sloan, the embarrassed doctor apologized and explained that he thought generals traveled in long black limousines; he never imagined he would encounter a general in such a vehicle as a jeep. The weight of training nonspecialists necessarily fell upon nonspecialist cadre NCOs. Of these, the medical battalion originally had only five. This number proved inadequate and increased fourfold during 1942. With greater numbers of NCOs, the training of the medical battalion progressed far more satisfactorily.[56]

Signal Corps was another service wherein cadre technicians were sufficiently numerous but cadremen to train nonspecialists were not. The NCOs who trained the draftee wiremen, radio operators, switchboard operators, and signal vehicle drivers were, for the most part, line rather than signal NCOs. Communications personnel were so directly integrated into the units they supported that the chains of command within those units assumed responsibility for them. This must have contributed to discipline, to a sense of belonging, and to the mastery of common skills, but it also must have reduced the exposure of these signalmen to signal-specific training.[57]

Collectively considered, shortages of trained logistical personnel and inequities in their distribution caused the 88th an array of reasonably manageable problems. Except in the case of automotive maintenance, the division was able to work its way through to satisfactory resolutions without much outside help. There was a great deal of talent among the draftees; personnel stability allowed that talent to surface and settle into appropriate slots. It also allowed the draftees sufficient time to be trained by someone—including themselves—even if that someone was not the cadreman initially designated for the task.

The physical quality of the Camp Gruber cantonment illustrates another type of logistical problem that troubled the new divisions: hastily built quarters. Between January 1939 and December 1941 the War Department's cantonment construction program kept pace with the then moderate expansion of the army. This prewar construction effort faced and for the most part overcame a number of difficulties, the most embarrassing of which was a feud concerning responsibilities between the Quartermaster Corps and the Corps of Engineers. On 1 December 1941, President Roosevelt signed a bill transferring cantonment construction from the quartermasters to the engineers. The transfer was to be effective on 16 December. The Japanese attack on 7 December placed radically increased construction demands squarely upon an agency in transition. At the time of the bidding on Camp Gruber, the engineers had not had sufficient time for the preliminary work their procedures required. They had not done the detailed planning that would have allowed them to define construction needs and costs accurately.[58]

Manhattan Construction Company–Long Construction Company, an organization with considerable experience in defense construction, won the Camp Gruber contract. Its bid was twenty-eight million dollars, four million dollars higher than the Corps of Engineers estimate. Manhattan-Long produced results quickly. In April 1942, Camp Gruber was 10 percent completed; by July the cantonment was finished. Construction moved along at a rate of one building constructed every forty minutes. The hastily assembled buildings conformed to a standard plan: large bays with little interior sectioning, unfinished pine board interiors, painted wooden exteriors, and virtually no insulation. Construction safety requirements had been abridged for the duration of the war although, curiously, a regulation issued by the surgeon general to minimize contagion prevented double bunking in troop billets. This considerably reduced the efficiency with which space could be used. The buildings themselves were comfortable enough during the summer of 1942, but somewhat less satisfactory in the winter that followed. The simple, wooden shells did house relatively sophisticated utilities and equipment; subcontractors installed an electrical system, plumbing, a telephone system, five motion picture theaters, and impressive arrays of modern kitchen equipment.[59]

Had the time necessary for detailed topographical research been available, it probably would have become apparent that the plans for Camp Gruber provided inadequate roads and parking. The access road connecting Camp Gruber with Muskogee and the outside world was too narrow for the volume of traffic moving over it, and it was impossible to keep well drained and repaired. Within living memory, the Cookson Hills wherein Gruber was located had been a favored hideout for outlaws and public enemies. For them the attraction had been inaccessibility. After heavy rains the camp was often cut off altogether. Within the camp, roads were of marginal quality and insufficient hardstand parking existed for the division's trucks, tractors, and guns.[60]

Sloan recognized these problems when he first visited the construction site in April 1942, but his efforts to redress them proved ineffectual. Manhattan-Long had no incentive to undertake construction in excess of that originally contracted for. Pressed by an accelerating construction program, the Corps of Engineers had little interest in further research or negotiation for such peripheral construction. The Oklahoma State Highway Department promised to improve the access road, then reneged. These oversights became an embarrassment to the 88th. The 2,149 vehicles of the new division put a severe strain on surface routes and motor parks. The condition of the access road led General Sloan and the Muskogee Chamber of Commerce—which also had an interest in routes to and from Camp Gruber—into heated confrontation with state highway officials. Mud in Camp Gruber's motor parks, and the attendant maintenance complications, came to the attention of Gen. Leslie J. McNair himself. Sloan enjoyed more flexibility with respect to construction needs when his own engineer batallion was trained and equipped. Until then he made do with the Camp Gruber he had received: a marginal facility that cost too much.[61]

The logistical problems faced by the new divisions were not the mere matters of scale predicted by Uptonian critics of a *levee en masse*. Far from being caught entirely unprepared on M-day, American legislators had funded preparedness measures that were well advanced by the time of Pearl Harbor. Supply *per se* was not a critical problem for the new divisions. Rather than choosing between a small, well-equipped army or a large, ill-supplied army in 1942, the War Department was able to achieve a large, well-supplied Army. Mobilization planners did not fully appreciate the implications of modernization, however. Logistical services that had changed little between the wars, such as weapons maintenance or food services, found themselves in less turmoil than did those most subject to the pressures of modernization, such as vehicle maintenance.

All factors considered, the American logistical mobilization for World War II must number among the greatest of the nation's military accomplishments. The problems and waste were vast; so was the achievement. Neither problems nor waste were inevitable, but they were readily enough resolved or endured as the nation prepared to exert its military might overseas.

5

The Movement Overseas: Keeping the Edge

The 88th Infantry, the first American draft division into combat in World War II, took over a sector of the Italian front on 5 March 1944[1]—twenty months after its activation and twenty-eight months after the Japanese attack on Pearl Harbor. The American draft divisions did not weigh heavily in the balance against the Axis powers until the summer of 1944, two and one-half years after the United States entered the war.[2]

Why did the United States take so long to deploy its newly mobilized divisions overseas? Some of the reasons for delay have already been discussed. The War Department considered the twelve-month training cycle an indispensable prelude to the entry of the draft divisions into combat. Divisions usually progressed from this into multidivisional maneuvers lasting about a month. Thus, a division moving on schedule through its training cycle was not prepared for deployment until thirteen months after activation. Additional delays might be caused by personnel transfers or failures to meet the exacting standards of tests administered at the conclusion of every training block. The 88th progressed through its training cycle on schedule and was designated deployable in August 1943, thirteen months after activation.[3] Seven months later it finally reached the Italian front. What did the division do during those seven long months?

Among the first issues to suggest themselves to War Department planners concerned with overseas movement was the problem of command supervision.[4] The War Department was ultimately responsible for overseas movement, but subordinate headquarters were more directly involved. In the Zone of the Interior the immediate subordinates of the War Department were the army's three great, often feuding, fiefdoms: the Army Air Forces, the Army Ground Forces, and the Army Service Forces. Each of these agencies had its own vast complement of installations, facilities, subordinate commands, units, responsibilities—and its own sense of prerogative. Because the Army Air Forces had little to do with the preparation and deployment of ground combat troops, the major headquarters most involved with the draft divisions were the Army Ground Forces and the Army Service Forces.

Throughout the war the Army Ground Forces and the Army Service Forces—the first responsible for personnel and training, the second for logistical support—worked in tandem. Their mutual cooperation was more effective, all factors considered, than one might have expected of two such bureaucratic behemoths, but differences could not always be easily reconciled. These differences were sometimes functional, since Army Ground Forces stressed training and Army Service Forces stressed logistics. Other times, they were related to the competitions for facilities, since the Army Ground Forces controlled training cantonments and maneuver areas, while the Army Service Forces controlled railways and ports of embarkation.[5]

The confusion that could develop during embarkation had been amply demonstrated in the autumn of 1942. The overseas movement of Task Force A, led by Maj. Gen. George S. Patton, Jr., became an administrative nightmare. Some of the difficulties encountered by Task Force A were inevitable, but most probably could have been avoided if the several agencies involved had cooperated more effectively. Whatever his merits as a field commander, Patton was not suited to the delicate task of developing habits of cooperation among supporting agencies.[6] The preparation of Task Force A was characterized throughout by defective coordination and indignant recrimination.[7]

After its sobering experience getting Patton overseas, the War Department set about developing a consistent program detailing the responsibilities of commanders and agencies involved in overseas movements. This activity resulted in a thirty-four-page directive, promulgated on 1 February 1943, labeled POM (Preparation for Overseas Movement). This established definite responsibilities and greatly facilitated planning and preparation.[8]

Insofar as command arrangements were concerned, POM subordinated units to different headquarters at different times during the course of their movements.[9] Draftee divisions served under the Army Ground Forces until the conclusion of their twelve-month training cycle. Army Ground Forces alerted a division three months prior to its proposed embarkation date. This alert notification initiated specific, detailed activity for which the division's responsibility was divided, part of it to its army headquarters (Army Ground Forces) and part to its service command (Army Service Forces). When embarkation was imminent, the designated port commander, a member of the Army Service Forces, called the unit to port. The port commander assumed supervisory responsibilities while the unit remained in the port of embarkation. Once the unit was on the high seas, it reverted to the direct control of the War Department until the receiving theater assumed command.

The details of POM represented an effective series of compromises between the training-oriented Army Ground Forces and the logistics-oriented Army Service Forces. On receiving the POM directives, a division undertook a specific sequence of activities, some of which favored training and some, logistics, regardless of the headquarters to which it was assigned at the time.

Once alerted, the 88th, in accordance with POM, undertook several weeks of training even more intensive than it had previously undergone. This intensive training was facilitated by the division's transfer to Fort Sam Houston, Texas, in the first week of September 1943. Here the 88th received priority in the use of the nearby Camp Bullis training area, a sophisticated facility featuring mock European villages, pop-up targets, live ammunition, and pyrotechnic training aids. Camp Bullis was famous not only for the innovativeness and realism of its training, but also for the size and persistence of its ticks. Here the draftees found "tick-picking" buddies indispensable; if they still retained any modesty they quickly shed it in their desperation to be rid of the pests. After a brief period of intense training, the attention of the division turned to logistics. During October the activity of the 88th was, for the most part, given over to inventory, issuance, maintenance, packing, shipping, and the turnover of property remaining behind.[10]

Maintaining reasonable standards of property accountability was difficult at best throughout World War II. The logisticians of the 88th had to account for millions of dollars of property, including far more T.O. equipment than had ever been issued in any army, anywhere. The 88th initiated its POM property accountability with a massive inventory—a "show-down inspection"—to identify "original shortages" within component units. Some of these original shortages were reconciled from stocks within the division. The remaining, or unreconciled, shortages were compiled into "initial lists of shortages" in sextuplicate. Of these six copies, one was retained and one was forwarded to each of five officers: the G-4 (supply officer) of the Third Army, the Eighth Service Command, the G-4 of the Army Ground Forces, the Stock Control Division of the Army Service Forces, and the appropriate chief of a supply service (quartermaster in the case of a boot, ordnance in the case of a gunner's quadrant, etc.). These agencies reviewed the initial lists of shortages to assure that they represented reasonable property losses during the course of the training cycle—assuming shortage items had been issued in the first place—then canvassed their own resources to assist in making the shortages good.[11]

During the period in which the division reconciled shortages of the property it was to take overseas, it also prepared to turn in property it was to leave in the Zone of the Interior. In addition to cantonment facilities, this property included the division's general-purpose vehicles. The Army Service Forces, conscious of the limitations of Allied shipping, had determined that such vehicles should be shipped separately, disassembled and in bulk. Bulk shipments were consolidated in depots overseas, then issued to incoming units as they arrived. Often this equipment was shipped directly from the factory and first assembled overseas.[12]

As did most draftee divisions, the 88th transferred the vehicles with which it had trained in the United States to the Army Service Forces, shipped without such equipment, then drew an entirely new issue of vehicles overseas. These arrangements had advantages for all concerned, but there were disadvantages as well. Units following the 88th through the training cycle had to use equipment increasingly worn each time it was passed on, or "bumped." Units such as the 88th, which transferred general-purpose vehicles and shipped organizational weapons, had to do without this equipment during the months required to move overseas.[13] This lack of equipment affected the state of training.

Equipment that was to accompany the division also had to be cleaned, serviced, packed, and stored. Soldiers served as packers, drivers, and stevedores, while officers assumed the responsibilities of overseers and shipping clerks in what proved a tedious process. This unglamorous logistical activity served the needs of the Army Service Forces far more than it furthered the training of the draftees and their cadremen. During October the division abandoned training efforts altogether while it met the logistical demands of POM. Inventories were necessarily repetitive since each major reconciliation initiated yet another listing of shortages. Division wags complained of "show down and short arms scheduled . . . daily." Preparing vehicles and weapons for turn-in was also a lengthy process; the packing details came to be compared with slave labor.[14]

The tedium was in part relieved by preembarkation furloughs. In accord with Army Ground Forces guidance, troops with homes in the Mississippi Valley received ten-day furloughs, while those from outside it were given fifteen days. Preembarkation furloughs staggered between 6 September and 24 October in such a manner that enough troops always remained available to provide fatigue details. Furloughs had an important effect on morale, since many of the draftees had not seen family since induction and few had been home since the Christmas season of 1942. They traveled in uniform and almost invariably encountered expressions of support for the war effort and their role in it. At home they were heroes to the children and recipients of unprecedented respect from their fathers and other older men. If they could get over their mothers' anguished looks upon parting, the trip was almost fun.

Even a document as detailed as POM could not have anticipated all requirements, so supplementary directives and hastily convened staff conferences were as much a part of the movement overseas as they were of training or combat. This unprogrammed activity was vulnerable to personalities. Unanticipated demands strain the time and resources of commanders who think their time and resources are already stretched to the limit. Staff officers and bureaucrats whose directives have been overlooked can never be sure that they are not being deliberately ignored. The effectiveness of coordination beyond that required by POM depended to a considerable extent upon the personalities of the officers involved. General Sloan and his chief of staff, Col. Robert J. McBride, consciously acted with an easy gentility that "made friends fast."[15] Their professional philosophies made no allowance for personality conflicts, and they did not permit their subordinates such indulgences either. Unlike Task Force A, the 88th Infantry Division enjoyed the personal goodwill of those in charge of the service commands to which it was assigned, supporting civil agencies, and the several installations in which the unit was based.[16] These good relations doubtless facilitated the many coordinations necessary as the division moved overseas.

As must have been the case with every other unit on its way to combat, the state of training of the 88th Infantry Division deteriorated en route. After the Louisiana maneuvers of July and August and the brief flurry of intensive training in September 1943, the 88th could do little unit-level training until it reassembled overseas. The month of October was given over to logistical preparations and furloughs, after which, without most of their equipment, the units of the 88th would trickle after each other along the rail lines to Camp Patrick Henry, Virginia, their port of embarkation.

During this period without meaningful unit training, the 88th's state of training suffered even further because of its second major instance of personnel turbulence (the surrendering of a cadre to the 11th Airborne Division being the first). This arose from requirements that the division embark at T.O. strength and that it release for reassignment men who could not meet the rigorous age and physical requirements of POM overseas screening physicals. These preembarkation losses were in addition to routine personnel losses accumulated during the course of the training cycle because of injuries, illnesses, selected reassignments, and discharges for cause. All sources considered, the personnel shortages of the 88th came to 2,057, or about

15 percent of the division's authorized manpower. Plans specified by POM called upon the division's parent army, the Third Army, to make up these shortages within fifteen days.[17]

Even under ideal circumstances the new men would have faced the usual integration problems of individual replacements. In addition to routine integration problems, however, the draftee divisions also risked receiving disproportionate numbers of undesirables in their preembarkation replacement contingents. Personnel shortages in fighting units or in those en route to combat were often reconciled by stripping men from units not yet prepared to embark. Troops thus gained were at various levels of training, and often they already identified with their original units. What was worse, commanders of the stripped units too often culled out their poorest troops for transfer. Contingents of "bolos" greatly aggravated integration problems in the receiving units. A replacement training center contingent tended to be a balanced cross-section of young men; the balance in stripped-off contingents depended upon the scruples of the commanders who gave them up.[18]

General Sloan was alert to the possibility he might receive undesirables from other units. Accompanied by the adjutants and personnel officers of the division, Sloan met the replacement train at the railhead on the day his preembarkation replacements were to arrive. He had guards posted and ordered that no one was to leave the train until the records of all had been screened. Technically, troops belonged to their original units until they debarked and were processed in. In a short time Sloan's adjutants and personnel officers established beyond doubt that the train was filled with the problem soldiers of the unit that had dispatched them. It was "wall-to-wall bolos" without one man in five "fit to pull KP." Sloan ordered the train to return whence it had come—without a man aboard ever having set foot in his cantonment.[19]

Sloan's flagrant act of refusing replacements precipitated stormy command and staff sessions in a number of headquarters. Commanders cursed and swore at Sloan's intransigence while the Third Army staff frantically attempted to gather another group of seventeen hundred replacements within their fifteen-day deadline. Fortunately, Sloan was good at mending fences and he avoided prolonging the controversy. He soon received seventeen hundred fully qualified replacements from the 86th Infantry Division—not, incidentally, the unit from which the rejected contingent had been drawn.[20]

Beginning 25 October 1943, the units of the 88th Infantry Division, including the partly integrated preembarkation replacements, traveled in relays by train from Fort Sam Houston, Texas, to Camp Patrick Henry, Virginia. Camp Patrick Henry was a secured area, which restricted movements because of space limitations and security precautions. The perimeter was heavily guarded and men were forbidden to move freely or to refer to unit designations, even when training. The post was suited for only the most basic sort of training; even this proved difficult because so much time had to be spent on preembarkation personnel actions, immunizations, inventories, inspections, and uploading.[21]

Army Ground Forces recognized that a unit's training deteriorated in transit and at ports of embarkation. It recommended speedy transit and a maximum of two weeks in the ports. Army Service Forces found these specifications difficult to meet, for shipping dates were approximations based upon the anticipated availability of transportation. Increments of the 88th departed for North Africa on 2 November, 3 November, 19 November, 23 November, 7 December, and 17 December. Thus the division phased its units through Camp Henry with less than a month in the port itself, although always with more than two weeks. This was somewhat better than average, as port movements went. All these increments closed to Casablanca by 27 December 1943.[22]

Once on the high seas, the division's opportunities for training did not improve. Troops bunked five high on canvas hammocks filling all the space available in the lumbering liberty ships. Deck space also was limited. Safety requirements kept men belowdeck except during daylight, so troops passed the long winter nights belowdeck in an atmosphere reeking of sweat, damp equipment, and sometimes vomit. The situation aboard ship would have offered few possibilities for meaningful training even had the troops been fit. As it was, the draftees of the 88th encountered the health hazards associated with major troop movements. The trip across the Atlantic took three weeks for all but those fortunate enough to cross in a week on the converted luxury liners *Empress of Scotland* and *HMS Andes*. Immediately before embarkation a virus swept through the congested Camp Henry cantonment and temporarily disabled thousands. Half the division eventually went to bed rest, ashore or at sea, and five hundred of its soldiers were hospitalized. Seasickness also set in. Soldiers could lie down on their hammocks through the worst days of seasickness, but the atmosphere was stifling and the power of suggestion so great that vomiting became contagious. Soldiers could also get up onto deck for fresh air, recognizing that they might have to make a run for the railing if the ship took a sudden lurch. Most troops took the latter alternative, and made what wags referred to as "the Atlantic crossing by rail."[23]

As if these temporary debilitations were not trying enough, the division narrowly escaped an outbreak of spinal meningitis. Division surgeons making daily inspections of the crowded holds identified the initial symptoms of two cases. They isolated these patients early enough to prevent further contagion. The patients received extensive doses of the not yet fully understood "wonder drugs" and survived both the disease and the treatment. An epidemic of spinal meningitis in the crowded holds would have been nothing less than catastrophic.

As the voyages wore on, the stateside virus ran its course and men gained their "sea legs" as well. Physical illness gave way to the tensions of prolonged confinement as the greatest threat to morale. Attempts to conduct training or calisthenics did little to relieve the monotony. A divisional parody of "Thanks for the Memories" rhapsodized: "Of training on the way, of decks that swing and sway / Of thieves and crabs and bayonet stabs / And a swell Thanksgiving Day."

Some of the fights that broke out in the fetid holds took an unexpected twist, for men began squabbling over the theretofore maligned fatigue detail of KP. Kitchen police duty provided temporary escape into the comparatively luxurious facilities reserved for the merchant marine crew. It also guaranteed more food to satisfy renewed, at times voracious, post-illness appetites. Shipboard provisions specified only two meals a day to the soldiers, this because of reduced physical activity, limited tonnage, and the administrative complications of serving three meals a day. Reduced rations were hardly a problem for the seasick, but when appetites returned even master sergeants pulled rank on lesser grades to make the KP list.[24]

Rather than shipping directly to Italy, the 88th would debark at Casbalanca, travel by rail to a staffing and training area about seventy-five miles south of Oran, then move by sea to Italy from Oran. The War Department considered the Gibraltar area too dangerous for the lumbering troop ships. Although the diversion through Casablanca required a 650-mile trip in boxcars through the Atlas Mountains, it had some redeeming features. Several days of rest and recreation at Casablanca were certainly welcome. Casablanca's camel caravans, wrecked French battleships, mysterious veiled women, colorful bazaars, and ostensibly off-limits sections received ample attention from the not-altogether-cosmopolitan assortment of draftees. Movies provided additional entertainment, and the mess halls of Camp Don B. Passage represented a considerable improvement over shipboard fare. When rest and recreation led to rowdiness, some of the new arrivals became familiar with Camp Passage's prison facility, Music Hill. Officers made the point that disciplinary standards would be even more severe overseas than in the United States.[25]

After those days of rest, recreation, exercise, and decent meals, troops crowded into boxcars for the trip to Oran, forty to a car. A single lyster bag provided water in each of the boxcars and meals consisted, for the most part, of unheated C rations. Many a soldier shivering under a single blanket and bumping along through the frigid winter nights of the Atlas Mountains may have longed for the warm, fetid holds and hot, if skimpy, meals of the liberty ships.

General Sloan was understandably unhappy with what he saw of his division as it off-loaded into the muddy staging and training area near Oran. In three months, two of them spent in actual transit, the division had lost the edge demonstrated in its Louisiana maneuvers. One soldier out of eight had never maneuvered with the division at all. The training of the others had suffered from the prolonged inactivities of transit, the time devoted to logistical preparation, and the recent lack of organizational equipment. To General Sloan, ever the stern ped-agogue, the condition of the division suggested only one response—the time-honored "big buck-up," an intense period of training and inspection to "whip a unit back into shape."[26]

Sloan realized that his division might be stranded for weeks be-cause of the vagaries of Allied shipping in the face of competing priorities and Axis threats. In fact, the 88th remained near Oran for more than a month. Seizing this opportunity for training, Sloan used the French Foreign Legion's Bedeau Cantonment south of Magenta. Here the empty vastness of the Atlas Mountains offered an ideal environment in which to retrain for the rigors of Italy. For weeks the infantry regiments maneuvered against each other through the rugged terrain while artillery, engineers, and logistical units struggled to render support. In particular, units reviewed land mine warfare, marksmanship, demolitions, small-unit operations, crew duties, and night operations. Even in the absence of organizational equipment—personal weapons were at all times available—the challenge of the terrain and the pace of the training whipped the division back into shape.

Soldiers again became hardened to life under canvas in inhospita-ble conditions, and they relearned the skills involved in caring for themselves and their equipment. Along with conventional field expe-dients, enterprising draftees discovered the properties of a local bev-erage called *Eau de Vie*. Versatile enough to drink or to serve as heating fuel, it relieved two shortages at once. One did have to take precautions against its fiery taste and unpredictable volatility, however.

Magenta exposed the division to many of the environment and leadership challenges it would encounter in Italy, including peddlers, pilferers, and camp followers. Theft seemed endemic, peddler and pilferer were often the same person, and local prostitutes were so degraded they virtually guaranteed infection. One wholesome alter-native to these temptations came with the arrival of the division's Red Cross Clubmobile. Attached from Magenta until the end of the war, this unit consisted of four attractive young women who provided soldiers with doughnuts, coffee, entertainment, and somewhat circumscribed feminine companionship. It was hoped that glimpses of the girl back home might help the draftees resist the temptations they would encounter in the fleshpots of the Old World. Four girls could hardly console fourteen thousand soldiers, but their smiles and services do seem to have exerted a disproportionate effect on morale.

The Magenta interlude, extending from the last week of December 1943 through January 1944, proved invaluable to the 88th. During this intensive training in rough terrain, the division recovered from the prolonged deterioration of overseas movement. Indeed, some participants considered the exercises in the wintry Atlas to have been the finest training the division ever had. Unlike many other divisions, the 88th debarked into the combat zone within two weeks of intensive retraining.

As the 88th prepared for its somewhat risky voyage from Oran to Naples, attention swung to the question of when, where, and under what circumstances it was to enter the front lines. The complete replacement of an entire division with another along the Italian front was no easy task, so sentiment developed in Fifth Army headquarters for detaching components of the 88th to reinforce the badly worn regular and National Guard divisions already in Italy. Even as General Sloan pushed his division across the Mediterranean, he unhappily reflected upon the fate of most World War I draftee divisions—liquidated upon their arrival in the combat theater.[27]

While at Magenta, Sloan dispatched an advance party to facilitate the division's deployment either as a unit or as piecemeal reinforcements. On 26 December this advance party, consisting of officers and NCOs from each component unit and led by the assistant division commander, Brig. Gen. Paul W. Kendall, scattered through front-line American units in Italy. The advance party was to become familiar with the actual front-line situation so that on its return it might carry a leavening of experience to each company, battery, and headquarters of the 88th.

The advance party gained experience quickly. General Kendall won the Silver Star when he became involved in the 36th Infantry Division's bloody attempt to cross the Rapido River on 20-21 January 1944. One advance party NCO, caught in a German air raid, was killed in action. By the time the 88th arrived in Italy, it already had seasoned "pilots" scattered along the Italian front.[28]

Once the main body was finally under way, its transfer from Oran to Naples went smoothly. One French and ten British ships shuttled the division in three convoys between 1 February and 21 February. On the first night out, German planes intercepted the first convoy as it cleared Oran's harbor defenses. One ship, containing no personnel or equipment associated with the 88th, went down. This was the only battle damage during the voyages. Once in Naples, units bivouacked overnight in the College of Costanza Ciano, then trucked to the vicinity of the 88th Infantry Division's new headquarters at Piedmonte d'Alife.[29]

Once all units closed to Piedmonte d'Alife on 21 February, the circumstances of the 88th's eventual deployment became a critical issue. Fifth Army headquarters had plans for the piecemeal deployment of the division's component units. Already on 9 February the 351st Regimental Combat Team (the regiment plus an artillery battalion and accompanying elements) had received orders for embarkation and shipment to the Anzio beachhead. Senior staff officers of Fifth Army now announced arrangements for the deployment of individual battalions to reinforce the battle-weary 34th and 36th infantry divisions near Cassino. Artillery units were to reinforce firing batteries all along the Italian front. Even as the 88th drew new organizational equipment from the Peninsula Base Section depots at Naples, it seemed that it could cease to exist as a unit.[30]

Alarmed by these developments, Sloan arranged to lay his case before the commander of the Fifth Army, Lt. Gen. Mark W. Clark, in a personal conference.[31] There were arguments for and against the dissolution of the 88th. On the one hand, the unit was fully trained, with an intact chain of command and a well-developed logistical apparatus. It had demonstrated high morale and had distinguished itself as far as it could short of combat. The value of unit integrity for the established divisions had always been taken for granted; why should it be any less important to a draftee division? On the other hand, hard-pressed Allied divisions around Anzio and Cassino, which already knew the ground, were badly in need of relief, yet their complete extrication and replacement would be difficult at best. Would the front not be better served by leaving the experienced divisions where they were and relieving their component units on a smaller scale?

While these rational arguments and doubts must have weighed heavily in General Clark's mind, it seems he considered the personal factor as well. Clark and Sloan were old friends whose acquaintance dated from the time Clark was Sloan's student at the Command and General Staff School. Both men had the highest regard for each other's personal integrity and professional competence. Both knew that Sloan had passed the army's overseas service age for major general and that the 88th Infantry Division afforded him his last opportunity to command in combat. Clark elected to favor Sloan's position.

On 27 February the 88th Infantry Division received orders to relieve the British 5th Infantry Division in the Minturno sector of the

Fifth Army line. This precedent repeated itself three weeks later when the 85th Infantry Division also moved intact into the line on the 88th's immediate left. The stage was set for the validation of the draftee division and the Army Training Program. As it happened, no other American draftee division would serve in combat until after these two went "over the top."

One does not ordinarily think of movement into a front-line position as combat, but such movement can be even more dangerous than the occupation of the front line itself. When a front is stable, risks are greater to a unit in motion within the range of enemy artillery than to units already settled into the entrenchments and bunkers of the front-line trace. As the 88th Infantry Division relieved the British 5th Infantry Division, it executed its first maneuver in the face of hostile fire.

While the front lines of Italy had reached an impasse, it was a more fluid stalemate than that of the Somme or Ypres in World War I. Contrary to conventional wisdom, the very roughness of the terrain lent the battlefield more depth and activity than it might otherwise have had.[32] A number of peaks provided positions from which observers could see well into the enemy rear. Even on the highest mountain, lines of sight often extended miles in one direction—but only meters in another. Draws, gullies, and dead space throughout the rugged landscape concealed the night patrols that scurried and skirmished through no-man's-land, gathering wisps of information concerning enemy dispositions or movements. Not even the front lines themselves were impermeable to enterprising patrols.[33]

Behind the Italian front's cat-and-mouse game of patrol and counterpatrol, intelligence and counterintelligence, stood the firing batteries of field artillery, the greatest man-killers of World War II. The skirmishing of the patrols in part represented infantrymen's continual efforts to locate lucrative artillery targets. Artillerymen of the Italian campaign—German, British and American—would reach the peak of technical competence. Located in one area for an extended period, they registered firing data on hundreds of reference points, correlated reports from numerous observers, repeatedly updated situation maps, and stood by to fire within seconds of a call for support. Artillery alone reached onto every meter of the Italian battlefield regardless of weather; it dominated the Italian battlefield in a way that no other arm could.

Among the most vulnerable artillery targets was an exposed column of infantry marching toward or away from the protection of front-line entrenchments. Mindful of the dangers that would attend their replacement of the British 5th Infantry Division, the commanders of the 88th undertook elaborate precautions. In an effort to create the impression that the British were not to be relieved, the draftees masqueraded as British and wore the traditional shallow "basin" helmet rather than the deeper American steel pot.[34] Because German spies were generally Italians who recognized a uniform more readily than an accent, the disguised draftees called little attention to themselves in the British sector. American movements in the British rear areas were staggered so that the numbers involved at any given time approximated those of routine movement. The Germans had little reason to believe that anything was afoot in the area of the British 5th.

The 88th needed to keep adequate firepower forward during the exchange, for the Germans were likely to exploit any weaknesses they detected in the Allied front lines. The 88th's infantry regiments spaced their movements forward over four nights, and always moved at night. On the first night a quartering party from each company infiltrated forward to reconnoiter and coordinate with British counterparts. On the second night heavy machine guns came laboriously forward, after which British heavy machine guns withdrew equally laboriously. On the third night the antitank platoons of the two armies furtively exchanged places. On the final, and most critical, night the infantry platoons themselves filtered past each other in the darkness.[35]

The assignment of guides from both armies to each platoon precluded delays, misorientations, or mistaken identities. Front-line positions were fully manned at all times and patrols maintained their usual levels of activity forward. Artillery batteries and rear echelon units found it somewhat less difficult to displace the British, but they, like the infantry, took extraordinary precautions to avoid being observed while moving forward or digging in; they wore British helmets, guarded against noise and light, and carefully planned and coordinated every phase of the relief. Even with these elaborate precautions, the relief was not accomplished without mishap. The 338th Field Artillery Battalion lost four men and one gun to an artillery barrage,[36] and elements of the 351st Infantry narrowly avoided heavy shelling on their fourth night of movement.

Despite the casualties, the relief was well executed and rated a "good show" from those British officers best in a position to observe it. A letter from Brig. Gen. L.L. Lemnitzer, deputy chief of staff of the Allied Central Mediterranean Force, informed General Sloan that the British officers "were much impressed by the quiet, efficient, and business-like manner in which your units took over their respective sectors and got on with the job. Not only were they impressed but they made it a point to express their views during their visits here."[37]

It is hardly surprising that British and, later, French officers made such a point of expressing confidence in the newly arrived 88th Infantry Division.[38] The British and French seem to have been, if possible, even more pleased to see the first American draftee division enter combat than were the veterans of America's own regular army and National Guard units. Among these Allied officers were some who could remember the agonizing delays that had preceded the forward deployment of newly arrived American divisions during World War I. In this new world war, the first American draftee division was in the line within two weeks of its arrival in Italy. America's vast reserves of conscripted manpower were at last coming into play directly, rather than through the filter of established prewar divisions.

Moving a division overseas during World War II was a lengthy and difficult process. The experience of the 88th Infantry Division amply illustrates the time and complexity involved. Identified as deployable in August 1943, the 88th gave over September to intensive training while awaiting specific instructions. October was spent in fulfilling the directives of POM; November and December, including delays, in transit to Africa; January and part of February 1944, including delays, in transit from Africa to Italy; and the remainder of February in drawing new supplies and making final preparations to enter combat. The 88th seems to have moved through this process as quickly and efficiently as the details of POM and the vagaries of available transportation allowed, yet seven months lapsed between the time the division was identified as deployable and the time that the division actually deployed. Some readers may be surprised that it took so long. Others, more impressed by the problems involved, may wonder that it happened so quickly.

6

Minturno: Baptism by Fire

On 4 March 1944 the draftees of the 88th Infantry Division at long last assumed responsibility for a sector of the Italian front. At that time the division's combat proficiency was unknown; it would in most respects remain an unknown until the 88th participated in its first major offensive, which began on 11 May. For officers and men anxious to share in great events, the nine-week interval may have seemed stale and inactive. Still, those weeks proved an important period of adjustment during which the division matured as a combat organization.

Across Europe the months of March and April 1944 stood in the shadow of greater events planned for May and June. In Italy, efforts to break the Gustav Line at Monte Cassino, the Rapido River, and, indirectly, through Anzio had all proven abortive in January and February. Now Allied commanders defended a stalemated front while gathering resources for yet another effort. In England two million men prepared for Operation Overlord, the invasion of France. In Russia the war ground on as one Soviet front and then another hurled itself at the Germans—Odessa finally fell on 10 April—but even in Russia lesser offensives were a prelude of sorts to the truly climactic Battle of White Russia, which began on 22 June.

There were differences between the war the draftees of the 88th had trained for and the war they first found themselves called upon to fight. While in the United States, the division's training had emphasized offensive operations. At Minturno, the division found itself initially engaged in a defense. Changing from an offensive to a defensive orientation—and learning to function in the peculiar climate and terrain of Italy—required adjustments in addition to those normally associated with "baptism by fire."

An overall evaluation of the 88th's performance during its first two months in Italy would be favorable,[1] but it should not be supposed that all developments were positive steps in the direction of ever greater combat proficiency. The division demonstrated the outlines of a cycle of growth, stagnation, deterioration, and conscious renovation that would be repeated, at varying intervals, through the balance of the war.

The 88th's initial performance at Minturno was unique, but not unprecedented. Other divisions had experienced or would experience similar periods of adjustment. The 88th was the first of the draftee divisions to do so. Both strengths and weaknesses in the preparation of these new divisions were revealed.

The reality of the Allied situation along the Gustav Line in March 1944 had little in common with the military ballet of regimental combat teams deftly maneuvering against each other through the expanses of Oklahoma, Texas, and Louisiana. Across the width of Italy and around the "stranded whale" of Anzio,[2] Allied and Axis troops lay frozen in stalemate. While the Western Allies gathered the resources necessary for yet another massive attack to break the deadlock, the 88th manned its small portion of a rigidly immobile front.

One of the unique features of a stalemate is the "no-man's-land" that tends to develop between the opposing sides. In a stalemate between worthy opponents, this no-man's-land is repeatedly threaded by patrols executing missions of reconnaissance, ambush, or general combat.[3] Reconnaissance patrols attempt to develop information concerning enemy positions, usually in order to bring them under artillery fire or to provide tactical information in the anticipation of larger operations. Ambush patrols attempt to intercept and wipe out small, moving enemy units—such as reconnaissance patrols. Combat patrols are somewhat larger bodies of men designed to inflict casualties upon moving or stationary enemy troops in order to increase the enemy's overall attrition. For inexperienced troops, patrolling provides an important opportunity for baptism by fire. To quote General Sloan on the subject:[4] "It's [patrolling] the only way to let the men get the feel of battle before being shoved into a hot fight. . . . They go up for a while, kill off a few Germans, and then come back feeling like veterans."

The draftees were not unprepared for the most purely "infantry" aspects of patrolling. The rifleman's training had emphasized stealth, markmanship and fire, and maneuver. This emphasis had been reinforced during the course of the rigorous small-unit training in the wintry Atlas Mountains. Even after the division arrived at Minturno it continued to sharpen patrolling skills by regularly sending personnel to the Fifth Army patrolling school.[5] Indeed, the division's patrolling proficiency was so polished that during its first week in the line the draftees killed or captured five Germans for every man of their own that they lost.[6]

The division's initial success seems to have resulted in part from an

enthusiasm for combat that caught the battle-weary Germans un-
awares. The draftees captured Germans sleeping in dugouts on several
occasions, and consistently initiated those engagements that did occur.[7] At least one of the 88th's patrols used knives alone to dispatch its
astonished adversaries.[8] Apparently the long-suffering British and
German soldiers in the sector had had a more relaxed relationship with
each other than that which the newly arrived draftee division was
willing to allow. Examples of German inattentiveness abound. Pfc.
George Zelinsky, on patrol, sat down for a self-appointed break on a
small mound. The clattering of mess cans underneath alerted him to
the fact he was sitting on a dugout occupied by four "krauts"; he
captured them all. Pvt. John Flores burst into a house to capture a Nazi
officer he observed writing a letter. The astonished German meekly
surrendered, as did fourteen others who overheard the commotion
from the adjoining room. Pvt. Leo Witwer got lost when carrying a
message to the 349th Command Post and inadvertently wandered into
German-held Castelforte. Rescued by a British patrol, he came back
with invaluable intelligence. His comment upon returning to the safety
of American positions was, "Ma will be pretty sore if she hears about
this." These draftees, far from being exemplars of the martial temperament, were ordinary men who summoned up the pluck to accomplish
extraordinary things. Witwer was lost; Zelinsky was taking liberties in
"taking ten"; and Flores later was court-martialed for laughing at a
warrant officer who told him to put on his helmet.[9]

The combat edge initially enjoyed by the 88th did not continue
uncontested. Once alerted to the presence of the new and enthusiastic
88th Division, the Germans of XIV Corps with its 94th and 71st infantry
divisions reacted with grim efficiency. The Americans had learned
patrolling as if it were uniquely the province of the rifleman. Their
lightly armed, fast-moving patrols soon found themselves outgunned
by German patrols relying upon the support of heavier weapons.
Speed and stealth would not enable the Americans to prevail in the face
of heavily armed, battle-hardened, terrain-wise German formations.
On the night of 12 March, a week after the division's arrival in the line,
the 88th lost seven out of twelve men in a combat patrol that encountered Germans supported by heavy machine guns and mortars.
Throughout the next week other American patrols suffered similar
losses. By 19 March, General Sloan was sufficiently alarmed by his
cumulative losses to direct that combat patrols—not to be confused
with reconnaissance or ambush patrols—were to be discontinued until
further notice.[10]

In part, the 88th's problems resulted from the long-term purpose
of its patrolling. Americans and Germans alike knew that eventually
the Allies would launch yet another attack against the Gustav Line.

American patrols sought to dominate no-man's-land and to develop intelligence concerning the nature and depth of German defenses. To the Germans, the domination of no-man's-land was far less critical than was the masking of their own defensive positions—to preclude the Americans from gathering intelligence. Thus the bulk of the patrolling took place closer to German than to American lines. This meant that German patrols consistently were closer to their own sources of combat support.[11]

The Germans maximized their advantages.[12] Heavy machine-gun positions watched over the movements and activities of their patrols. Mortar and artillery forward observers, with wire communications to firing batteries, assured additional fire support. German combat patrols of twelve to fifteen riflemen, reinforced by machine guns, mortars, artillery, and at times even tanks, proved far more lethal than their American counterparts. American reconnaissance and ambush patrols, while not as vulnerable as the combat patrols, proved ever less productive in the face of increasingly wary and well-supported opponents. These lighter patrols could not, of course, afford firefights of any duration.

The American riflemen needed supporting fires if the probing of the German lines was to continue. Heavy machine guns were too unwieldy for rapidly moving patrols operating through extended distances in rough terrain. Artillery and mortars were the logical sources of supporting fire. Infantry-artillery combined arms training had been one of the strongest features of the draftees' training program. This combined arms training had not, however, been conducted with patrolling in mind. Massive artillery preparations had been an integral feature of major maneuvers; the minutiae of fire support for patrols had never received much emphasis. When the 88th sought to provide artillery support to its patrols, it faced several limitations.[13]

Only a handful of the division's personnel was proficient in the techniques of calling for and adjusting artillery.[14] During the course of the division's training, calls for artillery fire had been referred through forward observers accompanying maneuver companies or through battalion artillery liaison officers. This practice worked well when companies were maneuvering *en masse*, but there were not enough trained personnel to allow forward observers to accompany each of the division's numerous patrols. Companies routinely sent out two or three patrols a night. Across the division, given that two out of three companies were ordinarily on the front line in a battalion, this translated to something between thirty and fifty patrols out at any given time.

Limitations with respect to tactical communications complicated this situation. The infantry's standard SCR 300 FM radio, which weighed thirty-two pounds, had a range of about three miles under the best of conditions. The radio combinations used by artillery forward observers or headquarters elements were more powerful, but two men were required to carry them, thus they were altogether unsuitable for rapidly moving patrols. These radios were also the first and most logical target of the astute German sniper. All radios were, of course, vulnerable to mechanical and electrical failures, not to mention degraded performance because of terrain or weather. Wire communications (field telephones, etc.) were more reliable, provided the tactical situation permitted one to lay wire behind one's advance.[15]

Three days after the embarrassing and costly encounter of 12 March, the patrols of the 88th began concerted efforts to tie into artillery and mortar firing nets. Reconnaissance patrols sent out on 15 March laid wire behind them until they reached positions on high ground from which the further movements of the patrols could be observed. At these overwatching positions, patrols established observation posts equipped with wire communications that reached back to an artillery forward observer on the front line. The patrols then moved forward without laying more wire and scouted through the terrain within several hundred yards of the observation posts. Patrols that located Germans without being observed withdrew to the observation posts and phoned artillery forward observers. In several instances artillery responded with telling effect.[16]

Unfortunately, the Germans could not be relied upon to remain stationary throughout such maneuvers, nor could the Americans always approach and observe German positions undetected. The overwatching positions usually lost visual contact with the patrols when they moved forward into the darkness, so they could not effectively bring in supporting fires until the patrols returned with the necessary information. In the case of firefights it usually proved impossible for those manning the observation post to distinguish friend from foe. A better technique was needed.

The next logical step, undertaken the following week, was to send an SCR 300 radio forward with the patrol while leaving another SCR 300 behind in the overwatching position. Despite range limitations, the SCR 300 could usually be relied upon to reach as far as the observation post. The observation post in turn could relay targeting information to the rear by wire. There were delays as this information passed from patrol to observation post, to artillery forward observer, to firing battery, but the system proved adequate in most cases. On occasion, patrols were close enough to friendly lines to allow for communications directly through front-line elements rather than through a forward observation post.[17]

The division's experiments yielded interesting results. At least one patrol crossed five hundred meters of open ground in daylight behind a radio-adjusted, mortar-delivered smoke screen. Other patrols pre-registered fires on positions within their proposed areas of operation, then called for fires on those positions they subsequently found actually occupied. This advance planning radically reduced the time necessary for artillerymen to respond to a patrol's calls for supporting fire.[18]

By the first week in April, the 88th's patrols were once again competitive with German patrols attempting to mask the German front lines. Despite delays, the communications relay system usually delivered supporting fires quickly enough to balance the advantages Germans gained by being closer to their heavy weapons. On 11 April, General Sloan underscored his renewed confidence by once again removing all restrictions concerning the size and mission of patrols.[19] After a relatively brief period of embarrassment and trial and error, the draftees of the 88th had adapted training and technology to the peculiar demands of no-man's-land in Italy. Their adaptation was not unique, but it was a creditable display of flexibility in the face of a demanding tactical environment.

No-man's-land was not the only scene of the maturation and adjustment experienced by the 88th Infantry Division. The front-line infantryman not on patrol endured the stresses often associated with positional warfare: shelling, physical hardship, boredom. Commanders faced particularly perplexing problems when evacuating casualties and bringing replacements forward. These considerations, taken together, all weighed heavily against that great intangible, morale.

During the 88th's first month of combat, hardly a day went by without a man being killed by snipers, mortars, or artillery. German artillery observers on the heights overlooking American positions enjoyed vistas stretching deep into the American rear. Nothing was safe. Infantry positions, artillery batteries, bridges, communications sites, logistical facilities—all came under fire. On the division's first day in the line an artillery battery lost three dead, four wounded, and a howitzer destroyed in a shelling. On the following day another shelling virtually buried the men and equipment of a battery dug into a sandy stretch of beach. A record for close calls seems to have been set by Pfc. Marvin Blake. Within fifteen minutes he was knocked to the ground by an artillery shell, had his rifle shot out of his hands by a sniper, lost his helmet to a machine gun bullet, and had the seat of his pants set ablaze by a phosphorous mortar round. He later said that fifteen minutes seemed like a long time. So it went, day after day. Smoke machines, camouflage, reinforced emplacements, restrictions on noise and light, movement control, counterbattery fires—all were used. Nevertheless, the death and damage went on. By the end of March the 88th had suffered 99 killed, 252 wounded, and 36 missing, a casualty rate three times that considered average for positional war-fare.[20]

As if shellings and snipings were not enough, the draftees too often became noncombat casualties as well.[21] Close living in foxholes and dugouts contributed to the spread of infection, as did exposure to spring rains, snowmelt, and the chill of the mountain nights. Blankets alone were an insufficient answer to the chill and wetness. Wet-weather gear, overshoes, and insulated sleeping bags were not yet items of general issue. There seemed to be no effective way to keep everyone warm, dry, and healthy. Hepatitis, respiratory ailments, and trench foot inflicted significant casualties. Extensive inoculation pro-grams and liberal doses of penicillin reduced the numbers of noncom-bat casualties somewhat, but only warmer April weather and a massive dry-socks program eventually brought health problems under control. The dry-socks program included command directives that soldiers, supervised by their superiors, would change socks daily and receive sufficient laundry service to keep them in dry socks. The overall noncombat casualties of the 88th during the month of March came to about seven hundred men requiring hospitalization. Compared with other divisions under similar circumstances, this was about average.

The evacuation of casualties, whether combat or noncombat, proved difficult in the broken Italian terrain.[22] It could hardly have raised the morale of the draftees to know that if severely wounded, they probably would die before reaching a surgeon. Medical evacua-tion proceeded from litter trail to wheeled ambulance, to aid or clearing station, to field or evacuation hospital. Company aid men gave the ill or wounded emergency first aid, then turned them over to litter bearers (each battalion was assigned twenty-two), who rushed over carefully delineated litter trails to the wheeled ambulance pickup point. Italian roads were so few and so poor that this pickup point often was thou-sands of difficult yards from where the soldier was wounded. Once the patient was aboard an ambulance, his evacuation was likely to be further delayed by congested vehicular traffic. Ideally, echeloned med-ical facilities and the traffic between them would have organized along routes separate and distinct from those supporting other logistical traffic. In Italy the terrain rendered this impossible; all traffic funneled into a few narrow roads. Not only were ambulances delayed, they also tended to come under German artillery fire targeted on other traffic.

One response to the time involved in medical evacuation was to push medical facilities closer to the front. It was not uncommon for field hospitals to be within five miles of the front lines and within walking distance of divisional clearing stations. This arrangement had dangers as well as advantages. Field hospitals thus deployed were not altogether clear of the fighting and might well end up—because of the congested routes available to vehicular traffic—in close proximity to gasoline storage areas, ammunition dumps, headquarters, and other attractive artillery targets. When field hospitals were located close to the rear of one unit, flanking units found themselves forced to evacuate casualties along routes parallel to the enemy front rather than directly through their own rear. Lateral routes were more exposed and often more difficult than those going directly from front to rear. All factors considered, medical evacuation proved unpleasant for all concerned, particularly for those who watched and wondered, "Who's next?"[23]

Although less harrowing than the evacuation of casualties, a new, experimental method for replacing casualties had implications hardly less important to the morale of the draftees. Uptonian notions of replacement had paralleled the Uptonian notion of training; both were thought best done within the context of established units consisting largely of veterans. Units stayed in the line without replacement until a prearranged rotation date, or until excessive casualties rendered them combat-ineffective, then they withdrew to secure rear areas. Once in the rear, these units absorbed new men and undertook rigorous training to "work them in." Under the Uptonian replacement system, warfare was to be a cycle of front-line duty, rotation, and training, with two or three units on the line for every unit in the rear and, preferably, twelve-day tours on the line separated by four-day breaks.[24]

At Minturno the 88th spent six weeks in its first stretch on the line. In that time it was the first division to exercise the new replacement system, whereby units stayed in contact with the enemy and individual replacements came forward into them. Men were replaced through logistical techniques similar to those whereby expended ammunition and broken equipment were replaced. Theoretically, units exercising the new system could remain on the front line at full strength indefinitely. The 88th even received, shortly before offensive operations began, an overstrength of 1,037 personnel to insure that individual replacements would be immediately available.[25]

The new replacement system had advantages and disadvantages. On the one hand, units did in fact remain at full strength without withdrawing from combat. This was no small advantage when one had relatively few divisions to rotate, as did the United States in World War II; the U.S. Army had ninety divisions, compared to the Japanese with one hundred, the Germans with three hundred, and the Russians with four hundred. On the other hand, units remained on the front lines longer than was desirable for combat effectiveness, and replacements often did not immediately identify with or integrate into their new units.[26]

Understandably, the 88th began to encounter neuropsychiatric casualties. The combination of hardship, boredom, and tension for weeks on end proved to be more than many soldiers could bear. Minor pleasures—dry socks, a letter from home, or uninterrupted sleep—assumed an importance that survivors considered pathetic in retrospect.[27] Men snapped following the most minor of frustrations. All ranks experienced the strain. One regimental commander suddenly ordered his astonished subordinates to conduct an unsupported, full-scale attack that would have been nothing less than suicidal. Fortunately, the regimental staff had the good sense to prepare lethargically while one of its number apprised General Sloan. Sloan hastened to the scene, canceled the operation, and relieved the commander. During April alone the 88th evacuated eighty-five such neuropsychiatric casualties to the rear.[28]

Sloan's treatment for neuropsychiatric casualties was, characteristically, a four-day dose of rigorous training. Line officers administered a therapeutic program that emphasized strenuous physical exercise as the best single treatment for "anxiety neurosis." The program also featured adequate sleep, cleanliness, health habits, wholesome food, and an array of challenging classes. Patients were either busy or asleep twenty-four hours a day in order to insure that they had no time to dwell upon their misfortunes. More than half of the division's neuropsychiatric casualties returned to duty within a week.[29]

In the light of our now somewhat more sophisticated understanding of mental illness, it is probably safe to say that Sloan's neuropsychiatric program was successful for the wrong reasons. Most of his patients were probably exhaustion cases or malingerers rather than genuine neuropsychiatric casualties. Exhaustion cases got the rest they needed during the course of Sloan's treatment. Malingerers found his program more arduous than front-line duty. Bona fide neuropsychiatric casualties, on the other hand, probably remained unaffected.[30]

Along the front lines the soldiers themselves seem to have done more to secure their own psychiatric health than their commanders possibly could have. When not on patrol, on watch, or asleep, the draftees occupied themselves with improving their environment. "Deluxe dugouts" featuring pilfered or fabricated chairs, tables, and beds proliferated just to the rear of the front lines. One soldier even went so far as to build one of these dugouts around an abandoned, yet serviceable, grand piano. Mine detectors readily located wine casks buried by the Italians. After consuming the contents, soldiers cut the casks in half and used them as bathtubs. Enterprising mess sergeants developed or appropriated facilities and continued their timeless attention to the stomachs of their troops. Deluxe dugouts eventually evolved into elaborate recreational facilities featuring reading, letter-writing, card playing, bathing, snacking, bantering, partying, and the services of self-appointed lawyers, psychiatrists, and barbers.[31]

Not to be left unentertained, the draftees encouraged acts of bravado—which most of them comfortably enjoyed as spectators. One such act was an incendiary mission by a Piper Cub airplane billed as "epic, colossal, history making." On the day of the big event a ridiculously light artillery spotter plane swooped over German lines dumping five-gallon tins of gasoline upon flames caused by a white phosphorus round, then strafed the front with .45-caliber pistols. Entrenched American infantrymen whooped and cheered throughout the course of this ineffectual but daring display.[32]

Not to be outdone, the Germans came up with their own widely visible acts of bravado. A case in point was a daring motorcyclist who made a daily routine of racing along the length of the German front in plain view of the Americans. His tiny motorcycle was closely pursued by bursting shells, and soldiers of both sides cheered his progress and jeered the unsuccessful American artillerymen. The cat-and-mouse duel continued day after day—until the day the intrepid cyclist disappeared under a burst credited to the division's 338th Field Artillery Battalion.[33]

Their macabre quality notwithstanding, such displays represented an adherence to tacit rules of conduct whereby German and American soldiers found it easier to live in each other's presence. Along with acts of bravado there developed mutually-agreed-upon rules of engagement. Where lines were within rifle range of each other, neither side fired while food was being brought forward. The draftees occasionally played football games on exposed fields while the Germans quietly observed. "Axis Sally"—a prominent German agent whose radio commentaries sought to demoralize the American soldiers—growled that the contestants would not forever continue unmolested, but the Germans did nothing at the time. Both sides developed the habit of discontinuing barrages once ambulances or medics were observed in the target area. Prisoners tended to be well treated; even during the brutal skirmishing in no-man's-land efforts were made to capture, if possible, rather than to kill.[34]

Perhaps the most spectacular single instance of tacit rules of conduct was the Easter service of the 349th Infantry Regiment.[35] For nearly an hour all firing ceased while the division chaplain conducted services in English and German. Loudspeakers carried Protestant services, Catholic Mass, and nondenominational female vocal accompaniment along the length of the front. Services concluded with the notification that troops of both sides should return to cover, after which the firing resumed.

Tacit rules of conduct between American and German were a puzzling phenomenon. Skirmishing in no-man's-land retained its essential brutality. Everyone knew the restraints were off once the Allies began their major offensive. Yet, however ephemeral, the rules made it easier for soldiers of both sides to tolerate each other's presence. It was just as well, for the draftees of the 88th would see much of the Germans in the 94th and 71st infantry divisions who were, like themselves, collections of conscripts officered by small cadres of professional soldiers.[36]

No less than the rifleman, the logistician found it necessary to adjust to the realities of the Italian theater. In some cases stateside preparations translated readily to the rigors of actual combat, and adjustments were matters of detail. In other cases, adequate logistical support required important changes.

Supplies in all classes were readily available to the division. The Minturno positions were less than fifty miles from the enormous Peninsula Base Section depots around Naples. Naples had been damaged during the fighting preceding its capture in October 1943, but by the time the 88th arrived, port facilities were once again operational and supplies flowed unimpeded.[37]

Rations—A, B, or C—never seem to have been in short supply. Canned and packaged foods were increasingly supplemented by items locally procured as spring returned to the portions of the Italian countryside hastily overrun in the first rush of the Allied invasion. Spring thaws guaranteed ample supplies of potable water throughout the division's sector.[38]

Clothing and personal equipment also were readily available from the Peninsula Base Section depots, although the spring of 1944 still saw the 88th equipped with antiquated shoes and leggings. There also seems to have been no lack of petroleum products. Newly constructed pipelines carried fuel as far north as Sessa, less than ten miles from the division's front-line trace. Secondary issuance of fuel proved simple enough, largely because of readily available fuel pods and the ever-present five-gallon cans. The division trucked packaged POL products (petroleum, oil, lubricants) directly from the Naples depots or received them through higher support activities originating at those depots.[39]

Maintenance, repair parts, and the supply of major items of equipment also posed few problems throughout the division's tenure at Minturno. The vehicles and equipment were virtually new; there was rarely a need for any save the most minor of repairs. Combat losses were not yet significant in this respect, and the grueling maintenance demands of extended forward movements under inhospitable conditions were yet to come.

Ammunition in all calibers was readily available, although the expenditure of artillery was carefully rationed and controlled.[40] This parsimony with respect to artillery was a local manifestation of world-wide stockpiling in preparation for Operation Overlord and other offensives planned for the spring of 1944. Despite rationing, lucrative artillery targets do not seem to have gone unengaged for want of ammunition.[41]

Simply put, supply per se was not a problem for the 88th during its occupancy of the Minturno position. The real difficulty lay in the area of tactical transportation—that is to say, in the delivery of supplies into the hands of front-line troops. In its rush towards modernization the American army saddled infantry divisions with road-bound truck fleets not altogether suited for the peculiarities of the Italian terrain. Large sectors of the front could be reached only by mule or porter under even the best of circumstances. German artillery interdiction rendered even more of the front unapproachable to trucks. The division's table of organization and its training provided for nothing in the way of off-road transportation other than the backs of the troops themselves.

The 88th was not the first division to suffer from this inadequacy of transportation. Following the Salerno breakout in the autumn of 1943, American front-line troops repeatedly had found themselves under-supplied—even when mere miles away from enormous stockpiles. On occasion, strategic terrain seized in hard-fought battles was abandoned when victorious Allied troops could no longer be supplied. As a stopgap, infantry and engineer battalions had been diverted from combat roles to serve as porters for battalions more heavily engaged.[42]

Porters were not the long-term solution to transportation problems. By the time the 88th Infantry Division arrived in Italy, a Fifth Army program attaching Italian mule-pack companies to infantry divisions was well along. The now-Allied Italian army organized these companies and attached them to Allied divisions. Upon its arrival in Italy the 88th received four such mule-pack companies numbering some 450 muleteers and 1,400 mules.[43]

The Italian mule-pack companies could not operate within the division without liaison and supervision. American muleteers accompanied the mule-pack companies at a ratio of one American for every ten Italians. This increased the number of muleteers and assured that English-speaking personnel moved with each of the mule trains. During its first month at Minturno, the 88th undertook a somewhat frenzied recruiting and training of muleteers. The division established a muleteer training school; most of its older artillerymen had had experience with animal transportation. Indeed, General Sloan himself once had organized an ROTC program of instruction on the subject. The division also had hundreds of farm boys among its draftees. Many of these knew mules well and some had, in fact, been muleteers. The draftees also included dozens of bilingual Italian-Americans. The mixture of farmers and Italian-Americans proved a good one. Italian mule-pack companies integrated quickly and efficiently into the division's logistical establishment.[44]

Some logistical problems did develop out of the peculiar international status of the mule-pack companies. Technically speaking, the mule-pack companies remained part of the Italian army. Although under the operational control of the 88th, they reverted to Italian channels for matters of discipline, administration, and supply. Discipline seldom was a problem with the 88th's muleteers. The Italian major in charge and his officers proved an experienced and competent set of disciplinarians.[45] For similar reasons administration also posed few problems.

Unfortunately, mule-pack companies were plagued by shortages with respect to two critical items, boots and mules. Under the best of circumstances, boots wore out quickly in the rugged Italian terrain. Muleteers did more walking under more trying conditions than anybody in the theater. Although Italian muleteers wore out their boots quickly in support of U.S. troops, Allied military authorities refused to allow American divisions to supersede Italian supply channels and provide Italian muleteers with American-issued boots. The problems associated with keeping the muleteers in serviceable boots were never satisfactorily resolved, but local solutions ameliorated the situation. Corpses, in particular German corpses, were seldom evacuated or buried with their boots on. The boots of the living also proved highly pilferable. American logisticians seem to have exercised imaginative interpretations concerning the transportation of stockpiled boots. Some of the stockpiles were carried around on Italian feet rather than in trucks, ostensibly to reduce transportation and storage requirements. One way or another, the 88th kept its muleteers in boots.[46]

Keeping the muleteers in mules was even more difficult.[47] In deference to local sensibilities, the division could not directly confiscate mules. In deference to Italian and American procedures concerning the accounting of funds, the division could not directly buy or requisition mules either. Mules were purchased *en masse* by high-level procurement agencies, then distributed to the mule-pack companies. Centralization allowed for a greater control of markets and prices, but also reduced flexibility at the division level. The 88th's logisticians found it difficult to influence the procurement process and thus to keep the supply of mules at constant or even predictable levels.

These several bureaucratic obstacles notwithstanding, the mule-pack companies proved an invaluable asset. Without them, tactical resupply might have posed insuperable problems. With them, no terrain proved too difficult for the division's logisticians.[48] The division did not, of course, dispense with its wheeled vehicle fleet, so it enjoyed the benefits and suffered the costs of two separate extensive, and not entirely complementary, transportation establishments. This duplication may have been an expensive way of doing business, but what World War II American logistical activity was governed by its expense?

As the 88th settled into an extended occupancy of its Minturno position, General Sloan once again had reason to become concerned with the division's state of training.[49] A paradox of warfare is that a unit's general combat readiness often decreases while its readiness increases for the particular type of operation in which it is presently engaged.[50] The ultimate purpose of the 88th was to attack. At Minturno it was learning to defend.

The training of the 88th had emphasized operations more mobile and more offensive than those in which the division now found itself. Of Camp Gruber's eight regimental combat team blocks of instruction, only one included a deliberate defense—a defense conducted by one regiment in order that the other regiments would have something challenging to attack. Battalion field exercise tests and platoon combat firing proficiency tests were altogether given over to attacks. Battalion combat firing proficiency tests specified a thousand points for the defensive phase and two thousand points for the offensive phase.[51]

This emphasis upon offensive operations as the true measure of a division's worth arose from American military psychology and doctrine.[52] America intended, after all, to carry the war into the Nazi heartland. The big crusade and the knockout blow were hallmarks of the American military tradition. Imbued throughout its training with the much-desired "aggressive attack spirit," the 88th was now developing a character better suited for the antithetical experience of positional warfare. Could it still attack?

One of the division's growing limitations was, quite simply, physical fitness.[53] Prolonged periods of inactivity in forward areas afforded troops little opportunity for physical exercise. Infantrymen averaged less than one extended patrol a week. Rearward echelons, under the surveillance of Germans on the heights, got scarcely more exercise. Lack of stamina would have adverse physical and psychological effects if poorly conditioned troops attempted the rigors of an attack.

Physical deterioration complicated a more general erosion of soldierly skills. Marksmanship deteriorated because few soldiers saw the enemy within rifle range, much less engaged identifiable targets with rifle fire. As for maneuver, the division seldom moved more than a dozen men at a time throughout its stay at Minturno. An organization's efficiency with respect to maneuver deteriorates rapidly.[54] The units of the 88th once again fell away from peaks of efficiency demonstrated during the Louisiana Maneuvers.

Another potential weakness within the 88th concerned its facility for combining the several combat arms, artillery excepted, into a single coordinated attack. Reconnaissance troops, signalmen, engineers and antitank sections all suffered from a lack of recent practice.

The experiences of the armored reconnaissance troops at Minturno had not differed materially from those of the infantrymen.[55] The patrols they sent forward were comparable to those of the infantry in size and duration. Reconnaissance troops had not recently practiced masking the forward movement of larger formations because there had not yet been such larger formations to mask. Reconnaissance troops had not, of course, operated mounted in their scout cars since the division moved into the line.

The division's signalmen had established a respectable array of static communications and had developed proficiency in laying wire to support patrols. They had not had any experience pushing communications forward over significant distances at a pace commensurate with the progress of an attack.[56] The signalmen were conscious of the limitations of the SCR 300 radio and of shortages with respect to the SCR 536, but these were problems beyond their ability to resolve.

The division engineers had cleared mine fields left scattered around rear areas by the somewhat untidy British,[57] and their officers had gone forward with infantry patrols to get a feel for the terrain. The engineers had not, however, recently practiced such critical offensive skills as the breaching of mine fields and obstacles or route construction.

Antitank sections had the dual offensive role of fighting tanks and of providing direct fire support to forward-moving infantrymen. They were to maneuver with the infantry during the development of the attack. These sections had not had the opportunity to fire or maneuver while in the static Minturno emplacements. Reconnaissance, signal, engineer, antitank, and infantry units all needed to practice previously learned skills before they would be prepared for the spring offensive. The proposed integration of tanks into the offensive posed problems that were somewhat more complex. The 88th Infantry Division had no tanks of its own, nor had it previous training exposure to tanks. Indeed, it had no organic armored fighting vehicles at all, other than the sixteen armored cars of its reconnaissance troop. Army Ground Forces planners had determined that infantry divisions would be supported by independent tank and tank destroyer battalions if such support became necessary. To this end, independent tank and tank destroyer battalions had been activated and had undergone mobilization and training programs separate from those of the infantry divisions. The men of the 88th had never trained with the tankers who were to support them in Italy—or with tankers at all, for that matter.[58]

Beyond a simple lack of actual combined arms training, there were also problems presented by the lack of an agreed-upon combined arms tactical doctrine. Members of the fledgling armored force displayed an understandable lack of interest in supporting infantry attacks. Tankers saved their enthusiasm for a vision of tanks advancing rapidly *en masse*—a mechanized version of a medieval cavalry charge that was hardly practical in all circumstances. Limitations upon such tank employment were particularly severe in Italy. Vehicular movement was often restricted to roads or ridge lines. Battle-wise Germans rendered these restrictions even more severe through their judicious positioning of mine fields and antitank guns. The "lessons" of Poland and France notwithstanding, mass tank attacks against prepared German positions would have been suicidal. If tanks were to be of use in the rugged Italian terrain, they would have to operate in support of and at the pace of infantry.[59]

Although American tank commanders recognized that their vehicles must support infantry attacks on occasion, they had not yet agreed on how such an unwelcome mission might best be accomplished. By 1944 differing opinions had reduced themselves to three distinct methods.

The oldest and simplest method saw the tank as a mobile pillbox, behind which dismounted infantrymen would advance.[60] Tanks would push forward at three miles an hour along whatever routes were available, smashing barbed wire and obstacles, exploding antipersonnel mines harmlessly, suppressing enemy positions with volumes of fire, and shielding infantrymen huddled in their tracks. As enemy positions were breached, infantrymen would fan out and mop them up, then return to the shelter of the tank and push on to the next obstacle. If immobilized or knocked out, a tank would provide infantrymen a supporting pillbox and firing position until another tank trundled past to assume the lead.

The mobile pillbox method was easy to control and was apt to work reasonably well where engagements were close range, such as in urban areas or in the jungle, or where objectives were shallow, such as when seizing a small island. The method also would work well when one's opponent was ill-equipped with antitank weapons or unaccustomed to battling armor. Marines in the Pacific adopted this technique early in the war and used it successfully throughout their island-hopping campaigns.[61] Against Germans in the Mediterranean Theater, however, the technique worked less well.[62] Antitank mines, covered by antitank guns with interlocking fields of fire, blocked all vehicular avenues of approach, often from extended ranges. Antitank guns were usually concealed or sited on reverse slopes in such a manner that they were unobserved until they opened fire. After mines or antitank gunners halted the slowly moving processions, artillery observers called in fire that blasted infantrymen out from behind the shelter of the disabled tanks. Circumstances favoring the mobile pillbox method of tank employment rarely existed in Italy.

A second method, endorsed by Gen. George S. Patton, Jr., treated tankers and infantrymen as somewhat more loosely integrated.[63] Where circumstances or terrain dictated a dismounted pace, infantry provided a forward screen while tanks followed within about three hundred yards. Tanks defiladed themselves until the infantry made contact, then rushed forward to pummel enemy positions that the infantrymen had located. When these positions were knocked out, tankers resumed defiladed positions while the infantry once again led the advance. As infantrymen located mine fields or other obstacles, they probed for bypasses or breached them with the aid of engineers, all the while covered by the watchful gunners of nearby tanks. Tank-infantry teams advanced in successive bounds, or rushes, with infantry providing reconnaissance and security while tankers provided firepower, shock action, and mobility.

This second method for combining the efforts of tankers and infantrymen proved successful in France and has come to be the formula approved by current American doctrine. Insofar as Italy was concerned, however, the method had serious weaknesses. Tanks operating in such close proximity to infantrymen tended to become tied into the infantry battle to such an extent that they could no longer be conveniently extricated to deal with unanticipated threats or to exploit unanticipated opportunities. In Patton's case this posed few problems; he deployed such large numbers of tanks that he could commit tanks to the infantry battle and still have reserves available for counterattack or exploitation. In Italy an infantry division was usually supported by a single tank battalion, a situation that afforded commanders no such luxury.[64]

A third method for supporting infantry attacks with tanks had the tanks trail by five hundred to fifteen hundred yards—well clear of the infantry battle.[65] Tanks hung back until the infantrymen developed the situation sufficiently to identify a preferred objective or avenue of exploitation. Tanks then rushed forward, joined the infantry, pounded a selected array of targets, and withdrew or exploited.

This third method divorced infantrymen from continuous tank support but allowed for the most efficient use of a relatively few tanks. It also separated infantrymen from the artillery barrages that moving tanks tended to attract. This method of tank support was the one espoused by the commander of the 760th Tank Battalion,[66] assigned to support the 88th. Eventually the 88th used this method to integrate

Brig. Gen. John E. Sloan and his wife, Amy, riding a caisson at Presidio of Monterey, California, 1940. Author's collection.

1st Lt. Horace M. Brown and his wife, Lucia ("Chick") at a garden party in Muskogee, Oklahoma, June 1942. Author's collection.

Except where otherwise noted, photographs are by U.S. Army photographers.

Above, draftees arriving at Camp Gruber's Braggs, Oklahoma, railroad station. *Right,* troop ship moves overseas. Some made the crossing "by rail".

Chaplain Francis J. Pryor holding services near Minturno, Italy. Photo courtesy of O.U. Bay.

Italian neighbors bring tin pails to a field mess to receive handouts from sympathetic GIs. Photo courtesy of O.U. Bay.

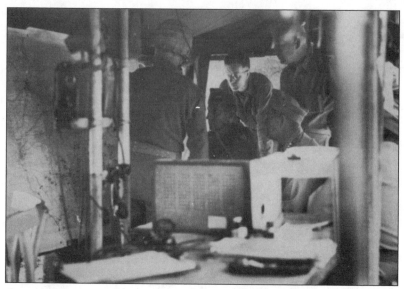

General Sloan (back to camera) confers with Lt. Gen. Mark W. Clark, Lt. Col. E.D. Beggs, Lt. Gen. Barney M. Giles, and Maj. Gen. Frank O. Hunter.

Muleteers prepare to bring up supplies. Photo courtesy of O.U. Bay.

Above, eight-inch howitzer shells German position. *Below,* a GI looks back toward Minturno from the heights just captured from the Germans.

After the breakthrough, the 88th advances through rocky countryside and shattered Italian village.

Above, General Sloan speaks to a resting infantry rifle company. *Below,* Blue Devils fighting in the outskirts of Rome.

Passing the monuments of ancient Rome, American infantry hurries through the city en route to further battles.

Romans celebrate their city's liberation, 5 June 1946.

Gen. George C. Marshall congratulates General Sloan after awarding him the Distinguished Service Medal.

Lt. Gen. Mark W. Clark awards Medal of Honor to Lt. Charles W. Shea.

Above, Secretary of War Henery L. Stimson reviews 351st Infantry Regiment at Tarquinia airfield shortly after the fall of Rome. *Below,* Generals Clark and Sloan leave the war room at the 88th command post near Volterra.

Communication wireman traces through a maze to restore a broken line.

Quartermaster struggles to keep the division in supply; the mule could go where the truck could not.

Alpine terrain faced the 88th before the Po Valley. *Below,* Blue Devils hurry across the beach after the Po crossing.

Captains Marvin L. Koehler left, and Ovid U. Bay, *far right,* 337th Field Artillery, meet Seventh Army staff officers at the Brenner Pass. *Below,* 337th officers, *from left,*: Captains Horace M. Brown, Ovid U. Bay, Hutchinson I. Cone, Taggart Whipple, E.F. Kennedy, James E. DeVaughan, Roland E. Palmer, and W.S. Brooks, Lt. Col. Wilson Hargreaves, and Capt. George H. Lester. Photos courtesy of O.U. Bay.

Maj. Gen. Paul W. Kendall, who followed General Sloan as commanding general of the 88th, bids farewell to the division at Ghedi, Italy, July 1945. Brig. Gen. James C. Fry is at right.

Four Blue Devils of Company L, 349th Infantry, homeward bound in the summer of 1945. *From left:* Donald S. Tonkin, Louis P. Casaccia, Albert J. Cheli, and Joseph Bielusiak. Photo by William E. Carnahan.

The American Cemetery in Florence, where many of the 88th Infantry Division dead rest. Photo courtesy of American Battle Monuments Commission.

tanks into plans and preparations for the spring offensive of 1944. This choice was not, as shall be seen, without its consequences.

The training of the 88th had not integrated close air support for reasons similar to those that left it without integrated tanks. With the Army Air Force altogether separate from the Army Ground Forces, the former contributed little to the training of the latter. Upon mobilization, the focus of the air force quickly shifted to its sustained campaigns overseas, and it never devoted time, resources, or interest to joint training with ground units in the United States. This disinterest was mutual. Ground commanders regarded artillery as a far more reliable means of close support and preferred to rely upon the familiar to get the same job done. Artillery was available in all weather and, most important for Italy, was efficient at night, when much of the fighting took place. Sloan, thirty-one years an artilleryman, was probably even less of an air enthusiast than most ground commanders. There is no evidence he ever considered close air support—as opposed to aerial interdiction of air interception—as much of an asset, yet he discovered the 88th was to receive a significant number of air sorties. His staffs at several levels would need the training necessary to coordinate them.[67]

As the month of April progressed, General Sloan found himself approaching the eve of a major offensive with his division not fully prepared to attack. A month of defensive warfare had eroded its offensive skills. The men were no longer physically fit and had not exercised such critical skills as marksmanship for some time. Major units had not maneuvered *en masse* and specialized elements had not recently exercised those aspects of their specialties appropriate to offensive operations. The soldiers had never trained with the newly attached tank and tank destroyer battalions, and his staffs had no practical experience coordinating air support. The only bright spot in this somewhat grim picture was the ever-increasing experience of the division's artillerymen. During April alone the artillerymen fired 43,940 rounds on an array of targets that would have been as appropriate for offensive as for defensive operations. During that period every artillery officer directed firing problems in concentrations ranging from highly flexible, independent battery missions through massive, division-concentrated fires.[68] Target arrays ranged from moving patrols through the most heavily entrenched of positions. Even relatively sophisticated control measures such as simultaneous time on target or rolling curtain fires had become familiar to the 88th's artillerymen. The recent experience of the artillerymen was comparable to that which they could expect in a major offensive. The rest of the division was not so lucky.

General Sloan's response to the 88th's condition was, characteristically, a brief period of intensive training. On 15 April the 88th—its artillery excepted—rotated out of the line and reconcentrated. The ostensible purpose of the rotation was R and R, rest and recreation. Sloan's soldiers more accurately described the objectives as R, R, and R—rest, recreation, and *retraining*. For two weeks the 88th undertook training as rigorous as it had ever experienced.[69]

Infantrymen reworked an abbreviated version of the entire program they had undergone at Camp Gruber. Day and night they sharpened tactical skills that had atrophied while in front-line positions. Maneuvers progressed from squad battle drills through battalion field problems. Physical conditioning received a special emphasis; each day the draftees marched prolonged distances through difficult terrain and practiced mountain climbing.

The retraining program put a special emphasis on the reduction of fortified positions. Fifth Army engineers constructed mock enemy strong points on the sides of mountains in the rest and recreation area. Platoons maneuvered against these pillboxes, while entrenched machine gunners fired noisily but harmlessly over their heads whenever they inadvertently presented targets. Dynamite charges simulating incoming artillery rounds added noise, realism, and confusion. Infantry platoons attacked, debriefed, and attacked again as they struggled to master techniques of maneuver and assault in the face of heavily fortified positions.

During this period the 88th exposed the draftees to new equipment. Assaulting squads used pole charges to breach obstacles and barbed wire entanglements. Recent graduates of the Fifth Army Flame Thrower School, a dozen men from each regiment, scorched dummy positions with their fearsome devices. Tankers from the 760th Tank Battalion integrated themselves into battalion-scale maneuvers. Each infantry battalion maneuvered at least once with a platoon of medium and light tanks attached. An exchange program brought pilots into the 88th's division and regimental headquarters. Here they exchanged ideas concerning close air support with operations officers and commanders. Perhaps some good was done, but there still was no practical training.

The 88th exercised its more familiar weapons in new and imaginative ways. Weather balloons attached to blocks of wood dropped into the Gulf of Gaeta became moving targets for 57-millimeter antitank gunners; prevailing winds and currents carried the balloons past firing positions. Antitank gunners, antitank grenadiers, and bazooka crews fired at destroyed German vehicles dragged onto ranges as hard targets. This firing was in addition to rifle marksmanship undertaken by all infantrymen, regardless of rank or duty position.

The reconnaissance troop undertook an intensive program similar to that of the infantrymen, save for its particular emphasis on infiltration, long-range patrolling, and mounted movement. Infiltration and patrolling were activities that might well precede or mask the movement of larger units. Mounted movements led by the reconnaissance troop's armored cars could be critical in exploiting the much-hoped-for general breakthrough.

Engineers also trained for the peculiarities of an offensive in Italy. Engineer officers who had gone forward to reconnoiter no-man's-land converted the knowledge thus gained into sand table reproductions of the division's front. Officers of all branches studied the obstacles, avenues of approach, and probable enemy positions displayed on the sand tables. The engineer units themselves practiced skills that ultimately enhanced the spring offensive. Engineer platoons breached one mock barrier after another. Engineer companies carved jeep trails along the sides of mountains, practice in pushing supply routes forward through inhospitable terrain.

When the 88th Infantry Division rotated back into the line during the first week of May 1944, General Sloan had more reason to be confident of its combat readiness. The leadership of the division was enhanced by assignment of two able and experienced combat leaders. Col. James C. Fry, who would become known as "Fearless Fosdick" to his devoted soldiers, took command of the 350th Infantry Regiment from the ailing Col. Charles P. Lynch. Col. Joseph B. Crawford, who had served as an infantry battalion commander and regimental executive officer throughout the North African, Sicilian, and present Italian Campaigns and had been dubbed "Krautkiller", took command of the 349th Infantry Regiment. These two new leaders with Col. Arthur S. Champeny—"Champ"—of the 351st would give the 88th a regimental leadership of a caliber enjoyed by few if any other infantry divisions. Also, once again the draftees were at a peak of training and readiness. Once again they had the offensive at the front of their minds.

Sloan was prepared for the supreme test along the lines of a promise he had made concerning veterans of earlier wars: "their faith will be sustained, their record maintained and the glory of the colors never will be sullied as long as one man of the 88th still lives." Sgt. Delphia E. Garris put it a little differently: "We have got to lick those bastards in order to get out of the Army. That's our main thought—to get rid of the Germans in order to get out of the Army." Sloan and Garris may have had differences in perspective, but both sought the same result and both were, as the saying went, leaning forward in the foxhole.[70]

All units are in part the products of training and combat experience. Trained to attack, at Minturno the 88th Infantry Division was first called upon to maintain fixed position. In its first month of combat the division grew accomplished with respect to the defensive realities of the Italian stalemate. Even while giving a good account of itself in front-line positions, however, its overall combat readiness eroded. The answer to such deterioration was retraining; in a frenzy of renewal the division shook off the lethargy of the bunkers and foxholes and prepared for the big offensive. Physiques hardened, tactical readiness improved, the "aggressive attack spirit" once again became pervasive. Even in this renewal, however, there were the germs of later disappointment. In particular, problems with respect to tanks and radios surfaced that were to reappear at a later time under more trying circumstances. March and April 1944 saw but the first of several cycles of growth, stagnation, deterioration, and conscious renovation experienced by the 88th.

The art, as opposed to the science, of war seems to include an element of timing. Units are not prepared to do everything equally well all the time. Units, like individuals, peak and decay. Some units are less radical in their fluctuations—perhaps because of combat experience, relative numbers of veterans, collective emotional temperaments, etc.—but all units peak and decay. It is science that prepares troops for war. It is art that assures their preparedness peaks at the moment when it is most needed.

The leadership of the 88th seems to have grasped some portion of that art. The draftees of the 88th, trained to a peak in North Africa, arrived in Italy eager to fight Germans and moved into the front lines smoothly. Although not fully prepared for the particulars of their initial role, they adjusted quickly and soon gave a good account of themselves. No one had the illusion that this respectable initial showing represented a validation of the draft division, however. That validation was to come, if it came at all, in the division's first major offensive. By then the draftees were once again trained to a peak.

7

Diadem: The First Three Days

As April turned to May, every soldier in the 88th Infantry Division knew the first major test was at hand. However creditably the division had performed during training or during the skirmishing of March and April, its ultimate worth would be measured not by virtue of training or skirmishing, but by performance in major battles. As a larger issue, the validation of the as yet untested draftee divisions depended upon this battlefield performance as well.

Each component of the U.S. Army made its World War II debut at different times and under different circumstances. The regular army first experienced combat in the unsuccessful, if courageous, defense of Bataan in the Philippines. The first major combats for the National Guard were the embarrassingly prolonged Buna campaign in New Guinea and the disaster at Kasserine Pass in North Africa. Draftee divisions were to go into their first major battle during Operation Diadem, an ambitious Allied offensive designed to break the Italian deadlock and sweep the Germans through Rome into the Northern Apennines. The first three days of a major offensive are generally the bloodiest and most consequential. The experience of the first draftee division during the first three days of its first major offensive held true to form.[1]

In April 1944, Allied Armies in Italy had been stalemated for six months on a line extending from Minturno through Cassino to Ortona on the Adriatic coast. Previous efforts to break the deadlock—bloody assaults on Monte Cassino, hotly contested efforts to break inland after landings near Anzio, and abortive attempts to force the Rapido River— had accomplished nothing. Now Gen. Sir Harold R.L.G. Alexander, the commander of Allied Armies in Italy, envisioned an even greater effort involving more than twenty-five divisions supported by two thousand guns and the absolute air supremacy of the Mediterranean Allied Air Forces.[2]

In Alexander's mind the offensive was to develop as a "one-two punch"—a main attack down the Liri River Valley linking up with a second major attack from Anzio to Valmontone.[3] Having thus trapped and dispatched a third of Generalfeldmarschall Albert Kesselring's Army Group Southwest, the Allies could then pursue the survivors through Rome and into Northern Italy. Alexander's plan envisioned the British Eighth Army conducting the main attack, closing the encirclement, and leading the Allied advance through Rome.

Alexander's ranking American subordinate and commander of the thirteen-division Fifth Army, Lt. Gen. Mark W. Clark, shared much of Alexander's vision but was skeptical concerning important details. Like Alexander, Clark favored a massive go-for-broke offensive and a one-two punch. Unlike Alexander, he did not believe the Germans could be trapped merely by seizing such strong points as Valmontone. There were too many lesser routes through the Southern Apennines for the Allies to enclose the Germans or to pin them neatly against the mountains. In Clark's mind it was better to attrite the Germans during hot pursuit, presumably in the direction of Rome with the American Fifth Army leading. Clark accommodated Alexander's guidance for a breakout from Anzio towards Valmontone, but supplemented that guidance with additional plans for a breakout from Anzio towards Rome.[4]

The appropriate direction of the Anzio breakout was not the only strategic particular wherein Clark differed with Alexander. In the south, Clark saw the British assault up the heavily defended Liri Valley past Cassino as no more likely to succeed than the sanguinary efforts of the previous winter. In Clark's view the thinly defended lunar landscape of the Aurunci Mountains offered better prospects for success.[5] Relying on the terrain itself, the Germans tended to defend such sectors lightly. Allied troops had discovered on several occasions[6] that defiladed routes, dead space, and trafficable ridge lines could be made to favor the attacker. Defending troops could organize level or modestly rolling terrain into tightly interlocking fields of fire. The Aurunci defied such neatly interwoven organization.

Clark's strongest asset in the case of an Aurunci offensive was the four-division French Expeditionary Corps (FEC). The FEC's commander, Gen. Alphonse Juin, was already legendary for his adept handling of a colorful mixture of French colonial troops, Moroccans, Algerians, North African mountain tribesmen, escaped French patriots, American tankers, and American artillerymen.[7] Insofar as Juin's polyglot troops possessed traits in common, they were fiercely eager, battle-hardened, and mountain-wise. If anyone could break through the Aurunci, it was the FEC.

General Juin did not, of course, intend to pierce the German defenses unsupported. He proposed that others should hold his shoulders while he himself effected the major breakthrough.[8] To his right, British frontal attacks up the Liri would tie down Germans in that sector. To his left, attacks by the American II Corps—to seize Mount Damiano initially and Spigno ultimately—could serve a similar purpose. Clark concurred with Juin's proposal and committed the II Corps' 88th Infantry Division to the objectives recommended by the Frenchman.[9] The II Corps' 85th Infantry Division was to make a further supporting attack along the coastal road. It was recognized that both divisions were composed of green draftees, but the limited objectives seemed commensurate with their known abilities.

At precisely 2300 hours on 11 May 1944, the Italian front from Cassino to the sea erupted with the first rounds of the most violent artillery preparation since El Alamein. Even before the shelling ceased, American, French, British, Indian, Polish, and Canadian assault troops stormed out of their foxholes and sangars and into the Gustav Line.

The 88th Infantry Division's 350th Regiment marked paths forward through the darkness with tracer lines—40-millimeter tracers for battalion boundaries, .50-caliber tracers to separate company sectors.[10] The 350th attacked with its 1st and 2nd battalions abreast, the 1st to seize Mount Damiano proper and 2nd to take its somewhat more distant appendage, Hill 316. When these were in hand, the penetration was to be broadened by taking Mount Ceracoli and deepened by seizing the village of Ventosa, then Mount Rotondo and Mount Cerri. The regiment was also to remain abreast of French units advancing along its right flank.[11]

The 1st Battalion's attack progressed quickly. Behind a curtain of preparatory artillery, Companies A and B advanced abreast through the cover of terraces and olive groves. The draftees took few casualties initially, largely because German mortars and infantrymen were so thoroughly suppressed by the American artillery. German flares signaled their own artillery to fire, but most of this fell well to the rear of the rapidly advancing American line. Within forty-five minutes the draftees were on the heights, swarming into German positions seconds after the American artillery shifted to deeper targets. Fighting became savage. German machine gun "zipper pistols," also called "burp guns," barked from the darkness of sangars and dugouts. These fires attracted the M-1s and hand grenades of the GIs in response. In places, fighting was so close that bayonets mattered.

After a few minutes of violence and confusion, the surviving Germans tumbled down the rear slope of Damiano in desperate efforts to escape. The draftees, hard on the heels of an earthshaking artillery preparation, were too formidable and too numerous for their grey-clad adversaries in the 194th Grenadiers. The Americans had taken casualties and had suffered consideable confusion. Company A was completely disorganized and Company B was too disorganized to continue the attack immediately. Company C, technically in reserve but in fact inching around the north face of Damiano towards Ventosa, was pinned down by heavy machine gun and mortar fire from German positions in the French sector. Nevertheless, the 1st Battalion's attack rated as a complete success. In the entire American sector Damiano was the single most critical piece of terrain. The 88th had seized it in just fifty-one minutes.

The 2nd Battalion's initial attack also combined success and confusion. Companies E and G were scheduled to advance abreast across the easterly slopes of Mount Damiano onto Hill 316. Company E failed to reach the line of departure on time and the battalion commander replaced it with his reserve, Company F. Immediately across the line of departure both companies encountered a mine field. Company G swung well to its right and bypassed the worst of the mines, while Company F inched carefully forward through the mine field using techniques of infiltration. In the darkness and confusion the two companies lost contact with each other. Both encountered heavy resistance when the Germans, no longer suppressed by preparatory artillery, emerged from their dugouts into the face of the American advance. Fierce individual battles developed between Germans, disorganized by the intense shelling, and Americans, scarcely less disorganized by mines and obstacles.

Here S. Sgt. Charles W. Shea won the division's first Medal of Honor. His platoon leader and platoon sergeant were casualties; he and a few other survivors were pinned down in a mine field by three machine guns. Inching carefully past trip wires and trigger plates, Shea made it over the lip of the first gun emplacement. Here he "had the drop" on four Germans. Three surrendered. The fourth, a diehard, went for a grenade and Shea shot him. Shea then inched his way carefully to the second machine gun position, where he captured two more Germans. The nature of the ground was such that he had to rush the last position, and he killed all three of the German occupants when he did so. Shea, a hot dog vendor from New York City, had not seemed all that likely a prospect as a major hero. In the darkness and confusion he rose to the occasion, and his platoon reorganized and continued its advance through the breach he had opened.[12]

By 0145, F and G companies had clawed their way forward to what they reported as Hill 316. Dawn's improved visibility revealed that instead they were in a saddle between 316 and Damiano proper. Heavy sniper fire from Hill 316 restricted individual movements and skirmishs developed elsewhere when German infantrymen desperately attempted to filter out of positions bypassed in the American advance. Company E, now under the command of a second lieutenant, finally fought its way forward to the lead companies. At daybreak the battalion commander attempted to reorganize and continue his attack.

In the 1st Battalion sector, renewed efforts after seizing Damiano led to heavy fighting for the village of Ventosa. Companies B and C continued the attack. Company A, the most severely disorganized during the attack on Damiano, was replaced by K Company from the 3rd Battalion, then in reserve. Fighting ebbed and flowed in fierce individual encounters until dawn, when the Americans finally shouldered their way into the village. The Germans did not retreat far. Their 71st Division launched a company-scale counterattack against the 2nd Battalion's forward elements just before dawn. This attack was repulsed without loss of ground, but it caused General Sloan to become increasingly concerned for the security of his right-flank units. Rather than expose these units to flank attacks before they recovered from the night's exertions, Sloan ordered the 350th to hold and reorganize on Damiano until the French came abreast north of Castelforte.

Once Damiano proper was in hand, the 350th was in a position to mop up Mount Ceracoli as well. Here the ground was rough and hilly, but nevertheless more suited for tanks than anywhere else in the regimental sector, so C Company of the 753rd Tank Battalion led the attack. The tankers kicked off at 0540, followed closely by the 350th's I Company. The tanks beetled foward against ineffectual opposition, all the while blasting Ceracoli with machine guns and 75-millimeter cannons. Two tanks hit mines; five threw tracks; one sheared a rear idler; and one suffered engine failure. The remainder gained the crest of Ceracoli and scattered the surviving Germans. The American infantrymen trailing the advance passed quickly through the tanks to sweep the objective. Twenty-five other Germans were killed or wounded. On Ceracoli, the Germans, their antitank defenses suppressed or destroyed by artillery and their positions overlooked by Americans on Damiano, proved helpless. The action lasted mere minutes before the defenders filtered out or surrendered.[13]

Through the remainder of 12 May, the 350th's sector was quiet. Units disappeared, or seemed to disappear, as infantrymen sought to exploit every shred of cover and concealment. Initial objectives achieved, or achieved in part, the battalions reorganized and shuffled intermingled units back to the control of parent organizations. Wherever possible, commanders evacuated casualties through the difficult terrain to the regimental rear. Some unfortunate casualties—German and American alike—could not be reached and endured a day of pain and exposure before rescue parties picked a way to them in the gathering darkness of evening. Evening brought a renewal of tactical activity as well. With its tactical organization and wire communications restored, the 2nd Battalion inched F Company along Hill 316. The 1st

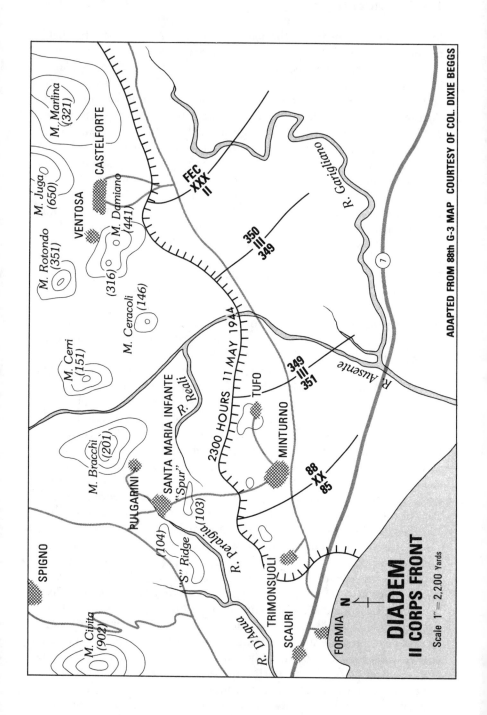

DIADEM
II CORPS FRONT

Scale 1" = 2,200 Yards

ADAPTED FROM 88th G-3 MAP   COURTESY OF COL. DIXIE BEGGS

M. Martina (321)

M. Juga (650)

M. Rotondo (351)

CASTELFORTE

VENTOSA

M. Damiano (441)

(316)

M. Ceracoli (146)

M. Cerri (151)

FEC
XXX
II

350
III
349

M. Bracchi (201)

SANTA MARIA INFANTE
"Spur"

R. Reali

2300 HOURS 11 MAY 1944

349
III
351

TUFO

MINTURNO

R. Garigliano

R. Ausente

7

PULGARINI

(103)

(104)
"S" Ridge

R. Peraigiia

88
XX
85

SPIGNO

M. Civita (902)

TRIMONSUOLI

R. D'Aqua

SCAURI

FORMIA   N

Battalion, also reorganized, straightened its line north of Damiano and tied itself into the French front-line trace.[14]

Two counterattacks caused momentary concern. One German company attacked F Company and temporarily stalemated the 2nd Battalion's advance. On-call mortars and artillery mauled the attacking German unit, and F Company resumed its tortuous advance By dawn on the 13th, Hill 316 was entirely in American hands. Another counterattack struck Mount Ceracoli. German tank killer teams found and exploited a gap in I Company's positions and nearly overran the American tanks. Just in time the tankers and infantrymen detected the infiltrators and drove them off, leaving nineteen Germans dead and three wounded, and taking eleven prisoners.[15]

Daylight on 13 May again quieted the 350th's battlefield. Casual sniping occurred along the line, including tanks on Ceracoli leisurely blowing up Italian houses—suspected enemy positions—with high-explosive super ammunition. The Germans, bent on covering their eventual withdrawal, shelled the 350th with greater intensity than before, but their capability to delay the 350th was weakening fast.

By 1700 hours the 350th was once again on the attack, this time to seize Mount Rotondo. The 1st Battalion, reinforced by Companies K and L from the 3rd Battalion, made the main attack, while the 2nd Battalion provided fire support from Hill 316. Moving quickly forward against weakening German resistance, the attack developed along textbook lines. The excitement of the event comes through in fortuitously preserved radio transmissions of an anonymous artillery observer. As the attack kicked off, the observer pleaded, "For God's sake, get some fire on Rotondo. The Krauts are running over it like rabbits. . . ." A little later the transmission was "We're killing plenty of Jerries. Keep it up. They're running like hell." Then came the exultant "Christ, there go our boys. They are going along just as if they were doing a maneuver at Gruber. Right up the side of Rotondo. Yea! Yea! We've got Rotondo!"[16]

By the morning of 14 May the 350th Infantry Regiment was firmly established on Mount Rotondo overlooking the Ausente Valley. In tough fighting the draftees had bested their German adversaries and knocked them out of formidable defensive positions—the Gustav Line had cracked. The regiment's next order would be to "pursue."

The 351st Infantry Regiment also attacked behind the violent artillery preparation of 2300 hours, 11 May. The regiment's objective was the small village of Santa Maria Infante, a hill town overlooking the Ausonia Valley and, more important, the single road providing the Germans lateral communications behind the XIV Panzer Corps front.[17]

Like the 350th, the 351st expected fierce resistance, but its terrain was more difficult: rolling countryside whose even slopes offered intervisible positions and interlocking fields of fire, precisely the type of terrain the Germans characteristically organized into their most effective defenses. As if this did not offer the five-hundred Germans of the 94th Fusilier Reconnaissance Battalion advantages enough, the front in the sector was masked by creeks that impaired off-road movement and, worst of all, confined tanks to a narrow strip along the road.[18]

The 351st's plan of attack called for its 2nd Battalion to lead along the road from Minturno to Santa Maria Infante. The 3rd Battalion covered the right flank and the 1st Battalion remained in reserve. To the 2nd Battalion's left, the 85th Infantry Division's 338th Infantry Regiment attacked S-Ridge, a long, low series of hills flanking the 351st's axis of advance. The 2nd Battalion attacked with E and F companies abreast, followed by G in reserve. Company F advanced on the left of the Minturno–Santa Maria Infante road; E Company advanced on the right of the road. The battalion plan of attack integrated artillery and mortar fires and provided for tanks and engineer support on call. Insofar as communications were concerned, the battalion and company commanders depended upon radio communications supplemented by visual contact, marking tape, and marking tracers.[19]

Company F's attack began on schedule, then disintegrated into four separate efforts. The platoons dispersed just across the line of departure when they came under fire from artillery, mortars, and machine guns firing from S-Ridge. One by one radios failed—the company commander's was among the first. Once dispersed, the platoons never regained their original configuration in the smoke, darkness, and confusion.

Picking separate ways forward through obstacles and mine fields, three platoon-sized groups—two of which consisted of squads from different platoons thrown together by chance—stalled against formidable emplacements along the crest and slopes of Hill 103. In confused and bitter fighting the draftees gave a good account of themselves but none of the individual groups proved sufficiently strong to work through more than one or two of the machine-gun positions in their line of advance. The Germans quickly replaced the fire from weapons knocked out with fire from other weapons whose sectors interlocked. Without communications, the separate groups of Americans could neither call for artillery and mortars nor support each other's efforts. Indeed, no group knew where the other groups were or what they were doing.

A fourth platoon-sized group from F Company—consisting of a squad from the 3rd Platoon, a squad from the 1st Platoon, three machine-gun squads from H Company (attached), and the company headquarters led by the commander himself, Capt. Carl W. Nelson—slipped by the otherwise preoccupied defenders of Hill 103 and penetrated to the outskirts of Santa Maria Infante. En route, this contingent overran a mortar position and captured fifteen half-dressed and completely surprised Germans. On the outskirts of Santa Maria Infante, Nelson's group came under heavy mortar and machine gun fire from the S-Ridge and under sniper fire from the village itself. Nelson decided it would be prudent to dig in until reinforced, so he converted a draw and culvert to the west of the village into a miniature strong point.

To the east of the road into Santa Maria Infante, E Company also encountered heavy resistance early in its advance. The array of emplacements that bedeviled F Company on Hill 103 extended across the road and along a spur that ran perpendicular to the American line of advance for five hundred yards. This German strong point in E Company's sector included no fewer than twelve machine-gun positions dug into the hillside or emplaced in the rubble of sturdy Italian farm houses. Company E retained its communications—and thus its artillery support and unity of effort—throughout the attack, but, like F Company, it also reached a stalemate in a thicket of mines, obstacles, and interlocking fires.

In an effort to restore momentum, the commander of the 2nd Battalion, Lt. Col. Raymond E. Kendall, added his own courageous feats to those already enacted. When E Company's commander was wounded, Kendall came forward and personally led attacks on the most troublesome of the machine gun emplacements. He personally destroyed a pillbox with bazooka shells and knocked out another machine gun with hand grenades. The reinvigorated attack gained another hundred years as the infantrymen, inspired by Kendall, renewed their roles. The attack stalled again when it ran into yet another string of German positions. Kendall himself fell mortally wounded when he rounded the corner of a house to throw a grenade and was struck in the face by a supporting machine gun seventy-five yards away. With Kendall's death, at approximately 0300, the 2nd Battalion advance mired in front of the spur. Company G fought through bypassed German positions to come to the relief of E Company, which by now had taken eighty-nine casualties, but G Company also was stopped by the formidable German defenses.

Company E had requested tank support during its first hour of fighting on the spur. After initial confusion, a platoon of tanks from the 760th Tank Battalion finally rolled down the Santa Maria Infante Road at about 0300.[20] The road was known to be mined, so the 351st's antitank company attempted to clear it before the tanks arrived. As the tank platoon leader approached the line of contact, an engineer officer advised him that the mine clearance was still incomplete; heavy interference fires had forced the breaching party to take cover. The tank platoon leader decided to take his chances, rolled forward, and lost his tank to a tremendous explosion. Even as this platoon leader was being evacuated, two other lieutenants, tank liaison officers spurred by desperate requests for support, decided to risk sending another tank into the mine field. The second tank also hit a mine and exploded. The regimental commander of the 351st, Col. Arthur S. Champeny, arrived on the scene and ordered the tank platoon sergeant to try again. This NCO, eyewitness to the two previous explosions and unimpressed with the 88th's mine clearance thus far, refused. Champeny declared him "relieved" of his command and after a fierce discussion cajoled another of the tankers into yet another attempt. This third tank also hit a mine. Champeny called to the rear and requested another tank platoon. He also left his supporting engineers instructions to complete a path through the mine field before tanks attempted another crossing, a course of action the surviving tankers firmly supported.

At 0420, Champeny fed his 3rd Battalion into the attack. Companies I and K swung wide to the left along the route successfully taken by Nelson's contingent from F Company several hours earlier. By now the Germans were alert to the dimensions of the Allied attack, however, so the path F Company's contingent had followed was no longer open. The 3rd Battalion stalled in its turn on the lower slopes of the hotly contested Hill 103. At daybreak the battalion found itself exposed to machine gun fire from the S-Ridge, still in German hands.

Throughout the night the Germans had been husbanding the resources necessary for local counterattacks. Captain Nelson's isolated contingent was their first target. In the late afternoon Nelson came under a determined attack supported by self-propelled guns firing at point-blank range. All appeared lost until American artillery observers, soaring high above the battlefield in a light observation plane, spotted his predicament and broke up the counterattack with heavy concentrations of artillery. These fires destroyed two self-propelled guns and scattered the rest. The artillerymen also annihilated a German reserve company they caught in an assembly area with a carefully coordinated time-on-target (i.e., simultaneous-impact) multiple battalion mission. Mauled by artillery and stubbornly resisted by Nelson's infantrymen, the initial German counterattack faltered.

While the men of F Company weathered German attacks, tanks from the 760th again tried to break through to relieve them.[21] By noon on the twelfth the 351st Antitank Company, assisted by heavy suppressive fires on enemy positions, cleared a lane through the mine field. A fresh tank platoon rolled through the breach and demolished the nearest machine gun positions with point-blank fire. Once the tanks crested the spur, however, they came under heavy and accurate antitank fire from Santa Maria Infante. In this exchange the Germans knocked out three tanks, after which the rest withdrew.

At about 1500 yet another tank platoon attempted to batter its way through to Santa Maria. These tankers were closely assisted by infantrymen—by this time intimately familiar with the layout of the German positions—who rode on the back decks and pointed out targets. Tank-infantry teams knocked out no fewer than twenty machine gun or sniper positions using this technique. In another duel with the German guns, the leading vehicles knocked out the first to fire on the advancing column. Unfortunately, this luck did not hold. Other German guns opened up and the array of antitank positions again proved too tough to break through. The Americans once again retired after having lost two more tanks to the stubborn Germans. Another tank platoon attempted to bypass the strongest German positions by following a trail winding across Reali Creek somewhat to the east of Santa Maria. The ground proved too soft for the vehicles; all mired. It took an engineer company a day and a half to get them out.

As darkness approached, the Germans again counterattacked. Limited visibility concealed them from American artillery observers as they assembled and moved forward. Again F Company was the initial target. The Germans used a ruse to get close. Six Germans moved forward with their hands over their heads shouting *"Kamerad,"* thus apparently attempting to surrender. This noisy distraction masked the forward movement of the German main body. Company F, by then almost out of ammunition and virtually without unwounded personnel, sent a contingent from its foxholes to accept the surrender. In a single rush the Germans swept through the American position, capturing the dazed defenders before they could offer effective resistance. Five enlisted men who pretended to be dead escaped capture.

Buoyed by success, the Germans moved on to attack the 3rd Battalion on Hill 103. This time their luck did not hold. The battalion was not in the exhausted condition of the contingent from F Company, and no conceivable ruse provided a means of approach. Although the initial attacks were hotly contested, American mortars and artillery soon swept the Germans back into the protection of foxholes and emplacements.

On the morning of the 13th, the 351st had little to show for two nights of exhaustive effort and heavy casualties. Nobody knew how badly they were hurting the Germans, nor could they know that the German line, unhinged by the successes of the FEC and the 350th to the north, could hardly afford to take further such punishment. An air of gloom pervaded a meeting between the commanders of the 88th and 85th infantry divisions as they once again resolved to batter their way forward.[22] They set a renewed attack for 1600. The 351st's boundary shifted west to include Hills 109, 126, and 128 on S-Ridge. This gave Champeny more room to maneuver and the opportunity to reduce the machine gun nests on S-Ridge that had so bedeviled his advance. Champeny's plan was to send the 2nd and 3rd battalions once more against the objectives in front of them—the spur and Hill 103, respectively—while swinging his 1st Battalion to the left onto S-Ridge. Once the 1st Battalion seized Hill 109, it was to advance along S-Ridge into Santa Maria. The critical attack on Hill 109 would be made by a battalion that was altogether fresh and without casualties.

The 1st Battalion did not attack at the scheduled time. Two thousand difficult meters separated its assembly area from its attack position. The battalion commander and his operations and training officer were isolated by enemy artillery fire when reconnoitering the assigned objectives, and they rejoined their battalion several hours later than planned. The route of advance to the attack position took the battalion through the knee-deep mud of Peralgia Creek. Heavy machine guns and cumbersome ammunition crates had to be manhandled across the width of the front. Preparations moved at a snail's pace.

Mindful of these delays, Champeny requested permission to defer his attack time. Sloan concurred with an 1830 attack time, but the 85th Infantry Division decided to conduct its attack at 1630 instead. In the confused radio traffic that followed, units came to dfferent conclusions as to when they were supposed to attack. The 85th's 338th Infantry Regiment attacked at 1630. The 351st's 2nd Battalion attacked at 1630. The 351st's 3rd Battalion attacked at 1830. The 351st's 1st Battalion, after experiencing further delays, did not attack until 2200. The Germans, having intercepted at least some of the radio traffic, prepared for an 1830 attack.[23]

Attacking at 1630, the 2nd Battalion's E and G companies made some initial progress. Their attack was assisted by supporting fire from tank destroyers on Tufo Ridge, almost two thousand meters south of the spur—well clear of the deadly fire of the German antitank weapons. The flat trajectory of the tank destroyers made them ideal for penetrating the embrasures of machine gun positions, provided such targets could be identified. To mark targets, E Company used .50-caliber tracers fired from its own positions.[24] Tankers on Tufo Ridge watched the tracers and followed the line of sight they described into the target, then blasted away at the positions thus identified. The 2nd Battalion worked its way to the opposite side of the spur, after which it became ensnarled in a thicket of machine gun nests invisible to the tankers on Tufo Ridge. The battalion knocked out some of these positions without being able to work through them all.

Shortly before the 3rd Battalion's attack, the Germans fired a preemptive barrage with four hundred rounds of carefully hoarded artillery ammunition.[25] When this subsided the 3rd Battalion advanced and made some progress knocking out the nearest machine gun positions. Without the support of the 1st Battalion's attack against S-Ridge, however, the 3rd Battalion was again doomed to stalemate in a crossfire from its front and flanks—Hills 103 and 109, respectively.

The 1st Battalion finally attacked at 2200. The Germans, who expected them earlier, had already exhausted their artillery in a preemptive barrage on the 3rd Battalion and on the not-yet-occupied attack positions of the 1st Battalion. One unit from the 338th had already mistakenly attacked Hill 109, so the Germans had reason to believe they had already experienced the anticipated attack.[26] Benefitting from this surprise and superior numbers, C Company worked its way quickly up Hill 109. In the darkness and confusion it initially attacked the misdirected contingent from the 338th, which had stalled halfway up the slope. These unfortunates quickly identified themselves as Americans, so little damage was done and the advance continued. At 0300, C Company evicted the exhausted Germans from Hill 109 and secured its invaluable crest.

Company B had remained in reserve. When C Company took flanking fire from Hill 131, in the 338th's sector, it crossed the regimental boundary and attacked Hill 131.[27] Initially there was considerable confusion as the Germans, mindful of the loss of Hill 109, struggled to extricate themselves and as troops from 338th and 351st mistook each other for Germans in the darkness. Ultimately both the Germans and B Company withdrew, leaving the hill to the 338th.

As 14 May dawned over the Italian battlefields, the 351st at last held the piece of terrain that would unlock Santa Maria Infante. The cost had been high: 84 killed, 284 wounded, and 93 captured or missing. Five of the regiment's nine rifle companies were at half strength or less. The Germans also had lost heavily. The 94th Fusilier Reconnaissance Battalion lost more than two hundred men in the bitter fighting along the direct approaches to Santa Maria, while the equally exhausted 267th Grenadier Regiment lost almost two hundred more on the slopes of S-Ridge. The brutal fact was that the two American fourteen-thousand-man draft divisions, with 10 percent overstrengths for replacements and entire battalions not yet engaged, could afford such losses; the thinly spread Germans could not.[28]

The logisticians of the 88th Infantry Division also found themselves taxed during the first days of the May offensive. Supplies in all classes rose to enormous levels of stockage prior to the attack. Peninsular Base Section issued 16,238 tons of ammunition alone in the fortnight before D day.[29] In an effort to avoid calling attention to extensive front-line depots, the division's logisticians forwarded most of this ammunition directly to the firing units. Mortarmen had one thousand rounds stacked by each tube. Artillerymen enjoyed similar largesse. In the push for Santa Maria, the 913th Artillery Battalion alone fired five thousand rounds. Contrast this with a "major" pre-emptive strike of the Germans: four-hundred rounds in front of Hill 103 on 13 May.

Rations, clothing, fuel, oil, lubricants, engineering items, medi-cines, repair parts, and major end items also had been prestocked in enormous quantities. Only extraordinary circumstances caused Allied units to experience supply shortages during the period 11-14 May. Indeed, throughout the II Corps sector only F Company of the 351st's 2nd Battalion—cut off, surrounded, and repeatedly subjected to heavy German attacks—ever found itself low on ammunition and medical supplies.[30]

Transportation posed more problems than did supply per se, but the 88th's advances from 11 May to 14 May were not yet so extensive as to make these problems serious. The division was serviced by fourteen hundred mules and four hundred muleteers. Railheads existed at Teano, Sparanise, and Carinola, and pipelines extended to Mignano and Sessa. From these points, routes that had been exercised for months extended to the initial attack positions, all of which were already well stocked. Several thousand yards more—through difficult terrain, to be sure—brought mule trains to the leading American units. The flow of supplies was uninterrupted and routine.[31]

Behind the new front lines engineers hastened to improve supply routes. Bailey bridges became permanent bridges; mine fields were marked, then cleared; goat trails were widened to support vehicular traffic; mired tanks were retrieved, then pushed forward along newly engineered routes. The front-line infantryman masked a frenzy of engineering activity.[32]

Insofar as maintenance was concerned, the 88th found it had few new problems to address, largely because vehicles were little-used initially and because firing batteries received little in the way of effec-tive counterbattery fire. There were, of course, small-arms failures and small arms damaged or destroyed. Small-arms repair was, for the most part, deferred. Men became casualties more quickly than did weapons, and replacement troops brought weapons forward with them. Indeed, the accidents of combat seemed to increase rather than reduce the small arms available to front-line infantrymen. One reads of assaulting troops picking up, using, and discarding weapons as if they were so many vegetables in an untidy garden.[33]

Only the tankers encountered serious maintenance problems. They mired, threw tracks in difficult terrain, lost suspension components to mines and obstacles, and suffered battle damage from anti-tank rounds. They also suffered routine mechanical failures. Infantry commanders became impatient with the array of mechanical difficulties;[34] tankers recognized them as the cost of doing business. All factors considered, the tankers and their supporting mechanics did a creditable job keeping as many tanks as they did in the action.[35] Most disabled tanks and many knocked-out ones were repaired in short order. Other tanks, even some with relatively minor damage, were simply replaced. The Peninsular Base Section depots included replacement tanks in their cornucopia of prestocked supplies.

Communications difficulties demonstrated a major weakness of American support apparatus. Attacking formations were overly dependent on radios, and the radios on hand were unreliable. Some radios failed altogether at critical times; others fell victim to the peculiarities of terrain, range, and interference. Units that took the time to lay wire enjoyed better communications, although wire presented its own special problems. Wire was easily cut by artillery fire, moving tanks, or simple clumsiness. Wiremen working their way back along the lines to restore communications found themselves bewildered by spaghetti snarls of entangled cable. Often it was quicker to lay entirely new lines rather than to attempt to restore old ones. This expedient in turn increased the total number of lines available to become entangled. After the first few days, experience and command attention led to improved communications. Commanders established radio relay stations and radio backup systems. Wiremen tagged lines where they came close to each other and began using the heavier 110 wire instead of the more fragile 130 wire. Couriers came to be more carefully and frequently used. The 88th would not master its communications for some time, but the experiences of the initial hours of the offensive spurred emphasis and improvement.[36]

It should not be supposed that communications problems were unique to the 88th. All Allied divisions suffered such problems to a greater or lesser extent.[37] The Germans, their rear areas and communications pulverized by artillery and air strikes, suffered even more. The 88th's commanders could talk to most subordinate and supporting units most of the time. German commanders were hard put to talk to anybody.[38]

During Diadem, American logisticians also saw further problems in the exercising of medical care. Casualty cases among the draftees benefited from a medical establishment as extensive as had ever been mustered. Benefited, that is, after they finally reached a medical facility. Evacuation schemes involving litter trails feeding into ambulance pickup points and clearing stations had been carefully thought out and rehearsed. Unfortunately, the sheer difficulties of terrain and circumstance made evacuation difficult. During daylight, casualties stranded between the lines suffered extended agonies until darkness concealed rescuers from enemy observation. Litter teams came under fire intended for other targets. Of sixty Italian volunteers who assisted in the evacuation of the 351st's casualties near Santa Maria Infante, twenty-three were killed in action. Medical evacuation probably could not have been much improved upon; it was difficult to extricate casualties quickly given the nature of the fighting and the evacuation means available.[39]

Fortunately, the overall division casualty rate for Diadem was low. This factor coupled with the on hand overstrength of 1,037 replacement personnel gave appearance of a successful individual replacement operation. But the apparent success of the 88th in replacing casualties led to misconceptions with unfortunate long-term consequences. Operation Diadem was not only a test of the draft division, but also a trial of the idea of replacing casualties as individuals, in a manner analogous to the replenishment of ammunition, spare parts, and irreparable vehicles. The division's successes in attacking ever wearier Germans with fresh men was misread—and continues to be misread—as a validation of the individual replacement system. In fact, the system of individual replacement did not work well during the actual combat itself. Replacements tended to be confused, frightened, and guided rather than led into combat. They often became lost or separated from the units they were to fill. They did not immediately identify with their new comrades, could not immediately be relied upon, and took time to settle in. There was nothing wrong with the replacements as individuals; in time they, too, became good soldiers. Replacements simply proved not to be interchangeable parts. The notion of a draftee division, trained as a unit from the ground up, and the notion of a drafted individual replacement, trained and deployed without unit identity, were confused in the aftermath of Diadem. The validation of one did not necessarily mean the validation of the other.[40]

The momentum of the 88th's attack was maintained not by fresh men, but by fresh companies.[41] During sledgehammer blows against the Gustav Line, companies wore out and were replaced by others not yet engaged. Increasingly weary Germans found themselves attacked by new American units on 13 May and again on 14 May. This was not because individuals came forward to replace the fallen, but because fresh companies attacked in their turn across the same narrow fronts.

What, then, can one conclude from the first three days of the 88th's first big offensive? In the strictest sense, the draftees fulfilled the promise of their training. What they had trained well to do, they did well. Techniques they had mastered through practicing time and time again in training or on maneuvers remained mastered in actual combat.

Unfortunately, the converse was also true. One could have predicted the strengths of the 88th by analyzing its training program; one also could have predicted its weaknesses by reflecting on that program's omissions.

Insofar as the riflemen themselves were concerned, nobody but the Germans had reason to complain. Their aggressiveness and determination were creditable, at times heroic. They moved well within ther squads: they alternated moving and supporting by fire, worked forward by bounds through formidable obstacles, rushed enemy positions after tedious approaches, and executed their most successful attacks with parade-ground precision. They seem to have handled personal weapons, rifles, pistols, grenades, light machine guns, competently and with effect. If anything, they were criticized for being too controlled in their use of weapons, for not being willing to fire blindly at targets they could not see.[42] Overall, the 88th's successes were, more than anything else, the successes of its riflemen; its failures were not failures on the rifleman's part.

The artillery of the 88th rendered a similarly creditable performance. The 88th's major training exercises had been exercises of an infantry-artillery combination. The proficiency thus gained had been sharpened in the two months of Minturno's no-man's-land. Practice paid off; dazed German prisoners commented on how closely American infantrymen followed the supporting barrages and on how effective American counterbattery fire was. German counterattacks were repeatedly swept away by hurricanes of American artillery. Whereas dismounted counterattacks traditionally had been an integral feature of German defensive technique, in the face of accurate, overwhelming American artillery the tactic proved suicidal in most circumstances. Some of the 88th's artillery actions were brilliant. Cases in point were the time-on-target annihilation of a German reserve company, the spotter plane–directed destruction of self-propelled guns attacking F Company, and the tracer-guided destruction of pillboxes during the final attacks on the spur.[43]

For a number of reasons, many of which were simply administrative, the 88th's training slighted the integration of air support and tanks as much as it emphasized the integration of infantry and artillery. These training omissions manifested themselves on the battlefield. There is no evidence that tactical air support made much difference in the 88th's front-line action. Indeed, the records reflect that maneuvering units were conscious of air strikes only in a general sort of way— this despite the fact that not less than one-eighth of the firepower assigned to the 88th's attack was to come from the air. It may be that the air support available to the Allied Armies in Italy served a useful purpose insofar as strategic bombing or interdiction were concerned, but in the much narrower field of vision of the 88th, air support came to serve little purpose at all. The technology existed to integrate close air support, and close air support had been effectively used by other divisions prior to Diadem. The 88th's underutilization of air support seems to have resulted from a preference for the familiar, a preference to use artillery to get the same job done.[44]

Tanks were somewhat better integrated into the division's attack than close air support, largely because of frenzied preparations after the division was in Italy. The tank-infantry training had not been extensive, however, and coordination proved to be far from smooth. The 760th Tank Battalion's preferred method of support was for tanks to trail infantry by a considerable distance, then to rush forward when suitable targets were identified. This technique requires masterful timing and reliable communications, attributes the 88th did not enjoy around Santa Maria Infante. Tanks arrived well after the 351st's attack stalled and plowed into a mine field the 351st had not yet cleared. From that inauspicious beginning the 351st's commanders ordered, cajoled, or browbeat the tankers into the teeth of a fully prepared enemy. The successes the tankers did have were testimony to courage and technical competence, not to imagination or tactical finesse.

On Mount Ceracoli the tankers had more luck, largely because German defenses had already been unhinged by the seizure of Damiano. Ceracoli was a well-executed, if minor, secondary attack. Even at Ceracoli, however, infantry and tanks were not fully integrated. In the consolidation, tankers and infantrymen each assumed the other was securing the ground masking the tank positions. In the confusion this ground remained unsecured and became the avenue of approach for a German counterattack that came within a hair's breadth of success.

One wonders how many lives would have been spared if tanks had been fully integrated into the first rush of the 88th's attack. The state of the art was illustrated by the 1st Armored Division's clockwork attack out of Anzio two weeks later. Armor represented more than a third of the firepower available to the 88th's attack. Employed late and largely frittered away, this firepower proved of little consequence on the immediate battlefield.[45]

Another handicap during the 88th's attack was faulty communications. Radios were not altogether reliable, nor did they always have the necessary range. Wire communications, while more reliable, were cumbersome and likely to be cut. Messengers were slow and often killed or wounded. These were technical problems that were not then and have not yet been fully resolved.[46] Commanders can improve their chances, however, by developing backup systems and previously agreed upon visual or acoustic signals. The Army Training Program did not emphasize techniques of battlefield communication, nor did the training of the 88th. Units went into the attack trusting their radios. Too often the result was confusion—each squad fighting its own little war. The 88th did learn from its experiences and eventually mastered tactical communications as far as was then possible. During the learning period of 11-14 May 1944, however, the division suffered some hard knocks.

Concerning logistics, one must conclude that the 88th was prepared to support itself to the limits of the technology of the time, for it never lacked with respect to a class of supply or a logistical activity. In light of the redundant mule and truck transportation establishments, one might argue that too many men were given over to logistical activities. If so, this did not leave too few riflemen available to fight the Germans, even though 50 percent of the division's personnel were given over to logistical activities. Only 40 percent of a comparable German division's personnel were thus used, but German rifemen were less well supported and far fewer in number than their Allied opponents.

An overall assessment of the 88th's first three days in its first big offensive must give the division high marks. In bitter, confused fighting the draftees penetrated some of the sturdiest defenses of the Gustav Line. Indeed, a recent and respected quantitative study identifies the 88th as Diadem's highest-performing Allied division.[47] Despite deficiencies in their preparation, the draftees proved adequately prepared to accomplish their doctrinal mission: to close with and destroy the enemy in extended ground combat. The War Department verdict concerning the performance of the 88th was, in fact, highly favorable.

Alas, the effectiveness of the draftees' performance was not immediately apparent. The War Department verdict would come only after several weeks of hindsight. On May 14 assessments remained confused. General Clark, somewhat removed from the fighting and not altogether conscious of its severity, had hoped to clear Sante Maria Infante by noon on the twelfth. In his disappointment he contrasted the successes of the "veteran" FEC with the frustrations of the "green" 85th and 88th. At the time, Clark did not know of the scantiness of the opposition in the face of the French, or of the strength of the defenses in the face of the draftees.[48]

The draftees themselves did not yet have a complete picture. Their sense of accomplishment or failure depended upon where they were. Some elements of the 350th had experienced easy successes, whereas others had been roughly handled. To the 351st, corpse-strewn hillsides around Santa Maria Infante initially smelled more of failure than of victory. The draftees of the 349th had not yet participated in their first battle at all. The verdict of 11-14 May is more clear in retrospect than it was to men at the time. One draftee could triumphantly cheer, "Yea! Yea! We've got Rotondo!" while another, with equal conviction, stared at the stump that had been his arm and sobbed, "We got the hell kicked out of us."[49] The facts were not yet clear. Only more fighting and greater success could bring them into focus.

8

Minturno to Rome: The Pursuit

Even as the 350th Infantry Regiment consolidated Mount Rotondo and the 351st inched cautiously from Hill 109 toward Santa Maria Infante, Allied chieftains shifted their attention from the immediate battle to wider vistas. Now breached in three places, the Gustav Line was but the first of a series of defensible traces separating the Italian southern front from coastal plains leading to Anzio and Rome. Of the other traces, the Germans had developed two—the Dora Extension, three miles behind the Gustav Line, and the Hitler Line, twenty miles to the rear of that—into formidable positions.[1] The Germans had long since proven themselves masters at improvisation, so the danger existed that they might redeploy enough units into the Dora or Hitler lines to once again halt Allied armies.

The Germans had uncommitted reserves. Anxiety concerning seaward flanks had caused Field Marshall Kesselring to retain sizeable forces to cover the Adriatic and Tyrrhenian coasts. Of these forces, four divisions—the 3rd, 29th, and 90th panzer grenadiers and the 26th Panzer—were first-rate, capable of significantly influencing the course of the battle. Kesselring now knew that the attacks on the Gustav Line represented the Allied main effort, so he could afford to divert these reserves to his southern front. A race of sorts developed as the German commander tried to cobble survivors and reserves into yet another line while Allied columns attempted to penetrate the most defensible traces before the Germans effectively manned them.[2]

In this race for position, the mountain-wise French Expeditionary Corps was the first out of the blocks. Having overrun Mount Majo on 13 May, the French threatened to push up the Liri River Valley on to Highway 6. Sensitive to the trafficability of the Liri Valley, Kesselring reinforced against this threat first. The 90th Panzer Grenadier and 20th Panzer divisions settled piecemeal into the path of the French drive.

Meanwhile, Generals Clark, Juin, and Keyes prepared to exploit through the thinly defended Aurunci Mountains. The Germans had reinforced elsewhere because they considered the terrain in the Aurunci too rough for the movement of major units. Allied commanders saw opportunity rather than obstacle in the crags and gorges, however. Here the Fifth Army would sweep on through the German defenses. Here the 88th Infantry Division would prove its mettle.

The 88th Division renewed its attack early on 14 May.[3] By 0900 the 351st Infantry Regiment, to its surprise, walked virtually unopposed into Santa Maria Infante. While the 351st mopped up Santa Maria, the as-yet uncommitted 349th Infantry Regiment passed through and led the advance across the Ausonia Valley. In quick succession the fresh regiment pushed the Germans off Mount Bracchi, Capo D'Aguo, and Mount Cirta. The somewhat wearier 350th advanced alongside the 349th toward Spigno. Early on the fifteenth the 351st, after a day of rest, passed through the 350th and seized Spigno itself.

The seizures of Spigno and Mount Cirta compromised the fortifications of the Dora Extension, the first of the defensible traces to the rear of the Gustav Line. The German 94th Infantry Division, battered by three days of fierce fighting, had suffered a near absolute breakdown of tactical communications. Leadership losses, the destruction of wire lines, bombings and shellings of key headquarters, and the fluid tactical situation all contributed to German confusion. On two separate occasions units from the 88th overran artillery batteries caught totally unaware by the pace of the American advance. One enterprising American captured by the Germans took advantage of the general confusion and convinced his captors they themselves had just been surrounded and should surrender.[4] He paraded them off, twenty docile "krauts" led by one swaggering GI. As the German 94th Infantry fell apart, surrender became contagious and prisoners of war—two thousand of them—soon overflowed the division's prisoner-of-war cages.[5] In part, Germans surrendered to Americans out of a fear of falling into the hands of the bloodthirsty North African groups of the French Expeditionary Corps. Resistance forward of the Aurunci Mountains faltered, then collapsed.

Once captured, Spigno became a gateway into the Aurunci. From the village, goat trails meandered into the Petrella Massif. Throughout 15 and 16 May, French and American troops poured through the village and up a tortuous road into the escarpment.[6] Guided by local peasants, the 351st led the 88th toward the village of Itri, an important junction of Highway 7 with the Germans' main lateral route, Highway 82.

Early on the eighteenth the 351st was in a position to cross the Itri-Pico road and seize Mount Grande, the height overlooking Itri. Here the Germans temporarily checked the American advance with a hastily assembled force of tanks and self-propelled artillery. The 351st was so far ahead of the main body that it could communicate only by a tedious radio relay system from mountaintop to mountaintop. The regiment had also outdistanced the range of supporting artillery. It needed artillery to break the Itri position, but artillery could not follow the route along which the infantry had advanced. Fortunately, the 85th Infantry Division also had been making progress along the more passable coastal road. Sloan's artillery trailed the 85th's advance until it was again within range of the 88th's forward units. On the morning of the nineteenth artillery near Maranola was within range of the 351st, near Itri. The 351st attacked to seize Mount Grande while the 349th cleared Itri itself.

General Keyes then directed Sloan to form a motorized task force and rush Fondi, a village the Germans had developed into a key strong point on their Hitler Line. A race developed between the 88th Infantry Division and the theretofore uncommitted 29th Panzer Grenadier Division, the latter ordered by Kesselring to Fondi on the nineteenth. Unfortunately for Keyes's plans, one could not readily make mechanized flying columns out of leg infantry units that were already committed. The narrow streets of Itri became a hopeless snarl of misdirected tanks, engineer vehicles, trucks, and self-propelled artillery.[7] South-bound units debouching from the Aurunci *north* of Itri and north-bound units debouching from the Aurunci *south* of Itri collided in the tiny village and further complicated a monumental traffic jam.

Fortunately for the 88th, its leading regiment did not await motorization. Deftly bypassing the chaos at Itri, the 349th skirted the mountains surrounding the town and marched on along Highway 7 towards Fondi. Battalions passed through each other in turns to assure that fresh troops always led the advance. Brushing through light resistance, the 349th reached Fondi a little after noon on the twentieth.

Here German resistance stiffened. A mixed bag of tanks, self-propelled artillery, and infantrymen from the 94th Infantry Division clung tenaciously to Fondi while awaiting imminent relief from the 29th Panzer Grenadiers. The 349th's I Company deployed abreast on Highway 7 in the face of heavy fire while a platoon of tanks, recently extricated from the snarl at Itri, added weight to their attack.

The attack of I Company faltered in the face of heavy resistance. The 3rd Battalion commander correctly diagnosed that the weight of the German defenses was directed down Highway 7. In a textbook maneuver he fixed the Germans' attention with I Company, while the remainder of his battalion worked its way through hills overlooking the town from the northeast. Once set, this spirited flanking attack poured down the slopes to make short work of the German defenders, then

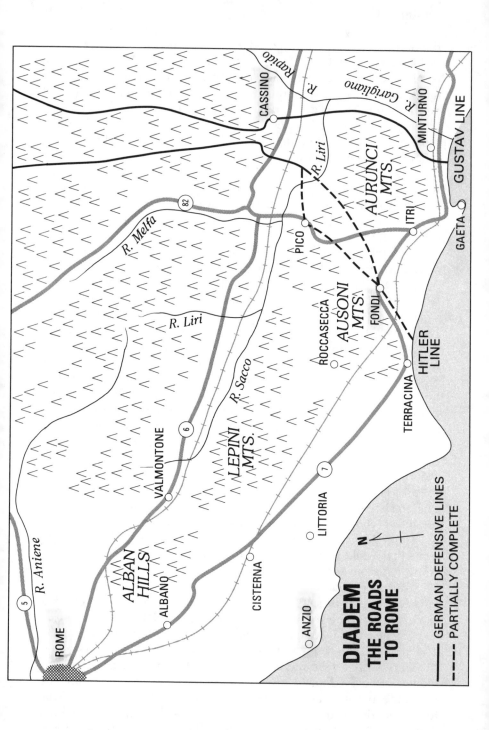

DIADEM
THE ROADS
TO ROME

——— GERMAN DEFENSIVE LINES
- - - PARTIALLY COMPLETE

N

ROME

R. Aniene

ALBAN
HILLS

ALBANO

VALMONTONE

CISTERNA

ANZIO

LITTORIA

LEPINI
MTS.

R. Sacco

R. Liri

R. Melfa

82

6

7

TERRACINA

HITLER
LINE

ROCCASECCA

AUSONI
MTS.

FONDI

PICO

AURUNCI
MTS.

R. Liri

CASSINO

R. Rapido

R. Garigliano

R. Minturno

GUSTAV LINE

MINTURNO

GAETA

ITRI

5

swept on through Fondi itself. The 88th had broken through the Hitler Line.

Having secured Fondi, the 349th moved rapidly on to Mount Passignano, a dominant feature a mile north of the village. This position anchored the 88th even more firmly inside the Hitler Line. Denied Fondi, elements of the newly arriving 29th Panzer Grenadier Division, moving south on Highway 7, reconcentrated around Terracina. Thus, the 88th found itself positioned between the arriving German reserves and the German line of resistance through Pico, Portecorvo, and Aquino. This separation of the German reserves from the German main line of resistance left the 88th with nothing but the battered remnants of the 94th Infantry Division to its front.

The 88th moved forward into the vacuum its success had created. The 350th assumed the lead and pushed along the spine of Mount Alto towards the village of Roccasecca del Volsci. Roccasecca overlooked an important lateral route between the Liri Valley and the coastal plain. Its seizure would establish the Fifth Army on terrain clear of the lunar landscapes of the Aurunci and Ausoni mountains. Encountering scattered resistance and accounting for more than one hundred Germans captured or killed at a cost of thirty American casualties, the 350th secured Roccasecca as light failed on the twenty-second. At dawn on the twenty-third, the regiment found the view from its newly won positions breathtaking. Spread panoramically beneath it was what appeared to be the entire German army—troops, tanks, trucks, trailers, mule trains—moving east and west along the valley floor. With some exaggeration, one American officer boasted that he could have ended the war in Italy if he had had sufficient artillery support available at that point. Col. James C. Fry, commander of the 350th, considered it imprudent to move off his commanding height onto the valley floor, but the regiment inflicted some damage when it opened up with the mortars and machine guns it had laboriously borne through the mountains. Surprised, the Germans made several ineffectual attempts to dislodge the 350th.[8]

Fry's advance had created a salient ten miles into the German rear and captured terrain overlooking an important lateral route of communications. Once the 88th's artillery drew within range of the 350th, the valley would become nothing less than a death trap for German troops and vehicles. German positions to the south and east of Roccasecca were no longer tenable.

Another development added to the German troubles on 23 May. The Anzio beachhead exploded as VI Corps hurled itself into the German Fourteenth Army.[9] The Third Infantry Division attacked towards Cisterna behind a wall of artillery fire while the First Armored Division clipped through the German lines to Highway 7 with a clockwise combination of artillery, breaching charges, smoke, mounted attacks, and dismounted mop-ups. The First Special Service Force began its spectacular assault up Mount Arrestina[10] while the 45th, 36th, British 1st, and British 5th infantry divisions engaged the Germans they found to their front.

Soon both sides were taking appalling casualties all around the beachhead. The Germans suffered more and could afford fewer. With daylight on 25 May, patrols from VI Corps' 36th Engineer Regiment linked up with a patrol from II Corps' 91st Reconnaissance Squadron. Shortly thereafter, officers from the 88th's G-2 (Intelligence) sat down to tea with the commanding general of the British 5th Division, the unit the 88th had relieved when it first arrived in Italy. One hundred twenty-five days after the Anzio landings, Allied forces in Italy had at last linked up.[11]

Despite their deteriorating situation south of Rome, most German units fought on tenaciously. In many cases shorn of leadership, or, more accurately, of effective communications with that leadership, the Germans instinctively defended their immediate positions. Rapid American advances bypassed German units that were still combat effective. The result was confusion when trailing American echelons collided with bypassed German positions or with German units attempting to work their way back to friendly lines.

In the case of the 350th, only the 1st and 3rd battalions glided easily through to Roccasecca.[12] Trailing to the left rear of the 1st, the 2nd Battalion stumbled upon a considerable body of Germans entrenched on favorable terrain near the village of San Biagio. The outcome was a five-day running battle as the Germans skillfully retired from position to position while the 2nd Battalion used artillery and flanking maneuvers with equal skill to extricate them from the successive positions they occupied. From 21 May to 25 May the 2nd Battalion killed 72 Germans and suffered 19 dead and 69 wounded. Another 198 Germans were captured during the course of this advance. Of these, a large number surrendered when the 2nd Battalion linked up with the 3rd Battalion sweeping rearward from Roccasecca to close a trap. The 351st and 349th infantry regiments also encountered resistance when they cleared the terrain forward to the 350th's positions. The Germans wiped out a mule train and a radio relay station before Sloan reestablished secure overland communications with Fry.

The fighting acquired a confused quality; combat, combat support, and combat service support elements found themselves jumbled together by terrain and circumstances. Germans were everywhere. One battalion commander was killed; one was wounded; and one escaped capture by playing dead while his boots were stolen. One intrepid muleteer was captured by nine Germans, who in turn were bypassed by American combat units. The muleteer then persuaded his captors to surrender—and to lend him a weapon so that the capture might appear creditable as he herded them down to the American lines. Persistence and numbers paid off. By the twenty-sixth the 88th's rear areas were in order, and the division prepared to continue the advance.[13]

Developing strategic considerations diverted the division to a mission other than continuing the advance, however. The Allied Armies in Italy commander, General Alexander, had envisioned the VI Corps breaking out to Valmontone and trapping the retreating German Tenth Army. General Clark had thought such a clean-out entrapment unlikely; he preferred to drive on Rome and destroy German formations by the pace of his pursuit. Alexander acquiesced, and in effect allowed Clark to treat Valmontone as a peripheral, rather than principal, objective. Alexander did not, however, transfer the right to use Highway 6 from the British Eighth Army, now trailing the French Expeditionary Corps by some distance, to the American Fifth Army. This forced Clark's divisions into an increasingly narrow frontage. Somebody had to fall out of the race for Rome. On 28 May, Clark pinched the 85th and 88th infantry divisions out of their sector of the front and brought the FEC abreast of VI Corps for the drive on Rome. The two draftee divisions were given missions to mop up the Lepini Mountains and the Anzio beachhead area.[14]

Whatever might be concluded from the draftees' performance in the first three days of Diadem, one could not avoid being impressed by their performance from 14 May to 28 May.[15] They outmaneuvered and outfought the Germans time and again. The division lanced through two successive defensive lines before the Germans could effectively defend them. Even the much-touted French colonials found themselves trailing the American advance through dusty Italian villages.

A number of factors accounted for the increasingly visible American success. The fluidity of the exploitation following the breach of the Gustav Line suited the draftees' training and temperament. There is little doubt that the battle-hardened British, French, Poles, Indians, Canadians, and even the Americans of VI Corps endured the appalling casualties necessary to breach the Gustav Line more philosophically than did the somewhat shaken draftees. Only time and experience would inure the 88th to losses on that scale. Once the Gustav Line broke, however, traits other than stoicism became the most important. Fourteen May began a week of furious marches punctuated by sweeping maneuvers and sharp, decisive engagements that could have been lifted bodily from the Camp Gruber scenarios. Frenzied artillery relocations also had been practiced repeatedly. Even the 88th's clumsiness with respect to tanks was in part offset by the speed with which those available were thrown into action.[16]

Nontactical factors further improved the 88th's tactical performance. Of these factors, one was physical fitness. Throughout their training and, in particular, during the last weeks before the offensive, the draftees benefited from a process of selection and exercise that left them among the most finely conditioned soldiers in the world. Certainly it left them in better shape than the Germans of the 71st and 94th infantry divisions, who had had little opportunity for exercise throughout the long Italian winter. Several American successes seem to have developed simply because the draftees covered ground more quickly than their opponents.[17] It remains unclear how many other successes, or how many stragglers and bypassed formations, developed because Germans were fatigued and Americans were not.

The 88th also frequently replaced leading formations, whereas the Germans seldom enjoyed such a luxury. One after another, fresh companies, battalions, and even regiments assumed the lead. Artillery, carefully surveyed into its firing positions, assisted infantrymen in land navigation during the rapid advance. In the tortured terrain one hill often looked like another to the struggling infantrymen, who often were unwilling to expose themselves to snipers in order to get a better view. With a quick radio call they could get a marking round from the artillery, set for a precise six-digit location from which the infantrymen could orient. In the low-casualty environment of exploitation, the experimental individual replacement system could be made to work. Whereas contingents of individual replacements only added to the confusion during the breakthrough of the Gustav Line, long marches and low casualties during the exploitation afforded platoon sergeants and squad leaders the opportunity to integrate new men effectively. Even the most severely depleted companies of the 351st regained former levels of combat effectiveness.[18]

As the pace of the 88th's advance accelerated, the demands upon its transportation establishment increased as well. The division's single abortive attempt to create a mechanized flying column has already been discussed. Although that effort ran afoul of restricted terrain and the infantryman's traditional heedlessness of keeping vehicles out of each other's way, trucking was used effectively to facilitate internal movements within the division area.[19] Some units coming out of rest cycles trucked forward to catch up with leading elements, while others sped by truck from one point to another behind the lines to keep up with the developing tactical situation. Of little tactical use in the front lines, trucks were of considerable value behind the lines.

Trucks played an even more important role in logistics, for they continued to forward supplies from as far away as the Peninsular Base depots in Naples. They replenished mind-boggling artillery expenditures and were the prime movers for the artillery pieces themselves.[20] Other supplies—rations, ammunition, engineer supplies, medical supplies, spare parts, petroleum products, even replacement troops—had to be trucked forward in enormous quantities. In Italy, as elsewhere, the redoubtable two-and-one-half-ton truck, or "deuce-and-a-half," proved an important instrument in the American success.

The truck, however, was *not* the dominant instrument of the 88th's logistical effort. That distinction belonged to the fourteen hundred mules plodding dutifully along in the wake of the American advance. Where the road and the truck ended, the mule took over. One must search hard for a logistical environment as challenging as that mastered by the division's muleteers.[21] The terrain alone was formidable. Quartermaster officers lamented that the goat trail behind Spigno was the steepest they had ever seen. In places the route barely admitted the passage of a man, much less a mule. Time and again mules plunged off cliffs to premature deaths.

As if terrain were not problem enough, muleteers often were not altogether sure where they were going.[22] The American advance meandered rapidly forward along paths of least resistance. Units took their orientation from key terrain features, but the easiest routes between those features proved to be anybody's guess. Muleteers in turn had to guess which of several possible routes the units they were seeking had followed. Another piece of guesswork was to anticipate a unit's logistical needs. Mule trains departed from staging areas hours and even days before they reached the units they supported.[23] By the time the trains arrived, the needs of the units might well have changed. Only rations could be predicted with reasonable accuracy. Finally, there was the problem of Germans. If a slowly moving mule train happened upon a bypassed enemy formation, it became a prime target for die-hard Germans. Several mule trains were attacked, and one forty-mule train was wiped out.[24]

Given the poorly known terrain, the uncertain locations and needs of supported units, and the presence of Germans, the task of the muleteers was akin to trying to paint a mural on the side of a moving train. The draftees did, however, come up with expedients that helped somewhat. Advancing units marked their trails with C ration litter. (The Germans had no C rations.) Rather than trying to find supported units directly, mule trains began to go forward to agreed-upon rendezvous points. There, representatives from supported units met them and guided them forward. Logisticians shepherding the mule trains increasingly insisted that ranking representatives from the supported units should traffic daily between units and mule-train staging areas. This improved the timeliness and detail of logistical information. At times, mule trains gained security from individual replacements moving with them or from trailing units moving to the rear of the leading elements. Radios (SCR 300s) were issued to the muleteers in an effort to give them some possibility of remaining in communication with friendly combat elements.[25]

The support and security of the mule trains, and thus of the division's logistical establishment, required more resources, thought, and effort than the division's planners had originally anticipated. At one point the 88th had one regiment forward and two struggling to keep supply lines open.[26] The division's engineers hurriedly blasted jeep trails through mountains, bulldozed rubble out of villages, and cleared away ever-present mines and booby traps. The price paid for security was necessary and had its rewards. Ambushes were thwarted or turned around. One spectacular shoot-out developed into a creditable American victory when F Company, 350th Infantry, countermarched to the rescue of a ninety-mule train and soundly defeated the Germans who had ambushed it.[27] Throughout this confused period the leading elements of the 88th Infantry Division remained in supply.

Medical evacuation proved as challenging as did supply forward.[28] Rapid advances through rough terrain rendered evacuation a long and difficult process. At one point, thirty additional litter bearers served in each battalion to support requirements logarithmically increased because the same number of casualties now had to be manhandled ten times the normal distances. In this effort, as at Santa Maria Infante, Italian volunteers proved invaluable.

The medical situation was further complicated by a widespread failure on the part of troops to use their halozone tablets, now more necessary than ever since they were on the march and drawing water from wells and springs rather than from mess teams. Attacks of diarrhea reached epidemic proportions. Instead of being hospitalized, the unfortunate victims were counseled on the value of halozone; they seldom made the same mistake twice.

The maintenance of communications during the advance also proved challenging. Radios were no more reliable than earlier, of course, but they came to be better used. The division continued its experiment of arbitrarily assigning numbers and letters to terrain features, a system now institutionalized in the army's use of target reference points and checkpoints. This abbreviated system reduced the length of radio transmissions and thus the probability of electromagnetic interference. Because letters and numbers are easier to hear and understand than words, messages in terms of letters, numbers, and a few key words proved more likely to survive the vagaries of static and distance. The use of code also reduced the possibility that eavesdropping Germans might garner useful information.[29]

Commanders also gave more thought to the development of radio nets and radio relay stations. Radio teams deployed in such a manner as to provide backups in the event of mechanical failure. Typically, the cumbersome yet powerful SCR 284 was located on prominent terrain near the tail of a regiment, while less-powerful SCR 584s and SCR 300s branched forward in a network of relays to the leading elements.

In addition to wire and radio communications, the division made considerable use of pyrotechnic signaling devices (smoke and flares), couriers, and liaison officers. Artillery spotter planes proved particularly handy for delivering operations orders and critical correspondence. The planes would circle a leading element while displaying a previously agreed-upon panel identifying important correspondence. The command group on the ground, usually including the regimental commander, then fired an agreed-upon pyrotechnic that marked its location. The plane would make a low run over the position thus marked and drop the correspondence out its window.

All factors considered, the 88th seems to have developed its communications to the limits technology would allow during the weeks following the breach of the Gustav Line.[30] Communication problems had so dominated the first several days of the offensive that they received a command emphasis, which in turn led to more effective communications.

By 28 May the 88th Infantry Division numbered among the high achievers of the Allied Armies in Italy.[31] It had an impressive combat record and had proven its ability to support itself in the field. General Clark's decision to write it out of the script for the race on Rome was an unfortunate necessity; the Fifth Army front was too narrow to get all its divisions on line. Clark could hardly favor the newly arrived draftee divisions over the veterans of the VI Corps or the FEC in a race for the honor of reaching Rome first.

The mop-up of the Lepini Mountains proved confused and physically taxing, but not particularly bloody.[32] Companies and battalions marched back and forth over the broken terrain and experienced a sharp little firefight here or accepted a docile surrender there. The Germans had by no means given up, but most knew their time had run out south of the Alban Hills—perhaps, some must have suspected, south of Rome as well. After three days of patrols, skirmishes, prisoner sortings, and rest, the 88th was once again consolidated into assembly areas and available for further assignments.

As circumstances would have it, this happened none too soon, for the sweep toward Rome ran afoul of an unexpectedly stubborn German defense.[33] Despite Allied advances along their flanks, and their own evacuation of Cassino, Germans in the Liri Valley continued to contest the British Eighth Army's advance. By 30 May a combination of formidable terrain, blown bridges, and German tenacity had opened a twenty-five-mile gap between American and British units. What was worse, the Germans seemed to have put together a tenable defensive line running through the Alban Hills. Through 29 and 30 May the VI Corps advance decelerated in the face of increasingly stiff resistance. In Clark's view the best answer seemed to be to flank the Alban Hills with a push down Highway 6. This could be done only if the British, well to the rear, gave up their preemptive right to the use of Highway 6.

On 31 May, Alexander finally released the stretch of Highway 6 between Rome and Valmontone, the point at which the Fifth Army debouched upon Highway 6, to the use of the Fifth Army.[34] As a proviso, Alexander added that if it became necessary for the Eighth and Fifth armies to make a joint attack—that is, if the British caught up—the original boundary would be restored.

Clark's plans matured quickly. General Keyes's II Corps was to reorganize, pulling together the 3rd Infantry Division, the 85th Infantry Division, the 88th Infantry Division, the 1st Special Service Force, and Task Force Howze, a tank-heavy configuration built around the 13th Armored Regiment. Keyes intended to seize Valmontone on 1 June, then turn west and advance along Highway 6 with the 85th on the left, the 88th in the center, and the 3rd on the right. Task Force Howze was to lead the 88th's advance.

Even as these plans matured, another development reinforced the Allied hand. Enterprising patrols from VI Corps' 36th Infantry Division (Texas National Guard) discovered a gap in the German defenses that exposed a key terrain feature, Mount Artemisio.[35] Unknown to the Americans, the gap was an accident resulting from Artemisio's location on the boundary between the I Parachute Corps and the LXXVI Panzer Corps. During the night of 30 May, the 36th Infantry Division poured three regiments through the narrow gap, then fanned left and right to seize the entire ridge line. This brilliant attack unhinged the German position in the Alban Hills.

After preliminary shuffling on 31 May, the Fifth Army attacked along its entire front on 1 June. Fighting continued to be hotly contested, but the Germans now knew that Rome was lost. Rear guards fought on to maintain a continuous front and to buy time for an orderly retreat across the Aniene and Tiber rivers.

Redeploying from the Lepini Mountains, the 88th was not available for the initial attacks on 1 June. By the time it entered the battle the next day, Valmontone had fallen and the German rear guard was badly shaken. The battalions of the 349th Infantry Regiment were attached to the depleted 3rd Infantry Division and the tank-heavy Task Force Howze. The 350th and 351st trailed Howze along Highway 6. Howze led until stopped by strong antitank positions ten miles east of Rome. Here the 88th's infantrymen finally caught up. In a sharp, well-coordinated tank-infantry assault, the Americans turned the Germans out of their position.

The tank-infantry pattern repeated itself as the 88th skillfully expelled the Germans from one hastily occupied position after another along the course of Highway 6. The 88th had arrived at precisely the right time. With the Germans reeling and all other American units fully committed, the 88th's fresh battalions weighed heavily in this final push. The draftees seemed to be everywhere in a general stampede toward Rome. Two battalions of the 349th leapfrogged along the Aniene River with the 3rd Infantry Division. Battalions from the 350th and 351st reinforced Task Force Howze and the 1st Special Service Force. Sloan ordered the 350th to attack through the 351st. The commander of the 351st agreed that would happen as soon as the 350th caught up with him, then redoubled his efforts to reach Rome first.[36]

The air was electric with a sense of victory. Everywhere the draftees pushed ahead with growing strength and confidence. No longer facing the German 71st or 94th infantry divisions, the 88th now swept along, among others, the famed Hermann Goering Division. Dazed prisoners reinforced the draftees' self-esteem with laudatory comments that Sloan quickly publicized throughout the division. One prisoner cited the 88th's daring; another noted the effectiveness of its artillery. Yet another attributed the 88th's success to flawless individual marksmanship. The GIs added one feat after another to their inventory of anecdotes. At a hastily established roadblock Pfc. Asa Farmer made seven bazooka rockets count for as many fleeing German vehicles—two half-tracks, a light tank, four jeeps, and sixty prisoners. Sgt. Paul N. Eddy personally killed five and captured eight from the Hermann Goering Division while knocking out three machine-gun nests. Eight division military policemen, allegedly rear-echelon types, captured eighteen German prisoners when on a hastily organized patrol. It all seemed so easy that the GIs joked about how quickly the Nazi "supermen" had turned into mere "krauts."[37]

Every unit in the Fifth Army strained to be the first to enter Rome. The VI Corps faced well-organized opponents who, of all the German divisions, were freshest and best positioned. Resistance in the corps' sector remained stiff and the VI Corps fell behind. Clark's reallocation of the avenues of approach to Rome had given the FEC a wide arc to travel. Having farther to go and finding themselves embarrassed by the very shortages of heavy equipment, in particular tanks, that had proved such an advantage in the Aurunci, the French also fell behind. This left the race to the II Corps. The 3rd Infantry Division, exhausted by two weeks of continuous fighting to seize Cisterna and Valmontone, moved slowly. The terrain in front of the 85th was more taxing than that in front of the 88th, and the 85th had fought a day longer. The 1st Special Service Force was a hair's breadth from Rome when it collided with a determined German rear guard near the suburb of Centocelle. Task Force Howze's powerful column also stalled in a traffic jam caused by the size of its vehicles, the narrowness of the suburban streets, a misoriented artillery battery, and crowds that collected around a throng of newspaper correspondents attempting to cover the entry.

While all this was happening, the 88th Cavalry Reconnaissance Troop threaded its way neatly between the embattled 1st Special Service Force and the logjammed Task Force Howze. Once clear of both columns, the tiny contingent debouched upon a main east-west road, the Via Prenestina, and sped toward Rome. At 0715 on 4 June, transmissions from the 3rd Platoon of the 88th Reconnaissance Troop crackled with the news: the 88th Infantry Division was into Rome—and first![38]

The fall of Rome was a welcome climax to a hard-fought battle. It did not end the war or the Italian campaign, and it was overshadowed by D day in Normady two days later. It did represent a major victory for the Allies after ten months of frustrating and brutal combat on the Italian peninsula. Much remains controversial about Diadem and its aftermath. Was General Clark right in focusing on Rome? Could the Allies have bagged the German Tenth Army instead? Who really was the first into Rome?

Clark thought Rome important for psychological reasons, and was certain no scheme of maneuver could bag an entire German army in the porous Italian landscape. The experience of the 88th seems to support his opinion. Fighting over relatively narrow frontages, German and American units frequently bypassed each other in the confusion of terrain, battle, and darkness. Although the 88th could and did secure every road junction in its sector, it could not hope to entrap all the small German contingents filtering out under the supervision of battle-wise, company-grade leadership. When the Allies inflicted disproportionate losses on the Germans, they did so by the pace of their pursuit more often than by entrapment.

As Clark had anticipated, the capture of Rome did have important psychological effects. The final race for Rome electrified the entire Fifth Army. Every unit covered itself with glory at very little cost. Success intelligently publicized is the surest stuff of morale.[39] All units in the

Fifth Army were strengthened by virtue of their success. The 88th in particular assumed a new stature. The draftees had performed creditably in the assaults on the Gustav Line, even better in the exploitation that followed, and magnificently in the final race for Rome. The 88th's claim to have been the first into the city still provokes disputatious howls of rage from the veterans of other units;[40] what really mattered was that the draftees themselves believed they had been first. From that point they thought of the 88th as the best division in Italy.[41] Axis and Allied leadership alike came to agree that it was among the best. Could the capture of a few hundred more prisoners per regiment have meant as much to the morale of the unit as that triumphal prossession through frenzied, cheering, almost uncontrollable crowds?

With the capture of Rome, the 88th came of age. It would fight as well in other battles—on the Arno, in the Apennines, along the Po, and through the Alps. It would fight, take losses, lose its edge, rest, retrain, and fight again in a cycle that continued until the end of the war. All of these later battles and cycles were of great importance. It was the events of May and June, however, that were particularly held by the nation's leadership, the War Department, the newspapers, and the draftees themselves to have proved the mettle of the draftee division. The toughness of the 88th Infantry Division was no longer a question.[42]

9

Rome to the Alps—and Beyond

The performances of the 88th and 85th infantry divisions during the final battles for Rome provided striking vindication of the draftee and the draftee division. By the hour of this triumph the value of the draftee had ceased to be much of an issue—individual replacements and the suspension of voluntary enlistments had filled most divisions with conscripts well before June 1944—but all-draftee divisions had until then remained unproven. One lesson from Diadem was clear: small cadres of professionals had, in fact, been able to mold masses of American conscripts into proficient, modern fighting organizations. In time, the War Department labeled the initial successes of the 88th and 85th as "the first confirmation from the battlefield of the soundness of our division activation and training program." Other confirmations were to follow.[1]

Although the capture of Rome was a climax for the 88th and provides the climax for this study, it was not the last of the division's experiences. It should be useful to survey the 88th's subsequent operations and to discuss parallels between the experiences of the 88th and those of other draftee divisions. It may also be instructive to estimate the extent to which the postwar army has exploited—or failed to exploit—the lessons provided by its most recent conscripted divisions.

Field Marshall Kesselring's loss of Rome was a defeat, not a rout. With great skill and some daring he maneuvered to regain a continuous defensive line north of Rome and salvaged much of his army group from the wreckage.[2] Fresh German units from northern Italy reinforced his lines in the face of the now somewhat overextended and increasingly weary Allied columns. Within a week of Rome's capture, Generals Alexander and Clark realized that pursuit of Kesselring would have to be systematic rather than headlong.

As if Kesselring did not present problems enough, Allied efforts in Italy now stood in the shadow of the Normandy landings. Senior Allied commanders knew that a major fraction of their military resources would soon be diverted to France. Clark's Fifth Army was to lose its VI Corps, including the veteran 3rd, 36th, and 45th infantry divisions, and the French Expeditionary Corps. Clark elected to continue his advance with these units during June, while pulling the units he was to retain in Italy out of the line.[3] Thus, when the VI Corps and the FEC withdrew to refit and retrain for the invasion of southern France, he would at least have some fresh units with which to continue his pursuit of the Germans.

On 10 June the 88th Infantry Division withdrew from Bassanelio, following a creditable advance of fifty-six miles in eight days, to a rest area in the Alban Hills. After a few days of recuperation and ceremony, General Sloan launched himself on yet another of his retraining efforts. The affectionately critical draftees adjudged Sloan to have been even more uncompromising a pedagogue than ever during this period. Sloan had reasons for his rigor. He was afraid his men would grow cocksure or stale resting on their laurels. The division had lost 134 officers and 1,844 enlisted men—killed, wounded, or missing—during Diadem. Replacements for these losses were already in the ranks; thus almost a fifth of Sloan's riflemen were new to the division. The replacements had received individual training in the United States, but Sloan thought his units needed intensive training to settle their new men in. While in the Alban Hills, Sloan found yet another reason for rigorous preparation; he suffered the first attacks of a severe, undiagnosed, and ultimately debilitating dermatitis. As disease began to swell his limbs and wrack his body, he suspected that his next battle with the 88th would be his last.[4]

After a week given over to rest, reorganization, resupply, and medical rehabilitation, the 88th retrained in accordance with a memorandum exhaustively entitled "Training in the 88th During Reorganization Period Subsequent to the Minturno Through Rome Drive." In effect, this was a miniature version of the Army Training Program, progressing in maneuvers from squad through battalion scale. The training included half-hour blocks of close-order drill and platoon-size orientation classes, both designed to make new men feel they were part of the team. Ten hours a week went to physical training, including road marches of five hours length. Division engineers constructed elaborate assault courses of up to ten square kilometers each, through which units of up to a battalion in size maneuvered. These courses were realistic live-fire facilities and required a commitment of training ammunition, supervision, equipment, and time comparable to similar training in the United States. The 88th's infantry units undertook a great deal of rigorous training in a very little time, most of it designed as a rehearsal for their next attack. If the performance of new men indicated they had not integrated quickly enough, they fell into a special

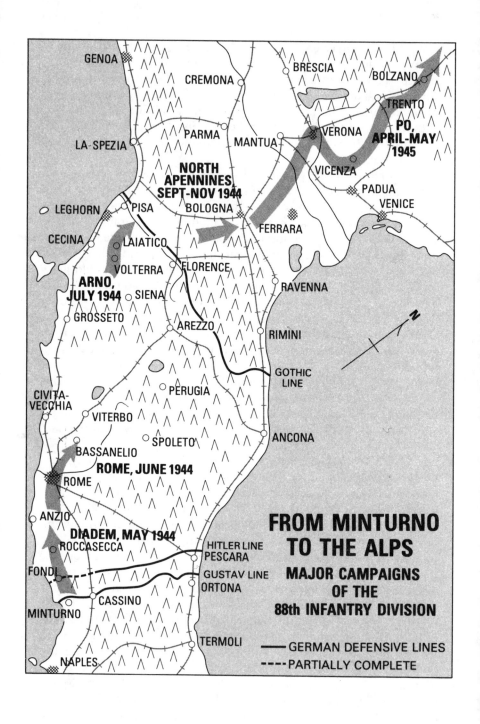

GENOA

CREMONA

BRESCIA

BOLZANO

TRENTO

PO,
APRIL-MAY
1945

LA-SPEZIA

PARMA

MANTUA

VERONA

VICENZA

PADUA

VENICE

NORTH
APENNINES
SEPT-NOV 1944

LEGHORN

PISA

BOLOGNA

FERRARA

CECINA

LAIATICO

VOLTERRA

FLORENCE

RAVENNA

ARNO,
JULY 1944

SIENA

GROSSETO

AREZZO

RIMINI

N

PERUGIA

GOTHIC
LINE

CIVITA-
VECCHIA

VITERBO

SPOLETO

ANCONA

BASSANELIO

ROME, JUNE 1944

ROME

ANZIO

DIADEM, MAY 1944

ROCCASECCA

HITLER LINE

PESCARA

**FROM MINTURNO
TO THE ALPS**

FONDI

GUSTAV LINE

ORTONA

**MAJOR CAMPAIGNS
OF THE
88th INFANTRY DIVISION**

MINTURNO

CASSINO

NAPLES

TERMOLI

—— GERMAN DEFENSIVE LINES

--- PARTIALLY COMPLETE

program for "backward men." This somewhat punitive retraining featured the denial of pass privileges to the slow learners and the requirement that veterans from platoons in question give up their own pass privileges to teach it. Thus, recruit and veteran alike had incentive for integrating new men quickly and showing well during the various field exercises.[5]

Sloan's principal purpose in retraining may have been the integration of replacements into his infantry companies, but he also wanted to polish skills that had eroded during combat and to improve tactical doctrine. Largely because of fatigue, carelessness, and casualties among junior leaders, the 88th's sharpness with respect to patrolling, night operations, and communications techniques seems to have eroded. To reverse those trends, Sloan prescribed complex and demanding night patrols as a dominant feature of the field problems, and also called for a day without telephones. The night patrols quickly honed the 88th's infantry squads back into the shape Sloan wanted. These patrols were also an excellent device for training junior leaders and allowing them to gain the confidence of their men. Sloan's day without telephones forced communications over radio nets carefully monitored by the signal battalion commander. Careful scrutiny polished the nets while emphasizing a command insistence upon improved communications. Insofar as improving doctrine was concerned, officer classes focused upon the "employment of attached units"—tanks and tank destroyers—reorganization upon the objective, breaching techniques, artillery control measures, and "soft spot tactics." When the 88th rotated back into combat, it benefited from four weeks of careful preparation for that event.[6]

Some observers consider the 88th's next battle, from Volterra to the Arno River (8 July to 25 July 1944), the best it ever fought. The Germans had finally stabilized their front on defensible terrain some twenty-five miles south of the Arno. A key position in their defenses was an ancient Etruscan hilltop fortress, Volterra. On 8 July the 88th seized Volterra with a textbook combination of heavy suppressive fires and engineer breaching parties, closely followed by assaulting infantrymen. Extraordinarily effective artillery-delivered smoke did much to compensate for lack of cover in the gently rolling terrain approaching the citadel. The 88th's reserve regiment, the 351st, passed quickly through the gap at Volterra to inflict another stunning defeat on the Germans near Laiatico. Here the Germans suffered 250 casualties and lost 400 prisoners in desperate efforts to extricate themselves from a closing trap, and the 3rd Battalion of the 351st earned the Distinguished Unit Citation for particularly outstanding efforts. The 88th's rupture of the defenses around Volterra forced the Germans to abandon their defenses south of the Arno. It was well conceived, well coordinated, and well executed.[7]

By this time the men of the 88th had come to speak of themselves as "Blue Devils." The nickname came from the Germans, who had taken to identifying these troublesome opponents by the color of their shoulder patch.[8] With an exercise of that logic which allows the translation of an opponent's opprobrium into a compliment, the draftees developed the epithet "blue devils" into a nickname. Sloan had always been disappointed that his division had no nickname. Indeed, he had tried several times to develop one, including the ill-fated effort to promulgate "Ranger" Division. The draftees had not liked that one; perhaps it sounded too military. Now that Sloan despaired of a nickname, the draftees found one they liked, and it stuck.

The campaign to close to the Arno (8 July to 25 July 1944) cost the 88th Infantry Division 142 officers and 2,257 enlisted men killed, wounded, or missing. Again the division needed a break in the action in order to rest and retrain. This time the 88th's hiatus lasted seven weeks, largely because of strategic shufflings of units as the invasion of southern France launched itself and General Alexander redeployed within Italy to favor a push along the Adriatic Coast. The 88th used this period to good effect, training with its usual intensity and rotating units through recreation centers as well. Medical authorities evacuated the ailing General Sloan in August, so the training period was of special value to the new division commander, Maj. Gen. Paul W. Kendall. Kendall was an obvious choice. He had been with the division since Camp Gruber as Sloan's assistant division commander, and had long since earned the respect of all ranks. Sloan recovered sufficiently to chair committees working for the War Department, most notably one concerned with awards and decorations, but he never returned to Europe. He retired to Weaverville, North Carolina, in 1946, where he lived happily as a gentleman farmer until his death, at age eighty-five, in 1972.[9]

The Germans made good use of these seven inactive weeks as well, absorbing replacements, retraining, and rushing ahead with the development of a heavily fortified "Gothic Line" along the tortuous North Apennines. When the Fifth Army once again attacked, it attacked into the teeth of well-prepared units in formidable defenses. Nevertheless, the Fifth Army's renewed drive began auspiciously enough. American units quickly seized key terrain features with clockwork combinations of infantry, engineers, artillery, and, where possible, tanks. Committed on 21 September, the 88th compromised strong German defenses on Mount Frena with a brilliant flanking penetration, then moved quickly on to secure one hilltop after another. Of these, the most savagely contested was Mount Capello, where the 2nd Battalion,

351st Infantry, won the division's second Distinguished Unit Citation.[10]

Kesselring had held substantial reserves back while diagnosing the locations of the main Allied efforts. Having identified these, he launched major counterattacks on his assailants, who were already somewhat disorganized because of the costs of their advances. On 28 September elements of four German divisions hurled themselves against the 350th Infantry Regiment's exposed holdings on Mount Battaglia. For seven days this embattled regiment beat off one attack after another in fierce close-quarters fighting. "Battle Mountain" became a symbol for GI toughness; heroism abounded. Capt. Robert E. Roeder's G Company was the linchpin of the defense during the early hours. Roeder was everywhere, encouraging men and giving direction, until knocked unconscious by a shellburst. Recovering conciousness but bleeding badly, he propped himself against a wall and picked off one German after another until a mortar shell killed him. T.Sgt. Manuel V. Mendoza, severely wounded and scorched by a flamethrower, held off a company until relief arrived. S.Sgt. Raymond O. Gregory and Pfc. Cleo Peck ran out of grenades and continued the battle by rolling boulders out of their commanding positions. Pfc. Felix B. Mestas doggedly hung on to his BAR (Browning automatic rifle) position and killed twenty-four Germans before they, in turn, killed him. 1st Lt. Edmund D. Maher killed four paratroopers with his bayonet. T.Sgt. Beni Mazzarella, on seeing the strongest Kraut attack of all overwhelm the castle on the crest, without orders picked up a handful of grenades and charged the castle. Pitching grenades like apples, he killed six invaders and wounded more. When the 350th was finally relieved, on 2 October, it had earned yet another Distinguished Unit Citation and had suffered 50 percent casualties—including all but one of its company commanders. Captain Roeder was awarded the Medal of Honor posthumously.[11]

Snow, fog, mud, and rain worked hardships upon the 88th's Apennines offensive as autumn shaded into winter, but the most pressing dilemma for the division was its casualties. As losses mounted, replacements pumped forward into units—some having flown in from as far away as England and France to redress the extraordinary personnel losses of the Gothic Line fighting. In its earlier campaigns the 88th had had an opportunity to rest and retrain every several weeks. The North Apennines offensive ground the division through seven long weeks of fierce combat and through more than six thousand casualties. The individual replacement system did not work out particularly well; it added more to lists of casualties than to lists of accomplishments. For the first time the division seems to have suffered more casualties than it inflicted. Units, depleted of combat-experienced personnel and restocked with whatever individual fillers were available, dutifully, if clumsily, attacked one hill after another at appalling cost. Well-executed German counterattacks whittled the division's gains and bedeviled its flanks in the jumbled terrain. The 88th painfully led the Fifth Army Advance to within nine thousand yards of the Po Valley before a masterful German counterattack wiped out its leading company at Vedriano. That ended the offensive; the next order from Fifth Army headquarters was to stop and dig in.[12]

Swallowing their disappointment, Clark, Kendall, and other American commanders undertook a conscious program of unit rest, rotation, and retraining. Again elaborate complexes in rear areas reproduced the combat environments units were expected to encounter during their next offensive.[13] Units trained intensely when in rear areas and patrolled extensively when once again at the front. During bitter winter weather the 88th sharpened its tactical skills at all levels of command. When spring returned to the North Apennines, the 88th was once again at a peak.

The Germans numbered the 88th among the most dangerous Allied units in Italy, and surmised that its location would define the Fifth Army's main effort. Shortly before its offensive of 15 April 1945, the Fifth Army played an elaborate shell game, shuttling units of the 88th around the breadth of its front so that the Germans would identify it in a variety of locations. Not particularly confused, the Germans settled their strongest defenses squarely in front of the actual location of the 88th, south of Bologna. In their efforts to contain the 88th Infantry Division, the Germans may have outsmarted themselves, however. If the 88th was the most dangerous American division in Italy—an immeasurable suggestion—its sister divisions were not far off its mark. While the 88th clawed its way through strong defenses near Monterumici, a newly arrived division, the draftee 10th Mountain Division, lanced through a more lightly defended sector and debouched into the Po Valley west of Bologna. When the Germans struggled to extricate themselves from this closing trap, the 88th and its flanking divisions refused to let them get cleanly away, and the withdrawal became a rout. The Fifth Army broke into the Po Valley on a broad front, seven divisions on line.[14]

The Germans hoped to hold successively at the lines of the Po and the Adige rivers or, failing in those efforts, to withdraw through the Brenner Pass past Verona and Bolzano. They moved too slowly for the hard-marching draftees. The 10th Mountain crossed the Po on 23 April, followed shortly by the 85th and within thirty-six hours by the 88th. These crossings reflected the careful integration of engineers and bridging equipment into the Fifth Army plans. Once across the Po the 10th, 85th, and 88th raced through sporadic opposition to be the first to close the door into the Alps at Verona; the 88th won by a hair's breath. Meanwhile, bridging and ferrying across the Po had advanced far enough to support the crossing of armored vehicles. Working frantically, the 88th's engineers restored a railroad bridge in Verona sufficiently to get armored vehicles across the Adige as well. The 350th Infantry Regiment quickly closed to Vicenza riding vehicles of the 752nd Tank Battalion and the 805th Tank Destroyer Battalion, then seized the town in house-to-house fighting. The Germans were now trapped in the Po Valley with the defensive lines of the Po and the Adige hopelessly compromised.[15]

On 28 April the 88th received orders to shift its axis of advance back into the Brenner Pass. Shadowy fears of a Nazi "National Redoubt" in the Alps prompted Allied chieftains to penetrate this fastness as quickly as possible.[16] The 88th did, in fact, encounter stiffening resistance as it closed on the SS headquarters at Bolzano; for a few anxious days the National Redoubt seemed a possibility. No one could be sure that this was the final offensive, the knockout blow. Then, on 2 May, the German army in Italy had had enough; it capitulated in the first of the mass surrenders that marked the disintegration of the Wehrmacht. On 4 May the 88th linked up with the southward-bound 103rd Infantry Division, another draftee division, from the American Seventh Army. Three days later Germany surrendered unconditionally. The Blue Devils' war was over.

It is doubtful that any modern armies, including those of the Wehrmacht at its height, could have outclassed the American Fifth Army of April 1945. The Po Valley campaign reflected masterful combinations of men, machines, maneuvers, and momentum. The several branches and services integrated themselves into one textbook operation after another, and a formidable opponent as numerous in personnel and with formidable defensive advantages disintegrated within eighteen days. The overall losses in the Po Valley campaign were 16,747 for the Allies to 67,000 for the Germans, which is not to mention the million who surrendered on 2 May.[17] The Fifth Army accomplished its final mission so well that retrospectively it seemed it must have been easy. It could have been otherwise.

The premier instruments of the Fifth Army's success were its battle-hardened, yet rested and retrained, divisions. Of these, none was more highly regarded than the 88th Infantry Division. In the fighting from Volterra to the Alps, the 88th deepened the lessons it had learned and the teamwork it had developed during the drive on Rome. Despite cycles of attrition and renovation, the division became ever more formidable as the war progressed.

The ability to coordinate artillery and infantry always had been a strength of the 88th. Extensive training in the United States had been reinforced during the efforts to provide fire support to patrols at Minturno. Proficiency continued to improve during the race for Rome, a race marked by frenzied artillery relocations to keep infantry spearheads under a protective umbrella of supporting fire. In the records of the battles for the Arno, one reads accounts of forward observers adjusting single artillery rounds to knock out individual machine gun nests. Such discrimination represented masterful use. Massive artillery preparations are not without effect, but well-entrenched defenders tend to emerge from them with much of their capability intact. Infantry close on the heels of preparatory shelling are likely to encounter determined pockets of resistance despite the most massive of preparations. At this point the well-directed artillery round is a priceless asset.

This precise use of artillery implies adequate communications. One striking aspect of a read through combat orders and related material generated by the 88th's several headquarters is the increasingly sophisticated attention given to tactical communications.[18] The 88th could not resolve the technical limitations of its equipment, but it could and did give attention to improving procedures. Radio relay stations, wired replacement of wireless communications as advances progressed, standard pyrotechnic signals, abbreviated codes, independent primary and alternate systems, detailed communications paragraphs in operations orders—all became increasingly familiar as communications techniques. Several techniques developed in the 88th—the use of checkpoints instead of place names on the radio, for example—are now accepted as doctrine.

Engineers proved as critical as artillerymen during the breach of prepared positions. Mine fields were a pervasive component of German defenses throughout the Italian campaign; they had embarrassed the 88th's first offensive in several ways. The unbreached antitank mine field before Sante Maria Infante had separated attacking infantrymen from armor support in the initial rush, and thus it had doomed the 351st Regiment to a grinding three-day battle. Elsewhere, infantry units, attempting to maneuver around mine fields, had become widely separated if they sought opposite shoulders of the same field, or congested if they gravitated into the same narrow channels. This latter possibility proved the most damaging, because openings that did exist were covered by enemy fire and units were already in echelons on narrow fronts anyway. Mine fields played a much less prominent role in the 88th's race towards Rome, so the problems they presented did not again receive detailed attention until the hiatus before the Arno offensive.

In part, the problem of mine fields was a training problem. The

Army Training Program stressed maneuver, and was somewhat super-ficial in the time given over to actually breaching prepared positions.[19] Commanders were taught that their first step upon encountering a mine field was to attempt to bypass it. Only engineers and a few special units received serious training in breaching mine fields; even these did not go through as much of the tedium of detecting, probing, digging, and disarming during training as they might have. In the first days of Diadem attempts to bypass mine fields shuffled units of their own narrow sectors into someone else's, and breaching expertise often was not present where needed.

General Sloan debriefed entire companies after Diadem and came to several conclusions with respect to mine fields. First, companies should not leave their sectors in efforts to bypass obstacles. Leading companies would attempt head-on breaches when they encountered mine fields; gaps that did materialize would be exploited by bringing companies up from the rear rather than by shifting leading companies sideways. Second, every assaulting company should have personnel skilled in breaching. If engineers could be provided to lead, they would, but commanders were expected to develop genuine breaching talent within their own units. To this end, each infantry platoon organized and trained its own breaching team; one team leader, one assistant leader and radio operator, two bazooka teams of two each, two flamethrowers, three pole and satchel demolition men, and five support and wire-cutting specialists. Finally, artillery should be inte-grated into breaching efforts on the finest possible scale, and all per-sonnel should be thoroughly briefed on the German's pervasive use of mine fields and booby traps.[20] Sloan's careful attention to breaching techniques paid off handsomely during the attack on Volterra. Combat engineers led the way through impressive obstacles and drew ac-colades from the infantrymen as instruments of the division's suc-cess.[21] From that time on practical exercises in breaching obstacles and clearing mine fields were an important component of training and retraining efforts. This type of training involved a great deal of tedium, but it proved to be time well spent.

Engineer construction also proved critical to the success of the 88th. Supply routes were constantly in need of attention, particularly in the aftermath of lengthy advances. Throughout the Italian campaign the support the 88th's front-line infantryman received from his engi-neers was creditable, at times brilliant. Cases in point are a resupply route engineers blasted out of the side of a mountain to support the flanking move on Mount Frena, and bridging feats across the Po and the Adige during the race to the Alps.[22]

Successful engineering efforts facilitated the integration of ar-mored vehicles into the 88th's tactical operations. The use of armor was not always practical in Italy, but over time frequent attachment led three independent battalions—the 752nd Tank, 760th Tank, and 805th Tank Destroyer—to become members of the division "family." This association proved invaluable when the 88th at last broke free of the Apennines and raced across the Po Valley. The crossing of the Adige and the assault on Vicenza involved classic combinations of armor, infantry, artillery, and engineers operating in a coordinated effort.

Transportation also achieved state of the art within the division as the war progressed. Transportation problems proved doubly perplexing because the worst of the fighting took place in tortuous terrain and because the Germans methodically disabled ports, rail lines, and bridges as they withdrew northward. Engineers rehabilitated bridges with dispatch, but advances often left the division at extended distances from a usable port or railhead. In the fighting to close to the Arno, the 88th received supplies from as far away as Naples; in the early stages of the Apennines fighting, from ports near Rome; and in the drive across the Po Valley, from railheads on the southern side of the Apennines. In this sprawling logistical environment the dual nature of the 88th's truck and mule establishment served the division well. Trucks sped supplies extended distances over marginal roads to rendezvous points at which mules took over. Some writers have supposed that the elaborate truck fleets of America's World War II infantry divisions were instruments of tactical mobility.[23] In the 88th they were not. The division's infantrymen made their advances through the time-honored technique of "picking 'em up and laying 'em down." Trucks could shift units behind the lines, but their principal use was the replenishment of the tons of supplies a division consumed in a day. Fully two-thirds of the 88th's truck assets were given over to replacing artillery expenditures alone.[24] Thus, trucks had far more to do with sustaining firepower than they had to do with mobility per se.

It was a good thing that the 88th's use of and support of artillery was well developed, because the division never did enjoy any particular luck using tactical air strikes. Part of the problem was—and remains—technical. Aircraft are limited in the time they can spend aloft and in the ordnance they can carry, so they cannot provide the luxury of working through successively smaller target errors until they finally hit the precise target the ground commander wants. Another portion of the problem stemmed from training and preference. The 88th had not trained with air units while in the States; during training it had relied exclusively upon artillery for indirect fire support and had brought artillery-infantry cooperation to about as fine an edge as it could have achieved without combat. Once overseas, commanders continued to prefer the familiar and to rely upon artillery, a reliance that proved well placed as long as artillery was in range. Even massive air strikes yielded disappointing results. On 15 April 1945, for example, 765 heavy bombers and 200 medium bombers raised a great deal of dust and smoke, yet did little substantive damage to the entrenched defenders fiercely contesting Monterumici.[25] When leading elements outdistanced their artillery—the ideal time to rely upon air support—effective strikes and effective coordination could not be readily conjured up. Indeed, during the drive on Verona the 88th's leading elements were shot up by friendly pilots who assumed that anyone so far north of the Po had to be Germans. One of the first casualties was the air-ground radio operator desperately trying to turn away the attacking planes. Air strikes along German lines of communications had considerable effect in Italy, but for close support only one type of aircraft ever seems to have been of much immediate value to the 88th: the light spotter planes used by artillery forward observers to identify and call in artillery targets.[26]

The vagaries of the personnel replacement system presented another array of problems to the 88th Infantry Division. As has been discussed, the War Department considered the successes of the 85th and 88th during Diadem as vindication of an experimental system in which individual replacements moved forward into units still in contact. An illusion that the system had succeeded dominated the War Department throughout the war, despite the fact that commanders at the division level and lower repeatedly expressed a preference for unit rotations rather than individual replacement.[27] The prolonged fighting in the North Apennines almost destroyed the 88th as an effective organization. Individual replacements did not work out well until they had had the time to settle in, and the fatigue prolonged fighting rendered ineffective those veterans still in the line.

Shocked by the erosion of their units, regimental commanders experimented with such replacement techniques as rotating battalions, timing offensives to allow for unit rest periods, and organizing replacements into small units sent forward as packages. Ultimately these half-measures failed. The only effective remedy was to call off the offensive altogether and to rest and retrain the entire Fifth Army. The rude fact was that only unit rotation could sustain prolonged combat, and the United States had not raised a sufficient number of battalions, regiments, or divisions to rotate them through a continuous major battle.[28] War Department planners excused America's relatively modest contribution of ground combat units by extolling the virtues of an individual replacement system that was to keep those units at full strength—even when in combat—indefinitely. The virtues of that individual replacement system were more apparent than real.

It should be noted that casualties did not wear evenly across the 88th Infantry Division. Artillery, quartermaster, ordnance, and head-

Table 7. 88th's "Old-Timers" as of 1 July 1945, by Unit Type

	Raw number	Percentage
Infantry regiments (3)	2,020	17
Artillery battalions (4) and DIVARTY	968	38
88th Recon Troop	82	51
313th Engineer Battalion	210	30
313th Medical Battalion	88	17
88th Quartermaster Company	122	60
Headquarters Company	119	99
88th Military Police	32	18
Division total	3,900	24

SOURCE: Derived from "Only 3,900 Old-Timers remain from 15,000 Who Started at Gruber," *The Blue Devil*, newsletter of the 88th Infantry Division, 14 July 1945.

quarters units took relatively few casualties; these deteriorated more from fatigue than from fatality during prolonged combat. Engineer, signal, and medical units exposed some personnel far more than they did others. Even in the rigors of the North Apennines fighting, artillery, headquarters, and logistical units remained intact, albeit weary. Only infantry units beneath the regimental level suffered debilitating casualties. An indication of the relative personnel stability of units by type can be gained from Table 7. The table depicts the relative numbers and percentages of "old-timers," men assigned to the division prior to 1 January 1943 who were still with the 88th on 1 July 1945.[29] Keep in mind that Table 8 reflects personnel losses from all causes, not necessarily casualties. Also note that although virtually all of the division headquarters company had been with the division since Camp Gruber, not all of them had been assigned to the headquarters company throughout.

Retraining efforts during interludes in combat were essentially crash programs to weld individual replacements, the products of thirteen weeks of individual training in the States, into the veteran infantry units. Given adequate support from the division's relatively undamaged logistical apparatus, some time for rest, and intensely supervised small-unit training, the infantry battalions regained combat readiness in less than a month every time the division pulled out of the line. The rest of the division was again ready for combat well before the infantry battalions completed this frenzy of retraining. An optimal cycle for the division seems to have been two or three weeks in combat followed by two or three weeks of rest and retraining. In part by accident, the 88th Infantry Division approximated this optimum throughout the Italian campaign, except during the near-crippling autumn of 1944. The 88th sustained its creditable reputation over time by virtue of what was, in effect, a unit rotation system. The War Department's cherished individual replacement system could not be made to work without a program for rotating units out of combat as well.

Of the ninety divisions with which the U.S. Army fought World War II, thirty-seven were draftee infantry divisions.[30] One might reasonably question the extent to which the experiences of the 88th Infantry Division reflected those of the draftee divisions taken as a whole. A cursory comparison suggests that there were some differences and a great many parallels.

The 88th Infantry Division was uncommonly fortunate with respect to personnel stability during its training in the United States. This fact above all else accounts for its being the first of the draftee divisions shipped overseas. It has been suggested that four-fifths of the training time lost to American units while in the United States was lost because of personnel turbulence. Sandwiched in its activation between the most frenzied period of mobilization and the bloodiest demands for combat replacements, the 88th was spared the worst of this turbulence. This relatively stable condition was for the most part fortuitous, although that good fortune was improved upon by the expediency with which the 88th negotiated its training cycle and by wise decisions made by the division's leadership on several occasions. Other divisions generally took far more time to assemble the team with which they finally deployed. Contrast the 88th's record of sixteen months between activation and deployment with the average time requirement for draftee infantry divisions, twenty-two months; this despite the shortening of divisional training cycles from twelve to ten months for later divisions.[31]

The logistical experiences of the draftee divisions seem to have been strikingly similar. The first of these divisions was activated in March 1942, the last in August 1943. National mobilization was in all cases far enough along that the new units had ample food, clothing, fuel, shelter, and ammunition. They also had the table of organization equipment they actually needed to support training, although most were short of their full authorizations until well into 1943. The equipment that was available was distributed evenly throughout the new divisions initially, so at any given time all enjoyed about the same equipment posture unless on major maneuvers or declared deployable. The divisions activated in 1943 were better off than earlier divisions with respect to percentages of authorized equipment on hand, and they benefited from the logistical lessons learned during 1942. The divisions of 1943 had ordnance light maintenance companies and adequate automotive spare parts from the outset, and did not suffer the logistical cadre reshufflings experienced by their predecessors. On the other hand, the divisions of 1943 received hand-me-down training equipment from the earlier units, so they were not altogether without maintenance headaches. The logistical experience of the 88th seems to have approximated that of the other draftee divisions; all seem to have been relatively well off insofar as supply and support were concerned.[32]

As divisions moved overseas, each in turn faced deterioration in training standards as personnel and equipment trickled for extended periods along rail lines and across oceans to distant destinations.[33] Once a division deployed, its personnel situation stabilized; this could be a mixed blessing, because divisions departed with greater or lesser numbers of last-minute fillers who had not trained with their new units. Theater commanders overseas were justifiably concerned about the battle-worthiness of the newly arriving divisions; they attempted to stand them down for a two- or three-week training program overseas or to give them a month's experience in a quiet sector before sending them to major operations. Some divisions, such as the 88th, had the benefit of both a training stand-down and a tour in a less active sector.

Of thirty-seven draftee infantry divisions, eleven spent a month or more in England, then shipped to France; one stopped briefly in England, then had a month in a quiet sector in France; twelve went directly to France and spent a month in quiet sectors; three trained several weeks in North Africa, then spent several weeks in quiet sectors in Italy; one went directly to Italy and spent six weeks in quiet sectors; three went to the Pacific and trained several months, although the training of one of three was badly broken up; and one went to Hawaii and trained for the rest of the war without fighting at all. Of the thirty-seven divisions, only five did not receive some kind of major retraining experience overseas. These included the ill-starred 106th, sent to a "quiet sector" that ended up in the path of the German Ardennes offensive of late 1944; the 75th and 76th, whose retraining experiences were cut short when they were hastily thrown against the shoulders of the Bulge; and the 92nd and 93rd, black units committed piecemeal rather than as divisions, with predictable consequences.[34]

The importance of a gradual initiation to combat—of a "warm-up"—should not be underestimated.[35] Divisions with both a retraining period overseas and a tour in a quiet sector seem to have done the best of any during their first major battles.[36] Those with lengthy tours in quiet sectors but no retraining program did almost as well, and those with neither retraining nor tours in quiet sectors fared least well.[37] The importance to the 88th of the Magenta training and of the tour of March

1944 in the line at Minturno has already been stressed. The division refreshed itself on the Army Training Program and then gained considerable combat experience at the small-unit level while diagnosing and working out a number of training deficiencies. Tours in quiet sectors seem to have been of equal value to other divisions.

A comparison can be made, for example, between the 99th and the 106th infantry divisions during the first days of the Ardennes offensive. By December 1944 the 99th had trained briefly in England, had had a month of combat experience in low-casualty environments, and was considered prime for a major offensive undertaking. Deployed alongside the 99th, the 106th had come almost directly from the United States, without significant retraining in England, and was just beginning to sort itself out in the quiet Ardennes. Both divisions found themselves in the path of the German offensive. The 99th fell back on its haunches, then very creditably held the northern shoulder of the Bulge until help arrived; the 106th folded in a little more than a day. The 106th was more exposed, to be sure. Among other differences between the two divisions, however, one must number the previous combat experience of the 99th.

One reason that tours in relatively quiet sectors seem to have been of even more value than retraining programs overseas was that the army training programs, for all their comprehensiveness, did have weaknesses. Retraining overseas refreshed units on the army training programs while carrying forward their deficiencies; combat experience allowed units to diagnose and overcome those deficiencies. The army training programs focused upon individual skills and upon large-scale offensive maneuvers in which the integration of the several arms and branches took place at the company level and above. It was not until Minturno that the 88th really wrestled with a highly discriminate use of artillery, with the intricacies of breaching mine fields and obstacles in depth—with or without engineer support—and with the complexities of maintaining communications in a hostile environment. The 88th never trained with tanks or air support in the United States, and it had only a superficial exposure to them prior to Diadem. Army training programs had not utterly neglected air support, tanks, mines, communications, or the discriminate use of artillery; the practical training stressed other things, however, and units first tend to reproduce their training when in combat.

It is significant that the training deficiencies cited represent tasks that are crucial when rupturing prepared defenses. Mine fields and obstacles msut be breached so that carefully integrated teams of tanks and infantry can roll forward—with infantry facilitating the advance of tanks and tanks providing direct fire support to infantry. After initial bombings and shellings the advance no longer requires massive artillery preparations; it requires carefully directed rounds into precisely the right troublesome positions; for example, machine-gun nests. This entire clockwork combination of infantry, armor, engineers, and artillery is utterly dependent upon effective communications as the battle develops.

Rupturing a defensive line is the most challenging of military operations. The draftee divisions of World War II came out of the Army Training Program lacking with respect to some of the intricacies involved. Unfortunately, most were called upon to break through prepared defenses early in their careers. All divisions had initial troubles putting line-breaking routines together; those without practical experience in quiet sectors had more.[38] The fighting in the bocage of Normandy, for example, required the apotheosis of combined arms coordination at the lowest levels of command; inexperienced units fresh from England could not quickly conjure the necessary skills.[39] Their clumsiness contrasted with the greater efficiency of such veteran units as the 1st, the 9th, and the 82nd. Divisions that spent some time in combat prior to their first attempt at rupturing defensive positions— for example, the 88th, the 102nd, or the 104th—generally had more success in their initial efforts.

Once the battlefield broke open into mobile warfare, the Army Training Program came into its own. Virtually every draftee division had its Fondi or its Roccasecca, its moments of glory when hard-marching columns outmaneuvered their German opponents and swept them from critical objectives into prisoner-of-war compounds. Deprived of formidable defensive positions, German units of 1944 and 1945 were generally inferior to their American counterparts.[40] German soldiers were not only less numerous, they were also less physically fit, less experienced as marksmen, less thoroughly trained, less well equipped, less well supported, and less able to make a combination of arms work for them.[41] German counterattacks often proved suicidal;[42] the best the Germans could hope for from the mobile battlefield was to escape from it with enough strength to man yet another line of prepared defenses.

Despite defensive advantages and masterful leadership at the highest levels, the Germans in Italy lost 536,000—killed, wounded, and missing—to the Allies' 312,000.[43] Other indications of German deterioration included an increasing tendency to surrender in groups when in less than desperate circumstances, the repellent policy of retaliating against dependents and relatives of soldiers who surrendered, and the 25,000 Wehrmacht servicemen ultimately shot for desertion. On a number of occasions, most notably during the battle of Aachen, the discipline of line infantry units was maintained by terrorist campaigns directed against them by the SS and other Nazi fanatics.[44]

Mobile warfare allowed the American army, including its draftee divisions, to use material advantages to best effect. Truck fleets sped supplies of all types over extended distances to support advancing units; in particular, trucks made possible the replenishment of mind-boggling expenditures of artillery ammunition and fuel over the widening gaps that separated divisions from railheads or ports. Tanks bypassed pockets of resistance to strike at more vulnerable—and critical—targets deep in the enemy rear. Planes may have had severe limitations insofar as close support was concerned, but on the mobile battlefield free-lance air strikes did much to disrupt enemy troop movements and resupply efforts. Behind stable fronts, Germans could move during limited visibility and avoid aerial interdiction. When the fighting broke into a war of movement, time proved too critical to allow the wait for fog or darkness.[45]

A statement that American units fared better than German units during mobile warfare deserves qualification. The Germans concentrated what personnel and equipment advantages they did have into a relatively few units that could make a difference in a narrow sector, as at Cassino, or in a spearhead, as in the Ardennes offensive. These elite units—panzer, panzer grenadier, and parachute divisions—stood in stark contrast to the infantry divisions that constituted the bulk of the German army.[46] American divisions did not demonstrate such extreme variations with respect to equipment, personnel, training, support, or capability. The Germans did have a superior personnel replacement system, and this muted American superiorities that might otherwise have been more obvious.

The Germans raised more than three hundred divisions during the course of the war and did their best to rotate units out of the line as a means to provide rest, retraining, and replacement.[47] Even severely depleted units tended to have leadership and logistical cadres still intact, so there were always experienced divisional bases to build upon. The Germans gained impressive successes by ruthlessly holding the line with increasingly depleted units, in the meantime building others back up to acceptable levels of manning, training, and capability. The reserve built up for the Ardennes offensive is the most dramatic illustration of the process. Manteuffel's Fifth and Dietrich's Sixth panzer armies were probably as good as any the Germans ever fielded.[48] The usual German achievement was more modest: plugging a crumbling line with fresh divisions that were not yet capable of a wide range of operations but were capable of defending their own positions.[49]

The American individual replacement system, bastard stepchild of a paucity of units, yet "verified" by the 85th and 88th infantry divisions, did not work so well. Weary units remained in contact far too long. Bewildered replacements became casualties themselves before they trained into their units, often before they even arrived in those units. The divisions, draftee and otherwise, that fought in the North Apennines and in northern France suffered the worst ravages of prolonged conflict without relief. In France some divisions never saw a day out of combat from the point at which they were first committed. Highly regarded divisions, such as the 1st Infantry Division in the Hürtgen, rendered themselves "somnambulate," and newly arriving divisions could find themselves more efficient than the veterans of many campaigns.[50] Despite their inexperience and training deficiencies, green divisions had one advantage over the exhausted survivors and confused replacements comprising veteran divisions engaged in prolonged conflict: they were still units.

The damage done by sending forward individual replacements rather than units was uneven. Local commanders, such as Clark after Rome and Kendall in the Appennines, did what they could to rotate units out of the line. France had its quiet sectors and the pulse of combat could create rest and retraining periods for divisions. In the Pacific, frenzied fighting cleared one island or another, after which came a considerable lull while preparations for the next operation matured. North Africa, Sicily, and Italy prior to the Apennines saw American divisions alternating weeks of intense conflict with weeks of relative quiet. The Sixth Army Group's campaign from Southern France through Bavaria was somewhat more episodic in the demands it placed on units than was the fighting farther north. In these cases an accidental alternation between intense combat and rest and retraining provided benefits similar to those provided by a conscious policy of unit rotation.[51]

It should be noted that in infantry divisions somewhat more than 94 percent of all casualties came from subordinate infantry units.[52] Artillery, engineers, and other supporting arms and branches came through the fiercest fighting relatively unscathed. Thus, it was easier to sustain high standards of cohesion and training in supporting units than in infantry battalions. American artillery, for example, trained to high standards of technical competence in the United States, suffered relatively few casualties overseas, and remained unexcelled on the battlefield throughout the period in which the draftee divisions fought their way.

The 88th Infantry Division departed notably from the "normal" experience of the draftee division in a few ways. It enjoyed relative personnel stability during its training in the United States; it had a lengthy "warm-up" overseas featuring both a training stand-down and a tour in a quiet sector; and it fought in episodes alternating weeks of combat with weeks of renewal, the North Apennines excepted. With respect to these factors, the 88th's experience was more like that of the most celebrated of the regular army divisions, specifically the 1st, 3rd, and 9th infantry divisions, than it was like that of the bulk of the divisions that followed it overseas.[53]

Combat experience is a perishable characteristic. Within a decade of war's end few veterans are left below the battalion level, and none remain in the rank and file. The expertise that remains is drawn more from what leaders have read than from what they have experienced. Concepts and techniques developed in the crucible of war appear in a body of postwar literature, and that body becomes the basis for future military preparation. The experience of the World War II draftee divisions influenced the postwar development of the U.S. Army. Although most of the lessons to be learned from them were learned, some seem to have been overlooked.

Led by the 85th and 88th infantry divisions, the draftee divisions of World War II irrevocably laid to rest a century and a half of controversy concerning the value of conscripted soldiers. By the hour of the 88th's triumph, the fall of Rome, this had ceased to be much of an issue, however. Individual replacement and the suspension of voluntary enlistment had filled the ranks of all divisions with draftees well before the great victories of 1944. The further vindication of the draftee undoubtedly had some influence on mobilization planners and did exhilarate the public, but since World War I even Uptonians had been satisfied with American conscripts as individual soldiers.[54]

The 88th and its sister divisions also laid to rest controversy concerning the value of all-draftee formations; tiny cadres of professionals had been able to mold masses of erstwhile civilians into proficient fighting organizations. This triumph was more to the point: America did not need enormous armies in times of peace to efficiently field enormous armies in times of war.

The draftee divisions' initial performances reflected the success of an Army Ground Forces training program that was at once the most massive and the most centralized in history. Although technological developments such as films, innovative training equipment, electronic communications, and air transportation contributed to the degree of centralization possible, the heart of the centralizing process was the detailed, structured, and unit-specific Army Training Program (ATP). In pyramidal fashion, service schools trained cadremen who trained subordinates to train troops, all in accord with the ATP. Mass publication provided copies of the ATP to trainer and trainee alike; every man could know where he stood on the "checklist." Checklist training has prospered in the aftermath of World War II success. Whether the ATP of the 1940s and 1950s, the ORT (Operational Readiness Test) of the 1960s, or the ARTEP (Army Training and Evaluation Program) of the 1970s and 1980s, the basis of collective training within the army continues to be a single, comprehensive document for each type of unit. This dictates training tasks, the conditions under which they are to be accomplished, and the standards against which performance is to be measured.[55]

Postwar training literature addressed the shortcomings of the World War II ATP with respect to such items as the integration of tanks and infantry or the coordination of close air support. After World War II, additional inadequacies surfaced as the army encountered or imagined new situations; these in turn led to further revisions in training literature.[56] Re-editing has amended substance without disturbing the centralizing premise that an army-level staff composed of personnel with line experience can identify unit training needs and develop detailed programs to address those needs. Training in the army continues to run from the center, as it did during World War II.[57]

The draftee divisions could not have trained in the States, much less deployed overseas, without impressive logistical achievements. Despite occasional miscarriages, the sophistication and scale of American logistics remain unparalleled. World War II–vintage shortcomings with respect to logistical manning, maintenance organization, spare parts stockage, and off-road transportation have been revolutionized by new technologies and new techniques.[58] Since the Truman administration, a policy of "creeping," or continuous, mobilization has sustained relatively high levels of material readiness; contracted deliveries have been spaced over years and have been guided by follow-on contracts to replace worn or obsolescent equipment.[59] Insofar as the army is concerned, logistical controversy centers not so much on whether material superiority could be achieved in a future war as on whether it would be achieved during the initial battles of such a war.

The U.S. Army may have less equipment than it would need in the early stages of a major war, but it has more than it effectively mans. Harkening back to the Uptonian premonitions of a rabble in arms and the mobilization disorders of 1940 and 1941, postwar logisticians developed a doctrinal principle labeled "material precedence."[60] A two-edged sword, this principle dictates that one should have the materials of war on hand before mustering units to use them. Adherence to this principle has supported the efforts of those who have made continuous mobilization work for thirty years; it has also led us to arrays of equipment brought together and then manned, or partially manned, regardless of the vagaries of personnel strength. This was not the experience of the draft divisions; their organizations established and trained at full personnel strength regardless of the vagaries of equipment availability. Material precedence subordinated personnel precedence, and the American army characteristically handled things better than it handled people.

The greatest weakness of the U.S. Army during World War II was its turbulent personnel system, at home and overseas. The 88th was fortunate enough to avoid the worst excesses of this turbulence but, ironically, it set a battlefield precedent that "validated" individual replacement analogous to the replenishment of fuel or spare parts. As World War II ended, an individual point system based on such factors as time in service, time overseas, decorations, and dependents managed the redeployment of soldiers from Europe. The British solicited the use of the 88th, a unit they held in high esteem, to establish an American presence in the vicinity of Trieste. The 88th they received was a division whose faces had changed; soldiers had rotated, if units had not. Through several years of occupation duty in Italy, Yugoslavia, and Austria, years punctuated by civil strife and sporadic Yugoslav guerrilla forays, commanders of the 88th wrestled with personnel turbulence as much as they did with operational concerns. Sheer entropy guaranteed that units had some portion of their assigned strength in transit all of the time. This had serious implications for cohesiveness and morale, and for the maintenance of consistent training standards.[61]

The administrative convenience of individual replacement soon infected the army at large. Commanders attempting to train units found their efforts frustrated by unremitting hemorrhages of trained personnel. Soldiers rotated through the Korean and Vietnam wars like so many passengers on a bus. In these wars newly arriving units, trained in the United States or elsewhere, fought well enough initially. Once the entropy of the personnel system set in, however, standards of cohesion and training inevitably dropped. Soldiers, not units, rotated from divisions training without fighting in the United States, Germany, and elsewhere to units fighting without training in Asia; and vice versa.[62]

It is true that the demands of modern combat cannot be sustained without the replacement of individual casualties. Techniques for accomplishing this vary, however. One can send partially trained replacements forward into units hotly engaged. One can also hold replacements until units return from the front lines, then weld a team out of replacements and veterans with whatever training time is available. During the latter part of World War II, the U.S. Army adhered to the first technique unless local commanders found or fell into a way around it. The systematic use of the second technique would have required more units—some forward, some back—than America's mobilization had made available. The second technique also seems to have been, as the Germans demonstrated and some American analysts suspected, the more efficient in the long run.[63]

Modern warfare is increasingly demanding of the front-line units that participate in it; it seems that units will need to be relieved ever more frequently. However, the postwar army has been even less attentive to unit rotation than was the army of World War II. During the Korean War, units rarely enjoyed training stand-downs; during the Vietnam War they had virtually none.[64] Training exercises outside of the combat theaters or in peacetime naively carried units through one mission after another as if they would never need to be replaced.[65] Rather than anticipating extraordinary demands for new units, postwar mobilization planning has focused almost exclusively on the active and reserve components, the equivalent of the regular army and National Guard of World War II. Like their predecessors prior to each of the world wars, modern planners are unenthusiastic about cutting new units from whole cloth.[66] The 88th Infantry Division was the ultimate product of a great deal of prewar thought. For all their deficiencies, the mobilization plans of the 1930s were more sophisticated with respect to new divisions than those of a more recent vintage.

It is not difficult to envision a crisis in which the United States would require ground forces greatly in excess of its present means. This suggests that Americans might once again fall back upon one of their more curious national traits, the ability to conjure proficient combat units out of an unmilitary people quickly. Under those circumstances the factors that made the 88th Infantry Division outstanding— the carefully trained and organized cadre; the relative personnel stability; the well-thought-out, albeit lengthy, training program; the unexcelled logistical wherewithal; the conscious retraining and warm-up overseas; and the episodic combat laced with retraining efforts—would once again merit professional and public attention.

Like so many historical issues, the issues associated with manning the American army have evolved without ever having been resolved. Questions (for example, whether to have a regular army, whether to render that regular army expansible, whether to have conscription, whether to have conscripted divisions) have been answered without Americans ever having achieved a final blueprint describing how the United States can best remain a nation of free people in a troubled world. The experience of the World War II draftee divisions was refreshing; it demonstrated that masses of citizens could be welded into proficient modern fighting organizations in reasonable periods of time, that the United States need not endure enormous armies in times of peace in order to field enormous armies in times of war.

Despite overall success, American mobilization for World War II was not without significant flaws. The army's handling of personnel, training, logistics, and doctrine encompassed experiences that should carry the label "how not to" as well as those meriting the label "how to." Nations are not soon likely to grow beyond the use of armed force. Americans should understand how they have defended themselves in the past in order that they may more effectively defend themselves in the future. Within its corner of American history, the 88th Infantry Division offers considerable insight towards the development of that understanding.

APPENDIX 1 ⸻

Cumulative Personnel-Induced Training Time Losses (Infantry Divisions Only)

Each of the letter entries on the accompanying figures represents a keyed annotation of a personnel disturbance War Department authorities credited with the loss of a month's training time. For more details on training time lost as a function of personnel lost, see the Memorandum of General McNair to the Chief of Staff, Army Ground Forces, 7 March 1944, National Archives, MMRB (353/206). The key to the figures is as follows:

X. One X for every month of training lost because of a one-time stripping of greater than 50 percent.

S. One S for each month of training lost because of stripping of greater than 20 percent but less than 50 percent.

T. One T for every month served solely as a replacement training center.

O. One O for every month the subject division underwent the OCS/AGCT "raid" or mass officer stripping.

A. Four A's if the division was caught in the great ASTP/AGCT "raid."

D. One D for every month lost in excess of the time loss attributable to personnel turbulence.

Note that of the numbers assigned to divisions, numbers 1-25 were reserved for Regular Army; 26-45, for National Guard; and 60 and greater, for all-draftee divisions.

If we assume pre-1941 divisions should have been ready for embarkation within four months of Pearl Harbor, 1941 and 1942 divisions should have been ready for embarkation within sixteen months of activation, and 1943 divisions should have been ready for embarkation within fourteen months, 78 percent of the total time lost by infantry divisions between activation and embarkation can be credited to personnel turbulence.

For some examples to assist in reading the figures:

1. The 26th Infantry Division, a 1941 division, has eighteen letters on the chart, indicating it took eighteen months more than it should have (16 + 18 = 34 months total) to embark. Of these eighteen months, twelve were lost because of OCS or officer stripping (O's); four were lost when the division was

delayed enough to be caught in the ASTP/AGCT raid (*A*'s); and two were lost for reasons other than personnel turbulence (*D*'s).

2. The 100th Infantry Division, a 1942 division, has eight letters on the chart, indicating it took eight months more than it should have (16 + 8 = 24 months total) to embark. Of these eight months, two were lost because of stripping greater than 20 percent but less than 50 percent (*S*'s); four were lost when the division was caught in the ASTP/AGCT raid (*A*'s); and two were lost for reasons other than personnel turbulence (*D*'s).

Figure A1-1. Training Time Losses, pre-1941 Divisions

```
                                                          D
                                                          D
                                           —              D
                                  D                       D
                                  D                       D
                                  D                       D
                                  D                       D
            —                     D           —           D      D
    D               —             D      A    A           A      A
    D          D                  A      A    A           A      A
—   D          D                  A      A    A           A      A
D   D     D    A                  A      X    X           X      X
D A D     D    A                  X      X    X           X      X
D A D  D  D               X       X      X    X       —   X
D A D  D—D                X  —    X      X    X       D   X
O O O  O  O               X  O    X      X    X       O   X
O O O  O  O               X  O    X      X    X       O   X
O O O  O  O               X  O    X      X    X       O   X
O O O  O  O               X  O    X      X    X       O   X
O O O  O  O               X  O    X      X    X       O   X
O — O  O  O               X  O    X      X    X       O   X
O D O  O  O  D            X  O    X      X    X       O   X
O D O  O  O  D            X  O    X      X    X       O   X
— O D O O  O  D           X  O  — X      X    X       O   X
D O O O O  O  O           X  O    X      X  — X       O   X
D O O O —O  O  O  — —     X  O D  X   —   X      X  O  X

  1   2   3   4   5   6   7   8   9  27  32  35  36  37  30  41  44  45  31
```

Figure A1-2. Training Time Losses, 1941 Divisions

	—						
	D						
—	D						
D	A	—					
D	A	D					
D	A	D					
X	A	D					
X	O	O					
X	O	O					
X	O	O				—	
X	O	O				X	
X	O	O				X	
X	O	O				X	
X	O	O				X	
X	O	O				X	
X	O	O			—	X	
X	O	O	—		D	X	
X	O	O	D		D	X	
X	O	O	O		O	X	—
X	O	O	O	—	O	X	O
38	26	28	29	34	43	33	40

Figure A1-3. Training Time Losses, 1942 Divisions

```
               A                                  —
               A                     D
               A                     D
               A                     D
               S                     D
               S                     D          D
 __  __        S            __       D   __     S                               __
 D   D         S        D   __       D   D   S               __                 D
 A   A         T        D   D        D   D   T          D    __                 D
 A   A   __  A T    __  D   D        A   D   T          D    A                  D
 A   A __  A   T    D   D   D        A   D   T   __  __ D    A    __            D
 A   A  D   A  T    A   A   A        A   A   T   A   A  A    A    A    A         A
 O   O  D   A  T    A   A   A        A   A   T   A   A  A    A    A    A         A
 O   O  D   A  T    A   A   A        S   A   T   A   A  A    S    A    A         A
 O   O  O   O  T    A   A   A   __   S   A   T   A   A  A    S    A    A         A

 77  90 85  93 76   79  81  80  88   89  95  78  83  91 96   94   98          102
```

```
                    —
                    D
                    D            —
                    D            D
         __  __ __  D    __      D
 __  __  __  D  D   D    A   A   A
 D   D   D   D  D   D    A   A   A
 D   D   D   A  A   A    A   A   A   __  __
 D   D   D   A  A   A    A   A   A   D   D  __  __
 A   A   A   A  A   A    S   S   S   S   S   S   S   __  __
 A   A   A   A  A   A    S   S   S   S   S   S   S   D   D  __  __  __
 A   A   A   S  S   S    S   S   S   S   S   S   S   S   S   S   S   S
 A   A   A   S  S   S    S   S   S   S   S   S   S   S   S   S   S   S

104  84  92  99 100 103  86  87  97 106  66  75  69  63  70  42  71  65
```

The Mythos of Wehrmacht Superiority: Colonel Dupuy Reconsidered

The casual student of World War II does not need to read much to be exposed to a pervasive adulation of the Wehrmacht. Testimonies of German proficiency are generally reinforced by comparisons wherein other armed forces, including those of the United States, appear unfavorably. This might have come as a surprise to the World War II GIs who herded "kraut" prisoners by the thousands after every major European battle the American army fought. How many of our soldiers reviewed the parades of docile prisoners and thought they were looking at men better than themselves?

The current inflated image of Hitler's armies is complex in its origin. Like most mythologies, it contains some truth; the Germans were outstanding when in their prime and were formidable throughout World War II. The British and French exaggerated German capabilities, however, too often explaining their own ineptitudes in terms of German genius.[1] German prisoners, once they recovered from the shock of capture, added their own apocryphal stories suggesting prowess and expertise.[2] American humor widened the distance. Sad Sack, Beetle Bailey, and Bill Mauldin portrayed the American soldier as a lovable nincompoop without providing a similar service for the Germans.

Immediately after World War II, a historiographical bias set in. German sources available to English-speaking authors were dominated by official records and the testimony, and later memoirs, of captured German officers.[3] American sources were much broader, featuring monumental bodies of correspondence, anecdotes, interviews, and oral testimony from soldiers of all ranks. The lower in an institution one descends, the more inchoate its activities may appear. Postwar America had no lack of veterans with a pet story illustrating martial miscarriages. Many of the veterans' stories were humorous; some were not. Debacles such as Buna, Kasserine, and the Rapido engaged the attention of print media and historians. It is true that German botches also received some publicity, but many of these were conveniently blamed on Hitler alone and were generally of less interest to the American public.

Studies appeared favoring those who had a point to prove or an axe to grind. S.L.A. Marshall's famous *Men Against Fire*, for example, stimulated the acceptance of "Train Fire" infantry exercises by suggesting that most American

---

"Colonel Trevor N. Dupuy and the Mythos of Wehrmacht Superiority: A Reconsideration." *Military Affairs*, January 1986, pp. 16-20.

infantrymen spent World War II cowering in the bottom of their foxholes; Basil Liddell Hart vented his pique on Allied leaders who did not share his elevated impression of himself; behavioral scientists, simply by their choices of subjects, created candid documents hazardous when quoted out of context.[4] The cumulative effect of all this has been relative images skewed to favor the German soldier over the American. This condition is not at all ameliorated by the fact that a significant fraction of the public buying World War II books consists of enthusiasts who collect Nazi memorabilia, construct plastic panzers, and energetically seek to be the German player in hex-grid war games.

It is ironic that a focus for this adulation of the Wehrmacht is a distinguished World War II veteran and prolific military historian, Col. Trevor N. Dupuy. His *Numbers, Prediction, and War* represents a promising effort to refine the analyses of battles wherein numbers of troops and weapons are known.[5] With sufficient ventilation in and criticism from the academic community, this work could evolve into a useful historical tool. Now it simply demonstrates the intellectual intimidation wrought when complex calculations are unleashed upon a liberal arts community. Books have emerged based uncritically upon Colonel Dupuy's "proof" of German superiority as a launch point for further enlargements of the Wehrmacht.[6] The extraordinarily exact calculation that one German had the "score effectiveness" of 1.55 Americans has become a powerful arrow in the quiver of Wehrmacht enthusiasts. The purpose of this text is to reconsider the numbers that have given Colonel Dupuy his results.

Colonel Dupuy's comparison of German and American units emerged from an analysis of seventy-eight selected engagements during 1943 and 1944. His historical data seems valid; one would be hard put to fault the careful and exhaustive enumeration of troops, weapons, and circumstances. Unfortunately, the sample itself is misleading. It scrambles together different types of units, disproportionately overrepresents panzer and panzer grenadier divisions, and features the American as the attacker in almost all cases.

Within Colonel Dupuy's seventy-eight battles, a number of different types of units appear: British infantry divisions, British armored divisions, American infantry divisions, American armored divisions, American corps, German panzer divisions, German parachute divisions, German corps, and German armies. Theoretically, Colonel Dupuy's "operational lethality index" (discussed below) offers the means of making these different types of units comparable. Until his "Quantitative Judgment Model" is perfected, however, it seems best to break comparisons out by unit type—to avoid comparing "apples and oranges," as it were. Screening out the British because they are different, and omitting corps because they are not standard units, Colonel Dupuy's sample includes thirty-nine engagements pitting American and German divisions against each other. Remembering that Colonel Dupuy's "score effectiveness" came out as 1:1.55 in favor of the Germans, it may be instructive to break out his computations by unit type (see Table A2-1).

These are Colonel Dupuy's own results. The gradient in German effectiveness from a high with the panzers to a low with the infantry is what one might expect. The Germans tended to concentrate personnel and equipment advantages into their most mobile divisions.[7] In the thirty-nine engagements,

Table A2-1. Score Effectiveness Comparison by Division Type

	German panzer	German panzer grenadier	German infantry
U.S. armor	1:1.76	—	1:1.30
U.S. infantry	1:2.40	1:1.97	1:1.25

thirteen featured panzer divisions; eight, panzer grenadier divisions; and eighteen, infantry divisions. The German army of 30 July 1944 had 27 panzer, 12 panzer grenadier, and 142 infantry divisions (not counting mountain and parachute divisions). This is not to mention the 29 static divisions German commanders regarded as their least potent units. Based on these proportions, Colonel Dupuy's sample overrepresents panzer divisions at 224 percent and panzer grenadier divisions at 323 percent; it underrepresents infantry divisions at 58 percent. The American sample is better balanced; the ten armored and twenty-nine infantry divisions in the sample are roughly proportional to the sixteen armored and forty-nine infantry divisions deployed to Europe. Thus the American army at large is, in effect, compared with the best of the German army.

Another disproportion does even more damage to Colonel Dupuy's analysis than his selection of divisions. Of the thirty-nine engagements pitting American and German divisions against each other, the American is the attacker thirty-six times. This introduces the question of whether anything in Dupuy's analysis favors the defender. The answer is yes.

Numbers, Prediction and War approaches the task of weighing units against each other by two routes. The most easily understood of these is score effectiveness, computed as

$$SE_f = \sqrt{\frac{Cas_e}{.001 \times S_f \times V_f \times U_f}}$$

Cas_e represents the number of casualties inflicted on the enemy; S_f is friendly force strength, discussed below: V_f is a friendly vulnerability factor, discussed below; and U_f is a friendly posture factor. The value of U_f represents the advantage accrued by different operational circumstances. According to Colonel Dupuy, if the attack is 1.0, the hasty defense is 1.3, the prepared defense is 1.5, the fortified defense is 1.6, and the delay is 1.2.

These values seem low for all postures except the attack. Few battalion commanders' careers would survive the assertion their battalion could hold off only a battalion and a half from prepared defensive positions. It is true that the attacker can turn flanks or concentrate favorable odds upon a specific point, but that is a measure of command and control rather than of the intrinsic strength of the defense. On a reasonably narrow front a defender of comparable ability and mobility can force his attacker into frontal assaults. The battles of Colonel Dupuy's sample generally feature such narrow fronts.

Table A2-2. Alternative Values of U_f

	Attack	Hasty defense	Prepared defense	Fortified defense	Delay
Col. Dupuy	1.0	1.3	1.5	1.6	1.2
Traditional	1.0	—	3.0	6.0	—
ORSA	1.0	1.3	2.5	3.8	2.2
Blast vulnerability	1.0	—	3.2	7.1	—

Numbers, Prediction, and War does not explain how the values of U_f were derived. The most persuasive indictment of its choices is that of hundreds of accomplished analysts who have attempted, for one reason or another, to reflect the relative advantages of a defender, none have come up with figures as low as Colonel Dupuy's. Traditional rules of the thumb, verified by experience as planning factors and still taught at command and general staff colleges, assert that one needs a three-to-one advantage in effective combat power—not necessarily numbers of troops—at the point of decision to overcome a defender in prepared positions.[8] Another set of U_f equivalents has emerged from the much-refined equations of such seminal theorists as Bradley A. Fiske and F. W. Lanchester.[9] These mathematical models are the stock in trade of the Operations Research and Systems Analysis (ORSA) community.[10] A third source of equivalents for Colonel Dupuy's U_f comes from assessments of relative vulnerability. These originated with the designers of fortifications and are now most widely used by nuclear targeting planners. For circumstances in which the governing effect with respect to casualties is blast—as opposed to radiation or thermal effects—parallels with World War II can be drawn. That which protects against blast protects against direct and indirect conventional fires as well.[11] Table A2-2 summarizes alternative values for U_f insofar as the several schools of analysts have developed them.

Given the information in Table A2-2, one can recompute score effectiveness for each of the thirty-nine engagements and rework the comparisons of Table A2-1. In each of the cells of Table A2-3 the first entry is derived from traditional, the second from ORSA, and the third from blast vulnerability values for U_f. Where a school of analysts proposed no alternative values of U_f, I used Colonel Dupuy's. As a point of interest, of the thirty-six American attacks, fifteen were against fortified defenders, four against prepared defenders, nine against hasty defenders, and eight against forces involved in the delay.

The most important point made by Table A2-3 is not so much specific values as it is the demonstration of how radically choices of U_f alter the results. Virtually any analyst except Colonel Dupuy would take the same data and rate the Germans far lower than he did. All factors considered, the ORSA equivalents of U_f are probably the most comprehensive, time-tested, and reliable. They have been used with considerable success to reflect past battles and predict future ones.[12] Colonel Dupuy takes some pains to establish that his Quantitative Judgment Model (QJM) gets a better "fit" with respect to his chosen battles than does the ORSA standardized computer model, ATLAS.

Table A2-3. Score Effectiveness Comparisons by Division Type, Alternative U_f Values

	German panzer	German panzer grenadier	German infantry
U.S. armor	1:1.38	—	1:0.64
	1:1.23	—	1:0.74
	1:1.37	—	1:0.61
U.S. infantry	1:1.81	1:1.11	1:0.94
	1:1.44	1:1.14	1:0.89
	1:1.80	1:1.08	1:0.92

This seems to be a result of QJM steps 9c and 10, which allow the analyst to review results, identify discrepancies, and go back and change parameters in such a manner that historical results are more nearly achieved. It seems no accident that *Numbers, Prediction, and War* labels one of its subchapters "Fudge Factors."

Colonel Dupuy's equation for score effectiveness contains V_f and S_f as multipliers that might correct the skew caused by too-low values for U_f. Values for V_f come from a complex formula:

$$V_f = 1 - [N \times U_v \times (\sqrt{S_e/S_f}) \times V_y \times V_r]/r_u S_f$$

According to Colonel Dupuy, this formula for the "vulnerability factor" has "resulted from considerable experimentation with World War II data." It seems V_f is more the derivative of curve-fitting than it is the representative of a specific theoretical concept. The values for U_v, V_y, V_r, and r_u are parameters for posture vulnerability, air vulnerability, amphibious vulnerability, and terrain posture. In the mind of this author, the tabular values chosen for these in *Numbers, Prediction, and War*, like the values chosen for U_f, favor the defender as score effectiveness is calculated. Theoretically, values for V_f could range widely enough to offset the too-low values for U_f. Colonel Dupuy established a minimum V_f at 0.6, however, thus limiting the range of that parameter. In the selected battle analyses not even the ranges possible are achieved, and V_f does not moderate U_f significantly.

Another value contributing to the calculation of score effectiveness is friendly strength (S_f). In some respects S_f is the most important of Colonel Dupuy's contributions, for it allows one to compare units with different compositions and equipment. The basis for the comparison is Operational Lethality Indices (OLI) computed for each weapon. OLIs are multiplied by factors representing the effects of terrain, weather, or situation. The total of all the OLIs in a unit is the force strength, S (S_f for friendly force strength).

The concept of totaling OLIs seems simple enough, but the numbers chosen to represent specific weapons cause problems. Colonel Dupuy derives his OLIs from Theoretical Lethality Indices (TLIs) based on the rate at which weapons would inflict casualties on 100,000 arrayed one per square meter throughout a one-kilometer square. The OLIs developed through Colonel

Table A2-4. Score Effectiveness Comparisons by Division Type, ORSA U$_f$, Assumption of Artillery/Air OLI Reduced by Half

	German panzer	German panzer grenadier	German infantry
U.S. armor	1:1.05	—	1:0.63
U.S. infantry	1:1.22	1:0.97	1:0.76

Dupuy's analysis give far more weight to firepower than they do to discrimination, and they do not allow for the fact that dispersion erodes the effects of indirect or automatic-fire weapons far more rapidly than it erodes the effects of direct-fire weapons or weapons capable of aimed single shots. This results in curious relationships. A single 105-millimeter howitzer, for example, is worth 1,288 Springfield rifles. A World War II fighter-bomber is worth 250 machine gunners. A one-megaton nuclear airburst is worth 4,635,900 men armed with late-nineteenth-century rifles—a point that might well have been lost on Chairman Mao. Colonel Dupuy's computations of S$_f$ do allow for weapons degradations due to terrain, weather, or situation, but the basic illogic remains. A 105-millimeter howitzer under unfavorable circumstances is worth 820 riflemen under favorable circumstances.

It seems obvious that Colonel Dupuy's OLIs rate artillery and air support far too highly. If German and American units had had equivalent proportions of such firepower available, this would do little damage to comparisons. Americans typically had higher proportions of both assets in their inventories, however. This makes American strength calculate too high and thus makes their score effectiveness too low. Without quibbling about how many riflemen a howitzer is actually worth, let us assume Colonel Dupuy's figures for artillery and air support are at least twice as high as they should be. Working back through Colonel Dupuy's sample, we can estimate American force strengths are overrated by at least 15-30 percent and German force strengths by at least 5-15 percent. The easiest way to adjust this imbalance seems to be to multiply through the German results by about 0.85. Applying that multiplier to our ORSA U$_f$-derived figures, one comes up with Table A2-4.

Table A2-4 may represent an improvement over Table A2-1, but it is not really satisfactory. It implies a precision its subject does not warrant. Combat units do not really achieve a score effectiveness of .76; they fight better than, about the same as, or less well than their adversaries. Table A2-5 translates Table A2-4 into appropriate imprecision. In each of the cells of Table A2-5, the first entry is the number of engagements wherein—according to the calculations that led to Table A2-4—Americans outclassed Germans. The second entry is the number of engagements wherein they did about the same, calculated as having been within 10 percent score effectiveness of each other. The third entry in each cell is the number of engagements wherein Germans outclassed Americans.

Table A2-5 suggests that the effectiveness of American armor and German

Table A2-5. American "Victories" / Ties / German "Victories"

	German panzer	German panzer grenadier	German infantry
U.S. armor	4/0/3	—	2/1/0
U.S. infantry	2/0/4	3/2/3	10/2/2

panzers and the effectiveness of American infantry and German panzer grenadiers were roughly equivalent. American divisions, armor and infantry, outclassed German infantry divisions by a wide margin, and American infantry was not at its best when faced by German panzers. These assessments track with the narratives of sober historians. Because infantry divisions constituted such an overwhelming proportion of the German force structure, American divisions clearly were more efficient overall.

Colonel Trevor N. Dupuy's painstakingly acquired historical data is an invaluable contribution. Appropriately analyzed, it offers convincing evidence that American divisions of 1943-1944 were more efficient than their German counterparts man for man, weapon for weapon, and asset for asset. This opens a new paradigm. A conventional explanation for American World War II victories has been overwhelming quantitative advantages. Colonel Dupuy's data suggests quantitative advantages were not sufficient to offset the difficulty of assigned missions, and Americans summoned up a qualitative edge as well. Perhaps German excellence was the artful choice of positions defensible by mediocre divisions.

An assumption of American superiority suggests a search for cause. At this point let me suggest some questions. How far off their prime, if at all, were the Germans of 1943-1944? To answer this, one must balance degradation due to combat losses against advantages gained from combat experience and institutional reform during the period 1939-1942. Was the elaborate, lengthy, and centralized American divisional training program ultimately superior to the somewhat feudal German counterpart? Did the large body of publications associated with stateside training lend themselves to ad hoc retraining overseas? How much of an advantage was American equipment standardization? American doctrine was balanced with respect to operations, logistics, and administration, whereas German doctrine focused narrowly on operations alone.[13] American logisticians were more numerous, influential, and likely to be decorated than their German counterparts.[14] To what extent did better logistical support translate itself into greater combat efficiency? What was the best compromise between the overly elaborate German replacement system, which did not survive long, and the underdeveloped replacement system with which Americans first went to war? Were the techniques for integrating replacements that ultimately emerged in such outstanding American divisions as the 3rd, 30th, and 88th Infantry optimal?[15] What was the overall effect of the rivalries and animosities, at times descending to sabotage and murder, that set German officers and officials against each other? What was the effect on ordinary units of the German habit of concentrating personnel and equipment advantages into elite units? Second-rate status can become a self-fulfilling prophecy, particularly if one is used as cannon fodder. As Medal of Honor rosters attest, ethnic minorities have always numbered among America's best soldiers. Why did the Germans not have similar luck with such fillers as German-speaking Alsatians or Czechs?[16] This is not to mention allies. Who fought for them as well as Poles or Free French did for us? Perhaps there is some advantage in fighting for freedom and justice against racism and tyranny. The German knew he was hopelessly outnumbered. Whose fault did he think that was, and how did his conclusion affect him?

The mythology of German combat superiority is deeply rooted. It will be some time before it has been objectively reconsidered. Insofar as that mythos is reinforced by *Numbers, Prediction, and War*, I hope this text justifies such reconsideration. Colonel Dupuy has done invaluable research and innovative thinking. His contribution should initiate debate, not close it. To his assessment of why he and his comrades—our fathers and grandfathers—won World War II, I would like to propose an alternative. I believe they won because, man for man and unit for unit, they were tougher than their adversaries.

Abbreviations and File Numbers

The following abbreviations occur in notes or the text:

AAF	Army Air Force
AG	Adjutant General
AGCT	Army General Classification Test
AGF	Army Ground Forces
AGO	Adjutant General's Office
AOAC	Armored Officer's Advanced Course
AR	Army Regulation
ASF	Army Service Forces
ASTP	Army Specialized Training Program
ATP	Army Training Program
AUS	Army of the United States
AWC	Army War College
BTMS	Battalion Training Management System
CG	Commanding General
CS	Chief of Staff
DA	Department of the Army
DCS	Deputy Chief of Staff
DF	Disposition Form
G-1	Personnel (division and above)
G-2	Intelligence (division and above)
G-3	Operations, Organization, and Training (division and above)
G-4	Supply (division and above)
FM	Field Manual
MMRB	Modern Military Records Branch
MOS	Military Occupational Specialty
MP	Military Police
MTO	Mediterranean Theater of Operations
MTP	Mobilization Training Program
NATO	North African Theater of Operations
NCO	Noncommissioned Officer
NG	National Guard

NTC	National Training Center
OCS	Officer Candidate School
OCMH	Office of the Chief of Military History
OHF	Ordnance Historical File
OPD	Operations Division
OR	Organized Reserve
QM	Quartermaster
QMC	Quartermaster Corps
RA	Regular Army
RDF	Rapid Deployment Force
RDJTF	Rapid Deployment Joint Task Force
ROTC	Reserve Officers' Training Corps
RTC	Replacement Training Center
S-1	Personnel (brigade or regiment and below)
S-2	Intelligence (brigade or regiment and below)
S-3	Operations and Training (brigade or regiment and below)
S-4	Supply (brigade or regiment and below)
SOP	Standard Operating Procedures
SOS	Services of Supply
ST	Special Text
TC	Training Circular
TM	Technical Manual
TO	Table of Organization
TO&E	Table of Organization and Equipment
USAARMS	United States Army Armor School
USAHRC	United States Army Historical Research Center
UTP	Unit Training Program
WD	War Department
WDGS	War Department General Staff
WPD	War Plans Division

Many of the documents cited in the notes are further identified by the number under which they were filed. A complete listing of these file numbers exists in the *War Department Decimal File System* (Washington, D.C., The Adjutant General of the U.S. Army, 1943). The documents referred to in this study include those filed under:

210	Officers
220	Enlisted Men
311	Telephone Conversations (AGF)
319.1	Reports (AGF)
327.3	Inducted Men
333	Inspections
337	Conferences (AGF)
352	Schools

353	Training
	353.01 Training Directives
	353.02 Instruction Visits
354.1	Replacement Training Centers
354.2	Maneuvers
370	Employment and Movement of Troops
381	War Plans
461	Publications

Notes

Preface

1. Robert W. Coakley, "The United States Army in World War II," *A Guide to the Sources of United States Military History*, Robert Higham (Hamden, Conn.: Archon Books, 1975), 378-403.

2. See, for example, Col. Robert S. Anderson, ed., *Neuropsychiatry in World War II* (Washington, D.C.: Office of the Surgeon General, DA); Nolan D.C. Lewis and Bernice Engle, eds., *Wartime Psychiatry: A Compendium of the International Literature* (New York: Oxford Univ. Press, 1954); or S.A. Stouffer et. al., *Studies in Social Psychology in World War II*, vols. 1-4 (Princeton: Princeton Univ. Press, 1949).

3. Adam Yarmolinsky, *The Military Establishment: Its Impact on American Society* (New York: Harper and Row, 1971), 283-302.

4. *The Army Almanac* (Washington, D.C.: Government Printing Office, 1950), 545-72.

1. Draftee Divisions: The Historical Roots

1. *Biennial Report of the Chief of Staff of the United States Army (1 July 1943 to 30 June 1945) to the Secretary of War*, 22, J.E. Sloan Papers; *Stars and Stripes*, 3 June 1944; *Washington Post*, 29 May 1944; *Muskogee Daily Phoenix*, May 29, 1944; "The Blue Devils Stumped the Experts," *Saturday Evening Post*, 7 September 1946, 120.

2. The material in this paragraph is most easily located in the semiofficial division history, *The Blue Devils in Italy: A History of the 88th Infantry Division in World War II*, by John P. Delaney (Washington, D.C.: Infantry Journal Press, 1947).

3. See Jonathan Elliott, ed., *The Debates in the Several Conventions on the Adoption of the Federal Constitution* (Philadelphia: Lippincott, 1888), vol. 3, 378-412.

4. Henry Cabot Lodge, ed., *The Works of Alexander Hamilton* (New York: G.P. Putnam's Sons, 1885), 474-518; John C. Fitzpatrick, ed., *The Writings of George Washington from the Original Manuscript Sources* (Washington, D.C.: Government Printing Office, 1931-1944), vol. 26, 374-98.

5. A good discussion of these constitutional issues is in Russell F. Weigley's *History of the United States Army* (New York: Macmillan, 1967), 84-89. See also Richard H. Kohn, *Eagle and Sword: The Federalists and the Creation of the Military Establishment in America, 1783-1802* (New York: The Free Press, 1975).

6. A discussion of these campaigns is in Francis P. Prucha, *The Sword of the Republic* (New York: Macmillan, 1968).

7. Fitzpatrick, *Writings of George Washington*, 384; Emory Upton, *The Military Policy of the United States* (Washington, D.C.: Government Printing Office, 1912), 96-142.

8. Richard K, Cralle, ed., *Reports and Public Letters of John C. Calhoun* (New York: D. Appleton and Co., 1864), 25-39.

9. Russell F. Weigley, ed., *The American Military: Readings in the History of the Military*

in American Society (Reading, Mass.: Addison-Wesley, 1969), 77; "Scott's Fixed Opinion" in *Bugle Notes* (annual publication of the U.S. Military Academy, 1967), 115; see Justin H. Smith, *The War With Mexico* (New York: Macmillan, 1919).

10. *Historical Statistics of the United States, Colonial Times to 1970* (Washington, D.C.: Bureau of the Census, 1975), 1141.

11. Weigley, *History of the United States Army*, 199-200, 203-4; see also John Hope Franklin, *The Militant South* (Cambridge: Belknap Press, 1956).

12. Fitzpatrick, *Writings of George Washington*, 389.

13. The Confederacy with the Conscription Act of 16 April 1862; the Union with the Enrollment Act of 3 March 1863.

14. Albert B. Moore, *Conscription and Conflict in the Confederacy* (New York: Macmillan, 1924), 356-57; Neil C. Kimmons, "Federal Draft Exemptions, 1863-1865," *Military Affairs* 15 (1951): 25-33.

15. See George Washington Williams, *A History of Negro Troops in the War of the Rebellion* (New York: Harper, 1888); Charles A. Stevens, *Berdan's United States Sharpshooters in the Army of the Potomac* (St. Paul, Minn.: Price-McGill, 1892); Marvin A. Kreidberg and Merton G. Henry, *History of Military Mobilization in the United States Army, 1775-1945* (Washington, D.C.: DA, 1955), 115; D. Alexander Brown, *The Galvanized Yankees* (Urbana, Ill.: Univ. of Illinois Press, 1963); *Personal Memoirs of William T. Sherman* (New York: Webster, 1892), vol. 2, 388.

16. Upton, *Military Policy of the United States*, 257.

17. John A. Logan, *The Volunteer Soldier of America* (Chicago: R.S. Peale and Co., 1887), 578-80.

18. See Walter Millis, *The Martial Spirit* (Boston: Houghton Mifflin, 1931).

19. *Historical Statistics of the United States*, 1141.

20. More properly, the Militia Act of 21 January 1903; *United States Statutes at Large*, vol. 32, 775-80.

21. The turn-of-the-century military professional's view of essentially civilian soldiers is in the prizewinning 1906 essay by Lt. Col. James S. Pettit, discussed by Weigley in *The American Military*, xi-xix.

22. Leonard Wood, *The Military Obligation of Citizenship* (Princeton, N.J.: Princeton Univ. Press, 1915).

23. *United States Statutes at Large*, vol. 34, 166-217; Weigley, *History of the United States Army*, 356; *History of the First Division During the World War 1917-1919* (Philadelphia: John C. Winston Co., 1922), 1-13. Popular, but informative, discussions of this training experience are in Frazier Hunt's *Blown In by the Draft* (New York: Doubleday, Page and Co., 1918) and in Irving Crump's *Conscript 2989* (New York: Dodd, Mead and Company, 1918).

24. This information is drawn from Capt. Shipley Thomas's semi-official *History of the A.E.F.* (New York: George H. Doran Co., 1920), 103, 448-91.

25. U.S. Congress, 65th Cong., 1st sess., Senate Committee on Military Affairs, *Reorganization of the Army: Hearings Before the Subcommittee of the Committee on Military Affairs, on S. 2715*; John McAuley Palmer, *America in Arms: The Experience of the United States with Military Organization* (New Haven, Conn.: Yale Univ. Press, 1941).

26. *United States Statutes at Large*, vol. 41, 759-812; *Historical Statistics of the United States*, 1141; Weigley, *History of the United States Army*, 401.

27. Arthur A. Ekirch, Jr., *The Civilian and the Military* (New York: Oxford Univ. Press, 1956), 256-57; Harvey S. Ford, *What the Citizen Should Know About the Army* (New York: W.W. Norton and Co., 1942), 56.

28. *The Selective Service Act: Its Legislative History, Amendments, Appropriations, Cognates, and Prior Instruments of Security* (Washington, D.C.: Government Printing Office, 1954), vol. 2 of the *U. S. Selective Service System Special Monographs*.

29. Bell I. Wiley, "The Building and Training of Infantry Divisions," in *The Army*

Ground Forces: The Procurement and Training of Ground Combat Troops (Washington, D.C.: Historical Division, DA, 1948); War Department memorandum (subject: detailed troop unit basis), G-3 for chief of staff, U.S. Army, 3 January 1942, National Archives, MMRB (381); letter (subject: schedule of allotments and movements of enlisted men to replacement training centers and units for July 1942) to commanding generals, 27 May 1942, National Archives, MMRB (324.71). One can get much the same picture of old divisions by perusing appropriate divisional adjutant general office files, National Archives, MMRB, or by reading such unit histories as Donald G. Taggart, *History of the Third Infantry Division in World War II* (Washington, D.C.: Infantry Journal Press, 1947), or *The Sixth Infantry Division in World War II, 1939-1945* (Washington, D.C. Infantry Journal Press, 1947).

2. Personnel and Personnel Utilization: Bureaucratic Roulette

1. Bell I. Wiley, "The Building and Training of Infantry Divisions" (Study Number 12, Historical Section, AGF, 1946), 4, 29, USAHRC; idem, "The Building and Training of Infantry Divisions," in *The Procurement and Training of Ground Combat Troops* (Washington, D.C.: Historical Division, DA, 1948), 489-93.

2. Memorandum (subject: readiness of divisions for combat) from Gen. Lesley McNair to the assistant chief of staff G-3, 20 December 1941, National Archives, MMRB (314.7); Wiley, "Building and Training," in *Procurement and Training*, 434-41.

3. Wiley, "Building and Training," in *Procurement and Training*, 463; Delaney, *Blue Devils*, 9. Note that of personnel problems, the attachment of nondivisional units did not apply in the case of the 88th and is not further discussed. By July 1942 the newly established Army Service Forces had relieved the Army Ground Forces of much of this burden.

4. Robert R. Palmer, "The Procurement of Enlisted Personnel: The Problem of Quality," in *The Army Ground Forces: The Procurement and Training of Ground Combat Troops*, 1-86.

5. Ibid., p. 18.

6. Memorandum of General McNair to the chief of staff, AGF, 7 March 1944, National Archives, MMRB (353/206).

7. 88th Infantry Division Report (subject: personnel status), G-1, 88th Infantry Division (G-1 files), 30 July 1942, National Archives, MMRB (220); T.O.70, *Tables of Organization of Infantry Units* (Washington, D.C.: Infantry Journal, 1941); interview with Col. H.M. Brown (then Capt. H.M. Brown, until September 1942 the aide-de-camp to Maj. Gen. John E. Sloan; subsequently he was an officer in the 88th's 337th Field Artillery Battalion, and by December 1944 he was an officer on the 88th Division Artillery staff), 2 July 1977.

8. Memorandum of General McNair to the chief of staff, AGF, 7 March 1944, National Archives, MMRB (353/206).

9. Robert R. Palmer and William R. Keast, "The Procurement of Officers," in *The Army Ground Forces: The Procurement and Training of Ground Combat Troops*, 92, 103-107; memorandum (subject: selection of trainees for OCS) from the adjutant general of the War Department to the G-1 of the War Department, 6 June 1943; WD circular No. 48, 19 February 1942, National Archives, MMRB (352); memorandum (subject: detailed troop unit basis) from G-3 of War Department for chief of staff, U.S. Army, 9 January 1942, National Archives, MMRB (381); 88th Infantry Division memorandum (subject: OCS nominations), adjutant general, 88th Infantry Division (G-1 files), 27 December 1942, National Archives, MMRB (210/352); memorandum (subject: troop basis, 1943) from War Department to commanding generals, AGF and SOS, 24 November 1942, National Archives, MMRB (320.2); letter (subject: officers candidate quotas) from Army Ground Forces to commanding generals, 4 September 1942, National Archives, MMRB (352/301);

memorandum (subject: quarterly capacities of OCS for AGF) from War Department to commanding general, AGF, 28 December 1942, National Archives, MMRB (352); memorandum (subject: troop basis, 1943) from General McNair to deputy chief of staff, U.S. Army, 22 June 1942, National Archives, MMRB (320.2/31); memorandum (subject: surplus AA officers) from G-1 Army Ground Forces to chief of staff, AGF, 29 January 1944, National Archives, MMRB (353).

10. Joint statement of the secretaries of war and navy department, 17 December 1942, National Archives, MMRB (353); Palmer, "Procurement of Enlisted Personnel," 29. A testimony to the general resistance to ASTP within Army Ground Forces is the fact that a strongly worded memorandum (subject: ASTP) from General Marshall to commanding general, AGF, 1 April 1943, National Archives, MMRB (353/31), proved necessary.

11. War Department memorandum W350-198-43 (subject: general qualifications for ASTP), 17 July 1943, National Archives, MMRB (353/81); memorandum (subject: ASTP) from General Marshall to commanding general, AGF, 1 April 1943, National Archives, MMRB (353/31); memorandum (subject: number of men in ASTP institutions), 21 July 1943, National Archives, MMRB (353/91).

12. Memorandum (subject: disposition of ASTP eligibles upon induction) from G-1, AGF, to G-3 and chief of staff, AGF, 26 July 1943, National Archives, MMRB (353/96); see note 11, above; see also 88th Infantry Division memorandum (subject: Army Special Training Program), adjutant general, 88th Infantry Division (G-1 files), National Archives, MMRB (220/352); Delaney, *Blue Devils*, 14; interview with Col. H.M. Brown, 2 July 1977.

13. Memorandum (subject: service personnel shortages) from General Marshall to the secretary of war, 10 February 1944, National Archives, MMRB (353/100).

14. Army Ground Forces distribution form (subject: allotments of enlisted men), 13 May 1942, National Archives, MMRB (327.3/7); letter (subject: improvement of personnel in airborne divisions) from Army Ground Forces to commanding generals, 18 September 1942, National Archives, MMRB (201.31/106).

15. See note 7, above; also letter from Col. Robert J. Karrer (then inspector general of the 88th Infantry Division) to the author in response to author's inquiries, 13 December 1977.

16. Wiley, "Building and Training," in *Procurement and Training*, 14; Delaney, *Blue Devils*, 14, 17; 88th Infantry Division letter (subject: training scheduled for October 1942), from the adjutant general of the 88th Infantry Division (G-3 files), National Archives, MMRB (353.01); interview with Col. H.M. Brown.

17. Interview with Col. H.M. Brown.

18. War Department memorandum for the adjutant general G-3/6457 (subject: replacement training centers), 27 September 1941, National Archives, MMRB (341).

19. Memorandum from Brig. Gen. H.R. Bull for G-3, AGF, 3 January 1942, National Archives, MMRB (381).

20. Wiley, "Building and Training," 457, 472-74; letter (subject: replacement pools) from Army Ground Forces to commanding generals, 2 October 1942, National Archives, MMRB (320.12/105).

21. Memorandum (subject: report of Army Ground Forces activities) from commanding general, AGF, to chief of staff, U.S. Army, 10 January 1946, 8-10, J.E. Sloan Papers; War Department letter to commanding generals (subject: commissioned personnel of the 77th, 82nd, and 90th infantry divisions), 6 January 1942, National Archives, MMRB (320.2); letter from Col. F.W. Farrell (chief of staff, 11th Airborne Division) to Maj. Gen. John E. Sloan, 23 February 1943, J.E. Sloan Papers; memorandum from the assistant G-3, AGF, to the G-3, AGF, 2 April 1943, National Archives, MMRB (333.1).

22. "Brigadier General Stonewall Jackson Began Military Career in Oklahoma," *Muskogee Daily Phoenix* (19 July 1942), B9; Delaney, *Blue Devils*, 8.

23. Letter from Maj. Gen. J.M. Swing (commanding general, 11th Airborne Division)

to Maj. Gen. J.E. Sloan, 11 March 1943, J.E. Sloan Papers; interview with Col. H.M. Brown; Wiley, "Building and Training," 489-93.

24. Letter from Maj. Gen. John E. Sloan to Capt. Horace M. Brown (his aide-de-camp), 17 May 1942, J.E. Sloan Papers; conversations with General Sloan.

25. E.g., see "Sergeant Siling is Kept Busy by Paperwork," *Muskogee Daily Phoenix*, 19 July 1942, C2; or "Enlisting in March, Marcus Attains Rank of Supply Sergeant," *Muskogee Daily Phoenix*, 19 July 1942, C9; Martin Van Creveld, *Fighting Power: German and U.S. Army Performance, 1939-1945* (Westport, Conn.: Greenwood Press, 1982), 124-25; S.A. Stouffer et. al., *The American Soldier* (Princeton, N.J.: Princeton Univ. Press, 1949), 362-429.

26. Stouffer, *The American Soldier*, 54-81; "First Recruits Arriving at Gruber Get Thorough Goingover," *Muskogee Daily Phoenix*, 19 July 1942, E5; letter (subject: replacement pools) from Army Ground Forces to commanding generals, 2 October 1942, National Archives, MMRB (320.12/105); interview with Col. H.M. Brown.

27. This was true then and, despite a great deal of behavioralist hocus pocus, seems to be true now. For example, see *Forecasting Army Officer Retention Prior to Commissioning* (West Point, N.Y.: Office of Institutional Research, 1982) (OIR 82-011).

28. The material in this and the following paragraph is reconstructed from conversations with General Sloan, an interview with Col. H.M. Brown, and the letter from Col. Robert J. Karrer, 13 December 1977. Judge Richard C. Prassel of Jourdanton, Texas, shared the anecdote concerning his brush with Sloan at the 1982 reunion of the Blue Devils. See also Delaney, *Blue Devils*, 14-15.

29. Report of Statistics Branch, WDGS (subject: status of personnel), 15 December 1943, National Archives, MMRB (320.2/351); Palmer and Keast, "The Procurement of Officers," 92-103.

30. See note 24, above. See also War Department letter (subject: candidates selected to attend officers candidate schools) to commanding generals, 24 December 1942, National Archives, MMRB (3352/18); War Department memorandum (subject: acceptance and selection of applicants for OCS), 1 September 1943, National Archives, MMRB (352/471).

31. "Biographical Data of Maj. Gen. John E. Sloan, 03018," undated public information sketch apparently released sometime between 11 May and 1 October 1944, J.E. Sloan Papers.

32. Letter from Col. C.H. Mason (deputy chief umpire of the 1939 Fourth Army CPX) to Lt. Col. John E. Sloan, chief of umpire school section, 17 August 1939, J.E. Sloan Papers.

33. War Department letter (subject: commissioned personnel of the 77th, 82nd, and 90th infantry divisions) to commanding generals, 6 January 1942, National Archives, MMRB (320.2); War Department letter (subject: commissioned personnel for the 80th, 88th, and 89th divisions) to commanding generals, 8 April 1942, National Archives, MMRB (210.31); Wiley, "Building and Training," 434-41.

34. The material in this and the following three paragraphs is reconstructed from an interview with Col. H.M. Brown and appropriate entries in *Official Army Register* (Washington, D.C.: Adjutant General's Office, published annually from 1882).

35. See also "Wealth of Experience Behind Ranking Officers of 88th Division," *Muskogee Daily Phoenix*, 19 July 1942, B8.

36. E.g., see Van Creveld, *Fighting Power*, or Max Hastings, "Their Wehrmacht Was Better than Our Army," *Kansas City Star*, 26 May 1985, 3D; see Eli Ginzberg et. al., *The Ineffective Soldier: Lessons for Management and the Nation* (New York: Columbia Univ. Press, 1959), or Stouffer et. al., *The American Soldier*; see also John Sloan Brown, *Winning Teams: Correlates of Success in World War II Infantry Divisions* (Fort Leavenworth, Kans.: Combat Studies Institute MMAS, 1985), 40-57. A partial exception to writers' ignoring of personnel differences occurs in Stouffer, vol. 2, 3-58.

37. Stouffer, *The American Soldier*, 82-229. This last aspect may well be the genesis of a saying popular at the time: "A griping soldier is a happy soldier."

38. "Army's All Right if You Want to Be a Good Soldier," *Muskogee Daily Phoenix*, 19 July 1942, D5. For a discussion of overall support for the war effort, see Richard Polenberg, *War and Society: The United States, 1941-1945*, (New York: Lippincott, 1972), 1-4.

39. Stouffer, *The American Soldier*, vol. 2, 431-85; Karrer letter, 13 December 1977; Marshal J.B. Mascarenbas de Moraes, *The Brazilian Expeditionary Force, by Its Commander* (Washington, D.C.: Office of the Chief of Military History, U.S. Army, 1965), 18-63; Frank D. McCann, Jr., *The Brazilian-American Alliance 1937-1945* (Princeton, N.J.: Princeton Univ. Press, 1973), 405-39.

40. Memorandum for the assistant commandant of the Army War College (subject: action to combat spread of subversive doctrines in the military establishment) prepared by Maj. John E. Sloan, 18 January 1932; letter from Chaplain John D. Boren (Gruber camp chaplain), 28 June 1943; letter from Chaplain Hirsh Goldberg (chaplain, Fort Dix, N.J.), 22 April 1943; letter from J.W. Storer (pastor of the Tulsa, Okla., First Baptist Church), 5 March 1943; letter from Mr. Bob Sibrle (Stanolin Pipe Line Company, Tulsa, Okla.) to Mr. Richard C. Murray (Chamber of Commerce, Tulsa, Okla.), 7 November 1942; all documents in the J.E. Sloan Papers.

41. To develop this impression, peruse copies of the *Saturday Evening Post* dating from December 1941 through August 1945; also, letter from Mr. Tams Bixby, Jr. (president of the Oklahoma Press Publishing Co.) to Maj. Gen. John E. Sloan, 28 December 1942, J.E. Sloan Papers.

42. 88th Infantry Division report (subject: May 1943), 88th Infantry Division G-3 operational report (G-3 files), 2 June 1943, National Archives, MMRB; letter from Maj. Gen. Richard Donovan (commanding general of the Eighth Service Command) to Maj. Gen. John E. Sloan, 14 June 1943, J.E. Sloan Papers.

43. Anecdote related by Mr. Sam Lepofsky during the August 1983 reunion of the Blue Devils Association at Minneapolis, Minn.

44. Stouffer, *The American Soldier*, 362-429; Ginzberg, *The Ineffective Soldier*, vol. 3, 117-40.

45. This paragraph was reconstructed from my memories of a conversation with Maj. Gen. John E. Sloan in the months between my commissioning (9 June 1971) and my first assignment (August 1971), and from a letter (subject: Christmas 1942 and New Year's 1943) to the officers and men of the Rangers from Maj. Gen. John E. Sloan, 21 December 1942, J.E. Sloan Papers; "Society," *San Antonio Evening News*, 12 October 1943; letter from Maurine Everly (president of the Muskogee Business and Professional Women's Club, 15 June 1943), J.E. Sloan Papers; and Delaney, *Blue Devils*, 16-18.

46. T.O.70, *Tables of Organization of Infantry Units* (Washington, D.C.: Infantry Journal, 1941).

47. Van Creveld, *Fighting Power*, 68-71.

48. Delaney, *Blue Devils*, 19.

49. Positive external evaluations of the 88th include Headquarters X Corps letter (subject: comments of commanding general . . .) from Maj. Gen. Courtney Hodges to Maj. Gen. John E. Sloan, 22 January 1943, National Archives, MMRB (353.02); letter (subject: visit to Camp Gruber, Oklahoma) from Lt. Gen. Lesley J. McNair to the commanding general of Third Army, 31 December 1942, National Archives, MMRB (353.02/32); and memorandum for Gen. John E. Sloan from Gen. George C. Marshall, chief of staff, 26 August 1943, J.E. Sloan Papers.

50. 88th Infantry Division report (subject: April 1943), 88th Infantry Division G-3 operational report (G-3 files), 6 May 1943, National Archives, MMRB; see also Delaney, *Blue Devils*, 21-22.

51. See notes 15 and 17, above; see also Ginzberg, *The Ineffective Soldier*, vol. 2, 52-69;

and letter from William J. Jones (CPE staging area), to Maj. Gen. John E. Sloan, 2 June 1943, J.E. Sloan Papers.

52. Interview with Col. H.M. Brown; memories of my post-commissioning conversations with General Sloan; Group Headquarters letter (subject: training of newly activated infantry divisions) to commanding generals, 16 February 1942, National Archives, MMRB (353/21).

53. Letter (subject: visit to Camp Gruber, Oklahoma) from Lt. Gen. Lesley J. McNair to the commanding general of Third Army, 31 December 1942, National Archives, MMRB (353.02/32).

54. Van Creveld, *Fighting Power*, 41-60, 68-71, 74-79.

55. Delaney, *Blue Devils*, 98.

56. Luther Gulick, *Administrative Reflections from World War II* (Tuscaloosa: Univ. of Alabama Press, 1948), 51.

57. Wiley, "Building and Training," 487-88.

3. Training: Honing the Edge

1. Memorandum for the chief of staff, U.S. Army (subject: report of Army Ground Forces activities) from the commanding general, AGF, 10 January 1946, 17-38, J.E. Sloan Papers; also see Bell I. Wiley, "The Building and Training of Infantry Divisions," in *The Army Ground Forces: The Procurement and Training of Ground Combat Troops* (Washington, D.C.: Historical Division, DA, 1948); *Biennial Report of the Chief of Staff of the United States Army, 1 July 1943 to 30 June 1945, to the Secretary of War* (Washington, D.C.: Government Printing Office, 1 September 1945).

2. War Department memorandum (subject: detailed troop unit basis) G-3 for chief of staff, U.S. Army, 3 January 1942, National Archives, MMRB (381); letter from the adjutant general (subject: schedule of allotments and movements of enlisted men to replacement training centers and units for July 1942) to commanding generals, 27 May 1942, National Archives, MMRB (324.71).

3. This held true until personnel stripping and other turbulence blurred earlier distinctions between the personnel of new and old divisions. See 88th Infantry Division report (subject: personnel status) G-1 for chief of staff, 88th Infantry Division, 3 August 1942, National Archives, MMRB (88th G-1/220).

4. See, for example, the account of the program of inspections conducted by the Emperor Hadrian (117-138 A.D.) in Dio Cassius, *Roman History*, vols. 69 and 110, 1-5 (Loeb Classical Library).

5. "Commissioned Personnel, Infantry Division" (chart produced by the New Divisions Division, AGF), now in the Lieutenant Colonel King Papers, USAARMS Library, Fort Knox, Ky.; see T.O.s 100-1, 200-1, 70-1, 7-12, and 7-17 in *Tables of Organization of Infantry Units* (Washington, D.C.: Infantry Journal, 1941), now in the Infantry School Library, Fort Benning, Ga.; Army Ground Forces memorandums (subject: report of G-4 inspection trip) from the G-4 to the chief of staff, 5 August 1942 and 8 September 1942, National Archives, MMRB (333.1); Wiley, "Building and Training," 452-53; Army Ground Forces report with indorsements (subject: visit to Camp Gruber, Oklahoma) to commanding generals, 31 December 1942, National Archives, MMRB (353.02/32).

6. The material in this paragraph is drawn from a letter from Col. Robert J. Karrer (then inspector general of the 88th Infantry Division) to the author in response to author's inquiries, 13 December 1977. See also Army Ground Forces report with indorsements, 31 December 1942.

7. See the series of correspondence in File SP 451 originated by the letter (subject: automotive disability report of the 88th Division) from the inspector general to the commanding general, X Army Corps, 6 November 1942, National Archives, MMRB

(SP475); see also 88th Infantry Division report (subject: automotive disability report of the 88th Division), G-4 for chief of staff, 88th Infantry Division, 18 November 1942, National Archives, MMRB (88th G-4/SP475).

8. See note 6, above. The same holds true today, of course. The current expression is "gaining vis," or visibility.

9. T.O. 100-1, *Tables of Organization of Infantry Units*; John P. Delaney, *The Blue Devils in Italy: A History of the 88th Infantry Division in World War II* (Washington, D.C.: Infantry Journal Press, 1947), 15.

10. *We Left Home*, unit history of the 337th Field Artillery Battalion of the 88th Infantry Division (Milan: S.R. Grafitalia, 1945), 13, USAHRC, Carlisle Barracks, Pa.

11. See the records of the telephone conversations (subject: inspections by AGF staff officers) among staff officers of the Army Ground Forces, Second Army, Fourth Army, and XXII Corps, 21 August 1944, National Archives, MMRB (333.1); *Muskogee Daily Phoenix*, 19 July 1942, C4; interview with Col. Horace M. Brown (then Captain Brown, aide-de-camp to Maj. Gen. John E. Sloan), 2 July 1977.

12. Memorandum for the chief of staff, U.S. Army (subject: report on Army Ground Forces activities), 23-24, J.E. Sloan Papers.

13. Interview with Maj. Gen. John M. Lentz (then training officer of Army Ground Forces), 27 September 1977; *Muskogee Daily Phoenix*, 19 July 1942, B6 and E1. Some idea of the extent to which films were used can be gained from the memorandum for the chief of staff, U.S. Army (subject: report on Army Ground Forces activities), 23-24, J.E. Sloan Papers.

14. See *Regulations for the Army of the United States* (Washington, D.C.: Government Printing Office, 1892), provided courtesy of Col. Corwin A. Mitchell, director, Command and Staff Department, USAARMS, Fort Knox, Ky.; memorandum for the chief of staff, U.S. Army (subject: report on Army Ground Forces activities), 23-24; interview with Col. Horace M. Brown, 2 July 1977. There seems to be a lesson here. We still put a great deal of literature in the hands of individual soldiers, and we still find that it remains unread. Author's personal experience as a company commander, August 1978 through June 1980. See also 88th Infantry Division report (subject: inventory and shortages of field manuals), G-3 for chief of staff, 88th Infantry Division, 8 November 1942, National Archives, MMRB (88th G-3/353.02).

15. Memorandum for the chief of staff, U.S. Army (subject: report on Army Ground Forces activities), 18; see also Wiley, "Building and Training," 432-36. The lengths of time allocated to each of these blocks decreased somewhat as the war progressed.

16. Army Ground Forces letter (subject: training directive effective November 1, 1942) to commanding generals, 19 October 1942, Lieutenant Colonel King Papers, USAARMS Library, Fort Knox, Ky. (320.2); letters from Maj. Gen. John M. Lentz (then training officer of Army Ground Forces) to the author in response to author's inquiries, 18 September and 30 September 1977; see the file generated as a result of Army Ground Forces letter (subject: weekly radio reports showing scheduled tests and exercises) to commanding generals, 1 May 1942, National Archives, MMRB (353/1132).

17. Interview with Maj. Gen. John M. Lentz, 27 September 1977; letters from Major General Lentz; file generated from Army Ground Forces letter to commanding generals, 1 May 1942.

18. I say War Department plan here to avoid confusion. The actual proponent agency was General Headquarters, the direct predecessor of Army Ground Forces. Army Ground Forces per se was created on 9 March 1942. See Wiley, "Building and Training," 433-36.

19. Letter from Maj. Gen. John E. Sloan to Capt. Horace M. Brown, 17 May 1942, J.E. Sloan Papers; see also note 3, above. The material in this paragraph is drawn from the War Department letter (subject: commissioned personnel of the 77th, 82nd, and 90th infantry divisions) to commanding generals, 6 January 1942, and War Department letter

(subject: commissioned personnel for the 80th, 88th, and 89th divisions) to commanding generals, 8 April 1942. Both National Archives, MMRB (AG 320.2 and AG 210.31).

20. A good, if brief, account of the evolution and purpose of the army school system occurs in Russell F. Weigley, *History of the United States Army* (New York: Macmillan, 1967), 272-74, 287, 320, 325-26, 387.

21. Interview with Col. Horace M. Brown, 2 July 1977; see also Wiley, "Building and Training," 441-43.

22. The division had, for example, only two cadre mechanized cavalrymen, neither of whom was in a position to much influence training; *Muskogee Daily Phoenix*, 19 July 1942, B8. The newly organized armored divisions hoarded most mechanized experience and seem to have developed an attitude towards the other branches akin to that of the French knights at Agincourt; see the letters from Maj. Gen. John M. Lentz. The draftees of the 88th never trained alongside tanks prior to their arrival in Italy.

23. See William R. Keast, "The Training of Officer Candidates," in *The Procurement and Training of Ground Combat Troops*, 321-50; Infantry School pamphlet (subject: the selection system of the OC course, the infantry school, and an analysis of OC failures), undated, assumed 1943, National Archives, MMRB (314.7).

24. Memorandum for the chief of staff, U.S. Army (subject: report of Army Ground Forces activities) from the commanding general, AGF, 10 January 1946; training memorandum no. 10, Headquarters, 76th Field Artillery, Fort Ord, Calif., 6 September 1940, J.E. Sloan Papers; Group Headquarters letter (subject: training of newly activated infantry divisions) to commanding generals, 16 February 1942, National Archives, MMRB (353/21); 88th Infantry Division training report (subject: December 1942), G-3 for chief of staff, 88th Infantry Division, 5 January 1943, National Archives, MMRB (88th G-3/353.01); interview with Col. Horace M. Brown, July 2, 1977.

25. Army Ground Forces letters (subject: cadre personnel for new divisions) to commanding generals, 23 April 1942, 2 July 1942, 10 September 1942, and 9 November 1942. National Archives, MMRB (320.2).

26. Ibid.; also, interviews with Col. Robert J. Karrer, Maj. Gen. John M. Lentz, and Col. Horace M. Brown.

27. Letter from the adjutant general (subject: schedule of allotments and movement of enlisted men to replacement centers and units for July 1942), to commanding generals, 27 May 1942, National Archives, MMRB (324.71). For visual impressions of the arriving draftees, see Delaney, *Blue Devils*, 9 and 13, and the 19 July 1942 issue of the *Muskogee Daily Phoenix*. The Fredericks are the subject of "Father and Son from Olean, N.Y., in Same Regiment of 88th," *Muskogee Daily Phoenix*, 19 July 1942, D5.

28. This represents a paraphrase of what must be one of the army's oldest and most cherished maxims. See the U.S. Military Academy text *The Study of Leadership* (West Point, N.Y.: Office of Military Psychology and Leadership, 1970).

29. The material in this paragraph and following ones should be familiar to anyone who has undergone basic training in the United States during the past fifty years. Formal citations for this material would include the interview with Col. Horace M. Brown; Delaney, *Blue Devils*, 12-18; *The Basic Training Guide* (Harrisburg, Pa.: Military Service Publishing Co., 1948); *New Drill Regulations* (Harrisburg, Pa.: Military Service Publishing Co., 1941); General Headquarters letter (subject: training) to army commanders, 16 September 1940; and several articles on the 88th in the *Muskogee Daily Phoenix*, 19 July 1942.

30. See, for example, General Sloan's open letter to the citizens of Muskogee in the *Muskogee Daily Phoenix*, 19 July 1942, B1.

31. Group Headquarters letter (subject: training of newly activated infantry divisions) to commanding generals, 16 February 1942, National Archives, MMRB (353/21); see also Army Ground Forces indorsement (subject: mobilization training programs) to G-3, WD, October 1942, National Archives (461); letter from Maj. Harvey R. Cook (then

special services officer of the 88th Infantry Division) to the author in response to author's inquiries, 1 December 1977.

32. *Muskogee Daily Phoenix*, 19 July 1942, D5.

33. War Department guidance as to how a unit was supposed to march dated back at least as far as the *Regulations of the Army of the United States*.

34. Letter from Gen. George C. Marshall to General Sloan dated 26 August 1943, J.E. Sloan Papers.

35. Army Ground Forces indorsement (subject: mobilization programs) to G-3, WD, 30 October 1942, National Archives, MMRB (461).

36. See the series of interviews with veterans of the 88th published in *Yank*, 23 February 1945. Provided courtesy of Dr. Paul Richmond, former division surgeon of the 88th Infantry Division.

37. Replacement and School Command letter (subject: revision of MTP 7-3, 6-3, 2-2, 17-1, and 18-2) to commanding general, Army Ground Forces, 15 July 1944, National Archives, MMRB (461); *Direct Support* (history of the 88th Infantry Division's 338th Field Artillery Battalion, publisher unknown, 1945), 1, J.E. Sloan Papers.

38. Interview with Maj. Gen. John M. Lentz; William R. Keast, "The Training of Enlisted Replacements," in *The Procurement and Training of Ground Combat Troops*, 412-13.

39. See 88th Infantry Division report (subject: personnel status), G-1 for chief of staff, 3 November 1942, National Archives, MMRB (88th G-1/220); see also note 24, above.

40. 88th Infantry Division training directive (subject: planning for command post exercises), 17 April 1943, National Archives, MMRB (88th G-3/353.01).

41. Interview with Col. Horace M. Brown, 2 July 1977.

42. Ibid.; see also Delaney, *Blue Devils*, 22, and 88th Infantry Division Training report (subject: May 1943), G-3 for chief of staff, 88th Infantry Division, 3 June 1943, National Archives, MMRB (88th G-3/353.01).

43. Letter (subject: SPDDP 451 vehicles) from Headquarters, SOS, WD, to commanding general, AGF, 15 March 1943, National Archives, MMRB (SPAG 451); Delaney, *Blue Devils*, 26; interview with Col. Horace M. Brown, 2 July 1977.

44. See *Direct Support*, 3-5; *We Left Home*, 12; or Delaney, *Blue Devils*, 25-58.

45. The material in this paragraph is drawn from Army Ground Forces letter (subject: initial performance of new divisions on maneuvers) to commanding generals, 13 April 1943, National Archives (354.2/56); the letters from Maj. Gen. John M. Lentz; and Paul L. Schultz, *The 85th Infantry Division in World War II* (Washington, D.C.: Infantry Journal Press, 1949).

46. This anecdote was drawn from Delaney, *Blue Devils*, 26-27.

47. Letter from the chief of field artillery, WD, to Lt. Col. John E. Sloan, 27 April 1939, and letter of commendation from the adjutant general, Fourth Army, to Lt. Col. John E. Sloan, 10 February 1940, both J.E. Sloan Papers; letters from Maj. Gen. John M. Lentz.

48. Corps commander's critique of the Louisiana maneuvers, quoted from Delaney, *Blue Devils*, 27; Army Ground Forces report with indorsements to commanding generals, 31 December 1942; interview with Col. Horace M. Brown, 2 July 1977.

49. See the appropriate entries in Vincent J. Esposito, *The West Point Atlas of American Wars* (New York: Praeger, 1959).

4. Logistics: The Strongest Card

1. The central theme in Upton's *The Military Policy of the United States* is, of course, the danger of relying upon a hastily levied "rabble in arms." Upton's intellectual heirs, writing in an era increasingly dominated by logistical considerations, stressed his observations concerning logistics even more strongly. Note that the argument between those here labeled Uptonians and the advocates of a *levee en masse* was not the ultimate size of the post-mobilization army, but rather the rate of its growth. See Brevet Maj. Gen. Emory

Upton, *The Military Policy of the United States* (Washington, D.C.: Government Printing Office, 1911); Lt. Col. Marvin A. Kriedberg and Lt. Merton G. Henry, *History of Military Mobilization in the United States Army 1775-1945* (DA Pamphlet 20-212, 1955), 141-213, 310-43, 377-677; Elias Huzar, *The Purse and the Sword* (Ithaca, N.Y.: Cornell Univ. Press, 1950); or Mark S. Watson, *Chief of Staff: Prewar Plans and Preparations* (Washington, D.C.: Historical Division, DA, 1950). For a particular instance of the issues involved being aired, see *Hearings* before the Committee on Appropriations, U.S. House, 76th Cong., 3rd sess., on H.R. 9209, 1940.

2. Kriedberg and Henry, *History of Military Mobilization*, 1-175, 424-532, 695-97; Col. Jacques de Chambrun and Capt. de Marenches, *The American Army in the European Conflict* (New York: Macmillan, 1919), pp. 385-90; Lt. Col. U.H. Johnson, "The War Department General Mobilization Plan, 1924," text of a lecture given before the Army War College (Carlisle Barracks, Pa., Army War College, 1925), AWC 318A-4, USAHRC; War Department memorandums (subject: revisions of the six year War Department programs), War Plans Division to G-3 dated March 1934 and G-3 to G-4 dated 1934, AG 111 (6-5-36), National Archives, MMRB.

3. See *Hearings* before the Subcommittee of the Committee on Appropriations, U.S. Senate, 73rd Cong., 2nd sess., on War Department Appropriation Bill 1935; War Department memorandum (subject: status of preparedness for mobilization); G-4 to the chief of staff, (G-4/20052-89) both National Archives, MMRB; War Department letter (subject: development of the four field armies), from the chief of staff to the commanding generals, 22 October 1932, WPD 3561-3; War Department memorandum, War Plans Division to the chief of staff, 12 December 1939, WPD 3674-25; War Department memorandum (subject: priorities of the expansion of the Army of the United States during mobilization), from the G-3 to the G-1, G-2, G-4, and WPD, 18 June 1940 (G-3/6541; all National Archives, MMRB; see also the texts of the War Department mobilization plans themselves (AG 381, MMRB, National Archives); Kriedberg and Henry, *History of Military Mobilization*, 441-91, 518-32. For details concerning the treatment accorded the World War I draft divisions, see the narrative annexes sketching the history of each of these divisions in Capt. Shipley Thomas, *History of the A.E.F.* (New York: George H. Doran, 1920).

4. Kriedberg and Henry, *History of Military Mobilization*, 424-91, 541-42, 554-96; Watson, *Prewar Plans*, 15-57, 148-83.

5. See the texts of War Department mobilization plans 1923, 1924, 1928, 1933, 1938, and 1939; all (AG 381) National Archives, MMRB.

6. War Department memorandum (subject: priorities for expansion of the Army of the United States during mobilization) from G-3 to G-1, G-3, and WPD, 18 June 1940 (G-3/6541) National Archives, MMRB; Kriedberg and Henry, *History of Military Mobilization*, 574-75.

7. For the benefit of the layman and the purposes of this chapter, the five classes of supply are here defined as rations, clothing and personal equipment, petroleum products, table-of-organization equipment, and ammunition. This classification corresponds to the classification used during World War II insofar as divisions were concerned. It does not, of course, correspond to the somewhat more numerous and complex classification now used. See Richard M. Leighton and Robert W. Coakley, *Global Logistics and Strategy 1940-1943* (Washington, D.C.: U.S. Army in World War II, Office of the Chief of Military History, 1955), 318-19.

8. Erna Risch, *The Quartermaster Corps: Organization, Supply and Services*, vol. 1 (Washington, D.C.: U.S. Army in World War II, Office of the Chief of Military History, 1953), 35-38, 231-36; letter, Maj. Gen. Lucius D. Clay to Mr. Roy Kendrickson, director of Food Distribution Administration, 29 January 1943; Office of the Quartermaster General letter (subject: representative on inter-agency food subcommittees of requirements), 4 August 1945; both (0030-74), National Archives, MMRB; report (subject: army subsis-

tence and PX requirements, July 1942–August 1945) from the Requirements Branch of the Office of the Quartermaster General; Army Regulation 30-2210 (subject: rations), 15 March 1940; all National Archives, MMRB.

9. Army Regulation 30-2210 (subject: rations), 15 March 1940, USAHRC; Risch, *Quartermaster Corps*, 38-39, 174-77; Annual Report of the Secretary of War for 1933 (Washington, D.C.: War Department, 1933), 37, USAHRC.

10. Risch, *Quartermaster Corps*, 237; letter (subject: stockage levels) from the Office of the Quartermaster General to all depots, 11 May 1942, 400.291; report (subject: first preliminary report) from the Stock Control Board to the Office of the Quartermaster General, 22 January 1943, 140.2, both National Archives, MMRB; memorandum (subject: first report of requirements study 18) from the Office of the Quartermaster General to the Director of the Requirements Division, ASF, 17 May 1944, 430, National Archives, MMRB. The perennial problem in forecasting mess requirements is that one can never predict how troops are going to react to such menus as liver, creamed chipped beef, or casseroles. On the other hand, with hamburgers or steaks one can predict consumption rates with considerable accuracy. Author's own experience.

11. Risch, *Quartermaster Corps*, 39; report (subject: field rations) from the subcommittee on rations of the Quartermaster Corps Technical Committee to the Quartermaster Corps Technical Committee, 15 September 1939, 0030-74, National Archives, MMRB; *Tables of Organization of Infantry Units* (Washington, D.C.: Infantry Journal, 1941), appropriate T.O.s, The Infantry School Library, Fort Benning, Ga. It never proved necessary to increase the ratio of cadre to draftee cooks; compare the T.O.s with the figures in Army Ground Forces letter (subject: cadre personnel for new divisions) to commanding generals, 9 November 1943 (320.2/42), LTC King Papers, USAARMS Library, Fort Knox, Ky.

12. Letter from Mr. William N. Partin (then an officer of the 88th Quartermaster Company) to the author in response to author's inquiries, 17 September 1977; letter from Col. Robert J. Karrer (then inspector general of the 88th Infantry Division) to the author in response to author's inquiries, 13 December 1977; interview with Col. Horace M. Brown (then Captain Brown, aide-de-camp to General Sloan), 2 July 1977; letter (subject: reassignment of QMC functions related to petroleum and petroleum products, fuel containers and drums), Office of the Quartermaster General, 3 December 1942, 0025-22; letter (subject: establishment of fuel and lubricants division), Office of the Quartermaster General, 29 May 1943; Erna Risch, *Fuels for Global Conflict* (Washington, D.C.: QMC Historical Studies, 1952), 45-50; Risch, *Quartermaster Corps*, 34, 250; letter from Maj. Gen. Richard Donovan (commanding general of the Eighth Service Command) to Maj. Gen. Sloan, 15 November 1943, J.E. Sloan Papers; letter from O.L. Scott (traffic representative of the Missouri Pacific Railroad Company) to General Sloan, 7 June 1943, J.E. Sloan Papers.

13. Letter (subject: reassignment of quartermaster functions relating to petroleum) from the Office of the Quartermaster General, 3 December 1942, 0025-22, National Archives, MMRB; Risch, *Fuels for Global Conflict*, 10-21; letter (subject: establishment of fuel and lubricants division) from the Office of the Quartermaster General, 29 May 1943, 0025-37, National Archives, MMRB.

14. *Tables of Organization of Infantry Units*, appropriate T.O.s; Risch, *Quartermaster Corps*, 144; memorandum (subject: assignment of responsibility for handling liquid fuel equipment) from the Adjutant General's Office, 10 April 1943, W850-15-43, National Archives, MMRB; letter (subject: liquid fuels) from the quartermaster general to the adjutant general, 25 February 1941 (463), National Archives, MMRB; report (subject: history of the gas and water can procurement program), Office of the Quartermaster General, 27 October 1941, (463) National Archives, MMRB.

15. Army Ground Forces report (subject: report of Army Ground Forces activities) to the chief of staff, U.S. Army, 10 January 1946, 18, J.E. Sloan Papers; Harry C. Thomson

and Lida Mayo, *The Ordnance Department: Procurement and Supply* (Washington, D.C.: U.S. Army in World War II, Office of the Chief of Military History, 1960), chap. 4; Constance M. Green, Harry C. Thomson, and Peter C. Roots, *The Ordnance Department: Planning Munitions for War* (Washington, D.C.: U.S. Army in World War II, Office of the Chief of Military History, 1955), chap. 3; monograph, "How the Ordnance Department Aided Britain After Dunkirk," by Capt. Paul D. Olejar, 1 June 1944, Ordnance Historical File, USAHRC.

16. Memorandum (subject: production and requirements of small arms material) to the chief of the Industrial Service, 3 June 1942, T676A; letter (subject: review of production plans) from Small Arms Branch of the Ordnance Corps, 16 December 1942, T676A, both National Archives, MMRB.

17. Letter from Col. Robert J. Karrer (then inspector general of the 88th Infantry Division) to the author in response to author's inquiries, 13 December 1977.

18. Janice McKenny, "More Bang for the Buck in the Interwar Army: the 105-mm Howitzer," *Military Affairs* 42 (April 1978): 80-86; report of War Department Equipment Review Board to the chief of staff of the U.S. Army, 31 August 1943 (ASF 334); Report of the War Department Procurement Review Board to the chief of staff of the U.S. Army, 31 August 1943 (ASF 334), both National Archives, MMRB; Thomson and Mayo, *Procurement and Supply*, 144-50.

19. Risch, *Quartermaster Corps*, 75-88, 97-99; Office of the Quartermaster General letter (subject: reassignment of Quartermaster Corps Functions), 31 July 1942, 00184; see also the major changes in uniform items represented in the photographs accompanying the text of John P. Delaney, *The Blue Devils in Italy: A History of the 88th Infantry Division in World War II* (Washington, D.C.: Infantry Journal Press, 1947); Helen R. Brooks, *Development of the Modern Service Shoe* (Washington, D.C.: Quartermaster Department Historical Monograph, 1945); letter (subject: combat service boot, composition sole) from the Quartermaster Corps Technical Committee to the quartermaster general, 19 November 1943 (400.114), National Archives, MMRB; letter from Dr. Paul C. Richmond (then division surgeon of the 88th Infantry Division) to the author in response to author's inquiries, 3 December 1977.

20. Risch, *Quartermaster Corps*, 123-33, 166-73; letter from Dr. Paul C. Richmond; memorandum (subject: establishment of quartermaster climatic research laboratory) from the Adjutant General's Office, 4 February 1943, SPX 322.29, National Archives, MMRB.

21. *Tables of Organization of Infantry Units*, T.O.70; Kreidberg and Henry, *History of Military Mobilization*, 654-657. Examine these figures drawn from information available in Kreidberg and Henry, Risch, and Thomson and Mayo.

Total U.S. Production: Representative T.O. Equipment

	Production			
	1940-1941	1942	1943	1944
Rifle, M1	375,000	758,000	1,220,000	—
Machine gun	31,305	314,839	1,888,331	121,771
Machine gun, .50-caliber	54,654	347,492	641,638	677,011
Tank Medium	1,467	14,000	21,000	13,468
Truck, all types	250,000	619,725	621,502	596,963

22. Cross-reference T.O.70 of the *Tables of Organization of Infantry Units* with the divisional schedule of departure in *The Army Ground Forces: The Procurement and Training of Ground Combat Troops* (Washington, D.C.: Historical Division of the Army, 1948), 489-93,

to get some idea of the magnitude of the equipment demands involved. Green, Thomson, and Roots, *Planning Munitions for War*, chap. 3. Kriedberg and Henry, *History of Military Mobilization*, 674-79, 677-79; memorandum (subject: equipment for the 84th, 88th and 102nd infantry divisions) from the assistant chief of staff, Operations, SOS, to the commanding general of the VIII Service Corps (SP 475); memorandum (subject: authorized allowances of status report items for 85th and 88th infantry divisions) from the director of the Service of Supply to the adjutant general, 27 April 1944, MMRB, National Archives (AG 400); letters from Col. Robert J. Karrer and Mr. William N. Partin.

23. Memorandum from the assistant chief of staff, Operations, SOS, to the commanding general, AGF, 30 December 1942 (SP 475), National Archives, MMRB; Army Ground Forces letter (subject: training directive effective 1 November 1942) from headquarters, AGF, to commanding generals, 19 October 1942. LTC King Papers, USAARMS Library, Fort Knox, Ky.; letters from Col. Robert J. Karrer and Mr. William N. Partin.

24. See, for example, Winston S. Churchill, *Closing the Ring* (Boston: Houghton Mifflin, 1951), 487-88; *Tables of Organization of Infantry Units*, T.O.70.

25. Letter from Mr. William N. Partin; Army Ground Forces report (subject: report of Army Ground Forces activities) to the chief of staff, U.S. Army, 10 January 1946, 20, J.E. Sloan Papers; letter (subject: SPDDO, 451 vehicles) from headquarters, Services of Supply, to commanding generals, AGF, 15 March 1943 (SP 451), National Archives, MMRB.

26. Interview of Col. H.M. Brown; letter from Col. Robert J. Karrer; Army Ground Forces letter (subject: training directive effective 1 November 1942) from headquarters, AGF, to commanding generals, 19 October 1942, LTC King Papers, USAARMS Library; Army Ground Forces report (subject: report of Army Ground Forces activities to the chief of staff, U.S. Army), 10 January 1946, 18.

27. *Small Unit Actions* (Washington, D.C.: War Department Historical Division, 4 April 1946), 119-70, USAHRC.

28. See Martin Van Creveld, *Supplying War* (Cambridge: Cambridge Univ. Press, 1977), 142-48, 175-81, 199-202, 202-6.

29. Letter (subject: automotive disability report of the 88th Infantry Division) from headquarters, SOS, to the inspector general, 13 February 1943 (SP 451), National Archives, MMRB; see the reading file generated by the letter (subject: automotive disability report of the 88th Division) from the inspector general to the commanding general, X Corps, 6 October 1942 (SP 475), National Archives, MMRB.

30. See FM 29-2, *Organizational Maintenance Operations* (Washington, D.C.: DA, 1975).

31. *Armor Reference Data* (Fort Knox, Ky.: U.S. Army Armor School, 1978), ST-1-1, vol. 1, appropriate T.O.s.

32. *Tables of Organization of Infantry Units*, appropriate T.O.s, including T.O.s 5-75, 5-76, 5-77.

33. *Tables of Organization of Infantry Units*, T.O.s 70-1, 10-15, 10-16; letter (subject: summary of motor maintenance activities in the U.S. Army) from the Hertz Committee to the undersecretary of war, 18 November 1941 (OHF 41-42), National Archives, MMRB; interview with Mr. Bud Thomas (proprietor of Bud's Auto Supplies from 1940 to 1951) Cedar Hill Road and 31W, Elizabethtown, Ky. 42701, 23 September 1978.

34. Memorandum (subject: automotive parts) from the assistant chief of staff, G-4, to the quartermaster general, 5 February 1942 (G-4/22528-153), National Archives, MMRB; Maj. Gen. Edmund B. Gregory, "Army Motor Transport," *Army Ordnance* 22 (March-April 1942); letter (subject: standardization) from the chief of ordnance, Holabird Quartermaster Depot, to the quartermaster general, 16 December 1945 (QM 451), National Archives, MMRB; Thomson and Mayo, *Procurement and Supply*, 266-72, 300-319; Public Law 703, 2 July 1940; memorandum (subject: contracts for purchase of repair parts) from the quartermaster general to the assistant secretary of war, December 13, 1937 (QM 451.01), National Archives, MMRB; memorandum (subject: further inquiries in Truman

Committee) from the Ordnance Department to the undersecretary of war, 25 July 1944, 032/416; memorandum (subject: purchase of assemblies and parts for motor vehicles) from the chief of ordnance to the quartermaster general, 8 November 1940 (QM 451.01); both National Archives, MMRB.

35. Letter from Col. Peter L. Topic (artillery battalion executive officer and then G-4 of the 88th Infantry Division) to the author in response to author's inquiries, September 1977; letters from Maj. Gen. John M. Lentz (then training officer of Army Ground Forces) to the author in response to author's inquiries, 28 September and 30 September 1977; letters from Col. Robert J. Karrer and Mr. William N. Partin.

36. Compare *Tables of Organization of Infantry Units, 1941*, with Army Ground Forces letter (subject: cadre personnel for new divisions) to commanding generals, 9 November 1942, LTC King Papers, USAARMS Library, Fort Knox, Ky.

37. Letter (subject: summary of motor maintenance responsibilities in the U.S. Army) from Hertz Committee to the undersecretary of War, 18 November 1941 (00 020/47), National Archives, MMRB; letter (subject: transfer of motor transportation) from the commanding general, SOS, to commanding generals (00 020/47), National Archives, MMRB; Thomson and Mayo, *Procurement and Supply*, 316-18; Green, Thomson, and Roots, *Planning Munitions for War*, 108-13, 139-47.

38. George R. Powell, *The U.S. Army in World War II, Statistics: Maintenance*, unpub. ms., 1950, Ordnance Historical Files, Washington, D.C., 9-28.

39. Letter (subject: automotive disability report of the 88th Division) from headquarters, SOS, to the inspector general, 13 February 1943 (SP 451), National Archives, MMRB.

40. Memorandum (subject: observers report on Louisiana maneuvers) for the commandant of the field artillery school, 30 October 1942, National Archives, MMRB; letters from Col. Robert J. Karrer, Mr. William N. Partin, and Maj. Gen. John M. Lentz.

41. Powell, *Statistics: Maintenance*, 9-28.

42. Dulany Ferrett, *The Signal Corps: The Emergency* (Washington, D.C.: Office of the Chief of Military History, U.S. Army, 1956), 3-9, 70-95; *Tables of Organization of Infantry Units*, appropriate T.O.s.

43. *Tables of Organization of Infantry Units*, T.O.s 6-87, 6-97, 70-1; interview with Col. H.M. Brown; letter from Col. Robert J. Karrer; *Technical Manual 9-2300-257-10* (Washington, D.C.: DA, 1973) paras. 3-23 and 3-46.

44. Thomson and Mayo, *Procurement and Supply*, 154-87.

45. Risch, *Quartermaster Corps*, 144-66.

46. Army Ground Forces letter (subject: enlisted personnel classification and assignment in the activation of an infantry division), 1 December 1942, LTC King Papers, USAARMS Library, Fort Knox, Ky.; *Military Service of Employees* (New York: National Industrial Conference Board, 1940), 13-14, 15-18; letter from Col. Robert J. Karrer.

47. Letter from P.J. Lunquest (Manager of the Muskogee Veterans Administration Hospital) to Maj. Gen. John E. Sloan, 2 June 1943, J.E. Sloan Papers; *Muskogee Daily Phoenix*, 17 July 1942, E6, see also the advertisements and articles throughout the issue.

48. Letter from Col. Robert J. Karrer.

49. This inexperience resulted from the grade the positions called for and the rapidity with which promotion was achieved. See, for example, "Enlisting in March, Marcus Attains Rank of Supply Sergeant," *Muskogee Daily Phoenix*, July 19, 1942, C9; memorandum (subject: report of Army Ground Forces activities) from the commanding general of Army Ground Forces to the chief of staff, 10 January 1946, 23-24, J.E. Sloan Papers.

50. The behavior of these World War II first sergeants reminds me of my own first confrontation with a first sergeant, when I was a second lieutenant in 1972. Spurred by complaints from my platoon, I felt emboldened to point out to him that none of the company clerks pulled routine fatigue details. I can still visualize the color rising on his thick freckled neck as he explained the proper purview of second lieutenants. Apparently this included the company formation, the motor pool, and everything outside of

the cantonment gate. This did not, however, include "his" orderly room or the company clerks.

51. Letter (subject: inspection of postal facilities in the 88th Infantry Division), 31 August 1942 (AG 333.1), National Archives, MMRB; Army Ground Forces letter (subject: cadre personnel for new divisions).

52. Army Ground Forces letter (subject: cadre personnel for new divisions); interview with Col. H.M. Brown.

53. See, for example, memorandum (subject: action to combat spread of subversive doctrines in the military establishment), from Maj. John E. Sloan to the assistant commandant of the Army War College, 18 January 1932, J.E. Sloan Papers; or "Spiritual Life of Camp Gruber Men Cared for; 13 Chapels Built," *Muskogee Daily Phoenix*, 19 July 1942, C8.

54. "They Assembled Themselves Within the Church," *Muskogee Daily Phoenix*, 19 July 1942, C8; letter from Maj. John D. Boren (camp chaplain, Camp Gruber), to Major General Sloan, 28 June 1943, J.E. Sloan Papers.

55. Letter from Dr. Paul C. Richmond.

56. Letters from Col. Robert J. Karrer and Dr. Paul C. Richmond; *Tables of Organization of Infantry Units*, T.O.8-65; Army Ground Forces letter (subject: cadre personnel for new divisions).

57. *Tables of Organization of Infantry Units*, appropriate T.O.s; interview with Col. Horace M. Brown; letter from Col. Robert J. Karrer.

58. See Lenore Fine and Jesse A. Remington, *The Corps of Engineers: Construction in the United States* (Washington, D.C.: U.S. Army in World War II, Office of the Chief of Military History, 1972), 4-8, 152-320, 440-77, 563-85; Kriedberg and Henry, *History of Military Mobilization*, 666-70; *Congressional Record*, 77th Cong., 1st sess., 1 December 1941, 9005, 9400.

59. Office of the Chief of Engineers, *Military Construction Projects*, pt. I, Camp Gruber, 652, National Archives, MMRB; letter from Major General Sloan to 1st Lt. Horace M. Brown, 2 April 1942, J.E. Sloan Papers; *Muskogee Daily Phoenix*, 19 July 1942, A9, B6 (pictures and accompanying articles), C6; letter (subject: 63-man barracks) from the Army Air Force to the surgeon general's office, the quartermaster general, and the chief of engineers, 10 September 1941, (QM 621), National Archives, MMRB; Fine and Remington, *The Corps of Engineers*, 556-560.

60. Interview with Col. H.M. Brown; memorandum (subject: visit to Camp Gruber, Oklahoma) from Lt. Gen. Leslie J. McNair to the commanding general, Third Army, 31 December 1942, J.E. Sloan Papers.

61. *Muskogee Daily Phoenix*, 5 July 1942, B1.

5. The Movement Overseas: Keeping the Edge

1. 88th Infantry Division History of Operations, G-3 operational reports with associated memoranda, entry for 5 March 1944, Combined Arms Research Library (M-N 1029), Fort Leavenworth, Kansas.

2. See William R. Keast, Robert R. Palmer, and Bell I. Wiley, *The Army Ground Forces: The Procurement and Training of Ground Combat Troops* (Washington, D.C.: Historical Division, DA, 1948), 489-93.

3. 88th Infantry Division training report (subject: August 1943), G-3 for the chief of staff, 88th Infantry Division, 4 September 1943, National Archives, MMRB (88th G-3/333).

4. See Keast, Palmer, and Wiley, *Procurement and Training of Ground Combat Troops*, 573-80.

5. Ibid.; see also Army Ground Forces memorandum (subject: status of staging areas) from Lt. Col. William J. Eyerly to Gen. Leslie J. McNair, 19 August 1942; and War

Department letter (subject: training of units at staging areas) from the War Department to commanding general, AGF, 26 March 1942. Both (AGF 320.2), National Archives, MMRB.

6. Indeed, Patton presents the image of a self-proclaimed nonbureaucrat, as a sampling of the quotations attributed to him on the walls of the Patton Museum, Fort Knox, Ky., will attest. Among his peers, he had the reputation of being difficult to work with. (Author's discussion with Maj. Gen. John E. Sloan, July 1971).

7. See Army Ground Forces memorandum (subject: confusion at DTC over conflicting orders) from plans sections, AGF, to the chief of staff, September 1942 (AGF 370.5/134), National Archives, MMRB.

8. Army Ground Forces memorandum (subject: processing of task forces), 31 October 1942 (AGF 320.2/133), National Archives, MMRB; *Preparation for Overseas Movement* (Washington, D.C.: WD, 1 February 1943) (WD 370.5), National Archives, MMRB.

9. *Preparation for Overseas Movement*; see also War Department letter (subject: organization, training, and equipment of units for overseas service) from War Department to commanding generals, 5 January 1943 (AG 320.2); Army Ground Forces letter (subject: preparation and movement of units for overseas shipment) from Army Ground Forces to commanding generals, 19 February 1943 (AGF 370.5/171). Both National Archives, MMRB.

10. See note 9, above; *We Left Home*, unit history of the 337th Field Artillery Battalion, (Milan: S.A. Grafitalia, 1945), 12-14; John P. Delaney, *The Blue Devils in Italy: A History of the 88th Infantry Division in World War II* (Washington, D.C.: Infantry Journal Press, 1947), 28-29; *Direct Support*, history of the 338th Field Artillery Battalion (publisher unknown, 1945), 5, J.E. Sloan Papers.

11. *Tables of Organization of Infantry Units* (Washington: The Infantry Journal, 1941) courtesy of the Infantry School Library, Fort Benning, Ga.; See note 9, above; see also letter from Col. Robert J. Karrer (then inspector general of the 88th Infantry Division) to the author in response to author's inquiries, 13 December 1977; letter from Mr. William N. Partin (then an officer of the 88th Quartermaster Company) to the author in response to author's inquiries, 17 September 1977; and letter from Col. Peter L. Topic (artillery battalion executive officer, then G-4 of the 88th Infantry Division) to the author in response to author's inquiries, September 1977.

12. *Preparation for Overseas Movement*; letters from Col. Robert J. Karrer, Mr. William N. Partin, and Col. Peter L. Topic; Keast, Palmer, and Wiley, *Procurement and Training of Ground Combat Troops*, 606; Army Ground Forces memorandum (subject: second annual report, AGF G-4 Task Force Statistics Book) from G-4, Task Force Division, to G-4, 6 April 1945 (AGF G-4 Task Force Statistics Book) National Archives, MMRB; letters from Col. Robert J. Karrer, Mr. William N. Partin, and Col. Peter L. Topic.

13. Army Ground Forces memorandum (subject: movement of units from home stations) from Army Ground Force to War Department OPD, 22 October 1943 (AGF 370.5/939), National Archives, MMRB.

14. See note 9 above; Delaney, *Blue Devils*, 29.

15. Interview with Col. H.M. Brown.

16. Letter from Maj. Gen. Richard Donovan (commanding general of the Eighth Service Command) Major General Sloan, 7 June 1943, J.E. Sloan Papers; letter from O.L. Scott (traffic representative of the Missouri Pacific Railroad Company) to Major General Sloan, 7 June 1943, J.E. Sloan Papers; *Muskogee Daily Phoenix*, July 19, 1942, C2, B8.

17. *Preparation for Overseas Movement*; letter from Gen. Leslie J. McNair to Maj. Gen. E.P. Parker, 20 December 1943, McNair Correspondence, USAHRC, Carlisle Barracks, Pa.

18. War Department memorandum (subject: replacement training centers) for the adjutant general, 27 September 1941 (AG 341), National Archives, MMRB; Keast, Palmer, and Wiley, *Procurement and Training of Ground Combat Troops*, 380-408, 471-74; War Depart-

ment memorandum (subject: loss replacements) to the commanding general, AGF, 13 July 1943 (WD 354.1); Army Ground Forces memorandum (subject: loss replacement training) from the G-3 to the chief of staff, 20 February 1943 (WD 354.1), National Archives, MMRB; interview with Claude W. "Doc" Waters, a replacement and later rifleman in the 88th Infantry Division, Havertown, Pa., 2 July 1977; War Department letter (subject: utilization of personnel) to commanding general, AGF, 20 August 1943 (WD 320.2); War Department memorandum (subject: capacity of RTCs) to the commanding general, Army Ground Forces, 23 August 1943 (WD 354.1), both National Archives, MMRB; sections C and D (Personnel) of the Lieutenant Colonel King Papers, USAARMS Library, Fort Knox, Ky.; Army Ground Forces letter (subject: enlisted personnel classification and assignment) 1 December 1942, in the Lieutenant Colonel King Papers; Army Ground Forces memorandum (subject: report of Army Ground Forces activities), 10 January 1946, 33-37, J.E. Sloan Papers.

19. Interview with Col. Horace M. Brown, Jr.

20. Ibid.; see also Keast, Palmer, and Wiley, *Procurement and Training of Ground Combat Troops*, 475-79. The 86th Infantry Division was, incidentally, the source of "Doc" Waters, the dynamo who has done so much to make the Blue Devils Association the truly active body that it is today.

21. *We Left Home*, 14-15; Delaney, *Blue Devils*, 29-34; 88th Infantry Division of Operation, G-3 operational reports with associated memoranda, entry for 25 October 1943, National Archives, MMRB (88th G-3/370).

22. Memorandum (subject: continuation of training in staging areas) for the G-3, AGF, 2 June 1943 (WD 320.4), National Archives, MMRB; Army Ground Forces memorandum (subject: command of units ordered overseas) for the chief of staff, U.S. Army, 19 August 1942 (WD 320.2), National Archives, MMRB; Delaney, *Blue Devils*, 29-34; letters from Col. Robert J. Karrer and Mr. William N. Partin.

The actual composition of the increments was as follows: 2 Nov., General Kendall and advance party (arrive by air in Algiers, 10 Nov.); 3 Nov., 351st Infantry; 19 Nov., General Sloan and headquarters element (arrive Casablanca, 27 Nov.); 23 Nov., 350 Infantry, 88th QM, 313th Engineers, plus detachments; 7 Dec., 337th, 338th, 339th, and 913th Artilleries; 17 Dec., 349th Infantry.

23. The material for this and the following two paragraphs was drawn, in the main, from a letter written to the author in response to author's inquiries by Dr. Paul C. Richmond (then division surgeon of the 88th Infantry Division), 3 December 1977; see also Delaney, *Blue Devils*, 30-33; *We Left Home*, 14-16; and *Direct Support*, 7-9.

24. Delaney, *Blue Devils*, 30-33.

25. *Ordnance in the Mediterranean Theater of Operations* (undated World War II pamphlet discussing, among other things, Mediterranean logistical routes), courtesy of the USAARMS Library, Fort Knox, Ky.; Delaney, *Blue Devils*, 33-36; *We Left Home*, 15-18; *Direct Support*, 7-8.

26. The material in this and the following four paragraphs has been pieced together from the surprisingly vivid memories of the participants. I am particularly indebted to my interviews with Col. Horace M. Brown, Jr., and the letters from Col. Robert J. Karrer, Dr. Paul C. Richmond, and Col. Peter L. Topic. See also Delaney, *Blue Devils*, 35-37.

27. Interview with Col. H.M. Brown, Jr.; Lt. Col. Chester G. Starr, *From Salerno to the Alps: A History of the Fifth Army 1943-1945* (Washington, D.C.: Infantry Journal Press, 1948), 137-66; *Log of the 351st Infantry Regiment*, entry for 9 February 1944, unit histories, National Archives, Suitland, Md.

28. Delaney, *Blue Devils*, 37-38; *Log of the 351st Infantry Regiment*, 6 February 1944; see also note 27 above.

29. 88th Infantry Division History of Operations, G-3 operational reports with associated memoranda, entry for 21 February 1944, CARL (M-N 1029).

30. *Log of the 351st Infantry Regiment*, entry for 9 February 1944; see note 29, above; see also Delaney, *Blue Devils*, 44-47, *Direct Support*, 12; *We Left Home*, 18.

31. Interview with Col. Horace M. Brown, Jr., for the material in this and the following paragraph.

32. Accounts of the fighting in Italy are, of course, legion. Insofar as this section is concerned, I am particularly indebted to the often shared reminiscences of my father, Col. H.M. Brown, Jr.; my grandfather, Maj. Gen. John E. Sloan; the letters from veterans of the 88th already cited; the daily logs (National Archives) of the division's component units; Delaney; Starr; and Maj. Gen. James C. Fry, *Combat Soldier* (Washington, D.C.: National Press, 1968). My appreciation of this terrain has been sharpened by personal visits to the battlefields involved.

33. See the *Log of the 349th Infantry Regiment* for 9-11 May 1944, and the *Log of the 351st Infantry Regiment* for 12 March 1944, both unit histories, National Archives, Suitland, Md.

34. Delaney, *Blue Devils*, 47.

35. *Log of the 351st Infantry Regiment* for 4-7 March 1944.

36. *Direct Support*, 14.

37. Letter from Brig. Gen. L.L. Lemnitzer (then deputy chief of staff, Allied Central Mediterranean Force) to Maj. Gen. John E. Sloan, 9 March 1944, J.E. Sloan Papers.

38. Letter from Gen. Alphonse Juin (then commander of the French Expeditionary Corps) to Maj. Gen. John E. Sloan, J. E. Sloan Papers.

6. Minturno: Baptism by Fire

1. E.g., see Colonel Trevor N. Dupuy, *Numbers, Prediction, and War* (London: Mac-Donald and James, 1979), 106; or the personal letter from Brig. Gen. L.L. Lemnitzer (then deputy chief of staff, Allied Central Mediterranean Force) to Maj. Gen. John E. Sloan, 10 March 1944, J.E. Sloan Papers.

2. Sir Winston Churchill's term; Winston S. Churchill, *Closing the Ring* (Boston: Houghton Mifflin, 1951), p. 488.

3. The body of military doctrine generally accepted in the West places a high premium upon the maintenance of the initiative. In cases wherein the movement of major units is temporarily impossible, initiative is to be maintained by the virtue of internal movement and active patrolling. *Notes for the Course in the Military Art* (West Point, N.Y.: United States Military Academy, 1969), 3, 17-23.

4. "First Division of Drafted Men Get Taste of Chasing Germans," *Evening Star* (Washington, D.C.), 29 May 1944, B-2.

5. Quotas called for one officer and fourteen men per battalion in attendance at any given time. *History of the 349th Infantry Regiment, 88th Infantry Division, April 1944 to May 1945* (88th Infantry Division Association, Inc., P.O. Box A, Kensington, Md. 20795, July 1973)—an exact reproduction of the regimental log for the period in question, now located in the National Archives, Suitland, Md.—entry for April 1944, 3.

6. Entries for the period 5-11 March 1944 from *History of the 349th Infantry Regiment, 88th Infantry Division; the History of the 350th Infantry Regiment, 88th Infantry Division;* and the *History of the 351st Infantry Regiment, 88th Infantry Division*, all regimental logs located in the National Archives, Suitland, Md. The German side of the fighting in this sector during this period is best captured in the *[German] XIV Panzer Corps War Diary* the *[German] 71st Infantry Division War Diary*, and the *[German] 94th Infantry Division War Diary*, all World War II German files in the Washington National Records Center (National-al Archives), Washington, D.C.

7. Ibid.

8. Entry for 8 March 1944, *History of the 351st Infantry Regiment.*

9. See note 6, above. For the anecdotes, see John P. Delaney, *The Blue Devils in Italy: A*

History of the 88th Infantry Division in World War II, (Washington, D.C.: Infantry Journal Press, 1947), 51-53. The American draftees in turn, as we shall see, slipped into a somewhat more civil relationship with their adversaries. Eyewitness testimony to the relaxed front-line attitude of veteran British troops was provided by Col. H.M. Brown (then an officer in the 88th Infantry Division's artillery), 12 June 1978.

10. Entries for the period 12-19 March 1944, *History of the 349th Infantry Regiment;* the *History of the 350th Infantry Regiment;* the *History of the 351st Infantry Regiment;* the *[German] XIV Panzer Corps War Diary.*

11. See notes 6 and 10 above; see also *Small Unit Actions* (Washington, D.C.: Historical Division, War Department, 4 April 1946)—case studies of small unit actions provided for the purposes of postwar instruction, in this case an analysis of the 351st Infantry Regiment's efforts to secure Sante Maria Infante—124-25.

12. For the material in this paragraph, see regimental logs, above, and *The Advance on Rome* (G-3 Section, Headquarters, Fifth Army)—a restricted battlefield summary issued to senior commanders and staff after the capture of Rome—J.E. Sloan Papers.

13. Peter Chamberlain and Terry Gander, *Machine Gun* (New York: Arco Publishing Co., 1974), 47-54; Army Ground Forces letter (Subject: Training Directive Effective 1 November 1942) from Army Ground Forces to commanding generals, 19 October 1942, LTC King Papers, USAARMS Library, Fort Knox, Ky.

14. Interview with Col. H.M. Brown, 12 June 1978.

15. Signal Corps General Development Laboratory progress report (subject: project 10-3) September 1942, National Archives (SCGDL); George R. Thompson, Dixie R. Harris, Pauline M. Oakes, and Dulaney Terrett, *The Signal Corps: The Test* (Washington, D.C.: Office of the Chief of Military History, DA, 1957), 218-41; interview with H.M. Brown.

16. Entries for 15 March 1944, *History of the 349th Infantry Regiment,* the *History of the 350th Infantry Regiment,* the *History of the 351st Infantry Regiment.*

17. Entries for 15 March through 15 April 1944, *History of the 349th Infantry Regiment,* the *History of the 350th Infantry Regiment,* the *History of the 351st Infantry Regiment.*

18. Entries for 1 April and 6 April 1944, the *History of the 351st Infantry Regiment.*

19. Entries for 11 April 1944, *The History of the 349th Infantry Regiment,* the *History of the 350th Infantry Regiment,* the *History of the 351st Infantry Regiment.*

20. Ibid., entries for 5 March 1944 to 15 April 1944; *Direct Support,* (History of the 338th Field Artillery Battalion), 14-15, J.E. Sloan Papers; (Delaney, *Blue Devils,* 53; FM 101-10-1, *Staff Officer Field Manual: Organizational, Technical and Logistic Data* (Headquarters, DA, July 1976), 4-6 thru 5-14.

21. The material for this paragraph was drawn from a letter to the author in response to author's inquiries by Dr. Paul C. Richmond (then division surgeon of the 88th Infantry Division), 3 December 1977.

22. For the material in this paragraph, see 21, above, and Charles M. Wiltse, *The Medical Department: Medical Service in the Mediterranean and Minor Theaters* (Washington, D.C.: Office of the Chief of Military History, 1965), 292-295.

23. Letter from Dr. Paul C. Richmond; [German] XIV Panzer Corps Diary, entries for March and April 1944; surviving operations overlays in the J.E. Sloan Papers (author's possession).

24. Brevet Maj. Gen. Emory Upton, *The Military Policy of the United States* (Washington, D.C.: Government Printing Office, 1911), 416-22; Capt. John W. Appel, "Prevention of Manpower Loss from Psychiatric Disorders" (undated study of the chief of the Mental Hygiene Branch), J.E. Sloan Papers, USAHRC, Carlisle Barracks, Pa.

25. Delaney, *Blue Devils,* 60; entry for April 1944, *History of the 349th Infantry Regiment,* 4.

26. Appel, "Prevention of Manpower Loss"; interview with Mr. Claude W. Waters (then a rifleman in the 349th Infantry Regiment), Havertown, Pa., 2 July 1977.

27. See, for example, the discussion in Maj. Gen. James C. Fry, *Combat Soldier* (Washington, D.C.: National Press, 1968), 4-13.

28. Delaney, *Blue Devils*, 51; entry for April 1944, *History of the 349th Infantry Regiment*, 3.

29. Entry for April 1944, *History of the 349th Infantry Regiment*," 3; see also Appel, "Prevention of Manpower Loss."

30. Wiltse, *The Medical Department*, 314-16, 450-51, 483. The regimental logs even go so far as to cloud the two terms, using "exhaustion case" and "neurotic" interchangeably. E.g., see the entry for April 1944, *History of the 349th Infantry Regiment*, 3.

31. For the material in this paragraph, see note 6, above, and Delaney, *Blue Devils*, 46-58.

32. Delaney, *Blue Devils*, 57.

33. *Direct Support*, 16.

34. Fry, *Combat Soldier*, 4-11; Delaney, *Blue Devils*, interview with Col. H.M. Brown; regimental histories for the period 5 March through 11 May 1944.

35. Delaney, *Blue Devils*, 55-57. Apparently the phenomenon of tacit rules of engagement surfaced in World War I as well; see pertinent items in note 23, chap. 1.

36. TM-E 30-451 *Handbook on German Military Forces* (Washington, D.C.: War Department, 15 March 1945), I-2 to I-15, II-7 to II-33; *[German] 71st Infantry, Division War Diary, [German] 94th Infantry Division War Diary*.

37. Letter from Mr. William Partin (then an officer of the 88th Quartermaster Company) to the author in response to author's inquiries, 13 December 1977; letter from Col. Robert J. Karrer (then inspector general of the 88th Infantry Division) to the author in response to author's inquiries, 13 December 1977; letter from Col. Pete Topic (the assistant chief of staff, G-4) to the author in response to author's inquiries, 12 March 1978; Lt. Col. Chester G. Starr, *From Salerno to the Alps: A History of the Fifth Army 1943-1945* (Washington, D.C.: Infantry Journal Press, 1948), 36-37.

38. Letter from Col. Pete Topic; letter from Dr. Paul Richmond.

39. Starr, *From Salerno to the Alps*, see note 37, above.

40. Harry C. Thompson and Lida Mayo, *The Ordnance Department: Procurement and Supply* (Washington, D.C.: Office of the Chief of Military History, Department of the Army, 1960), 143-50.

41. Indeed, the division fired 43,940 artillery rounds during the month of April alone. Entry for April 1944, *History of the 349th Infantry Regiment*, 2.

42. See Starr, *From Salerno to the Alps*, 44-54.

43. Letters from Mr. William Partin and Col. Pete Topic.

44. Ibid; also the letter from Colonel Robert J. Karrer; Delaney, *Blue Devils*, 50; training memorandum no. 10, Headquarters 76th Field Artillery (by order of Col. J.E. Sloan), Fort Ord, Calif., 6 September 1940, J.E. Sloan Papers.

45. Letter from William Partin.

46. Letters from William Partin and Col. Pete Topic; interview with Col. H.M. Brown.

47. Letter from Col. Pete Topic.

48. Letter from William Partin.

49. Entries for the period 15 April through 5 May 1944, in *History of the 349th Infantry Regiment*, the *History of the 350th Infantry Regiment*, the *History of the 351st Infantry Regiment*.

50. E.g., see the discussion of the difficulties involved in maintaining a general-purpose armored force in Vietnam in Gen. Donn A. Starry, *Mounted Combat in Vietnam* (Washington, D.C.: DA, 1978), 33-37.

51. Army Ground Forces letter (subject: training directive effective 19 November 1942) to commanding generals, 19 October 1942. In the LTC King Papers, USAARMS Library, Fort Knox, Ky.

52. E.g., see the discussion of the traditional American crusading mindset in Robert E. Osgood, *Limited War* (Chicago: Univ. of Chicago Press, 1957).

53. Material in this and following paragraphs is drawn from a review of the entries for the period 5 March through 11 May 1944, in *History of the 349th Infantry Regiment*, the *History of the 350th Infantry Regiment*, and the *History of the 351st Infantry Regiment*.

54. Lt. Gen. Arthur S. Collins, Jr., *Common Sense Training* (San Rafael, Calif.: Presidio Press, 1978), 146-163.

55. Delaney, *Blue Devils*, 58; *History of the 349th Infantry Regiment*, 1.

56. Thompson, et al., *The Signal Corps*, 218-41; interview with Col. H.M. Brown.

57. *History of the 349th Infantry Regiment*, 3; *History of the 351st Infantry Regiment*, entry for 10 March 1944.

58. *Tables of Organization of Infantry Units* (Washington, D.C.: Infantry Journal, 1941), T.0.70, courtesy of the Infantry School Library, Fort Benning, Ga.; Army Ground Forces memorandum from Gen. Leslie J. McNair to Brig. Gen. John M. Lentz (AGF, G-3), 10 March 1943, (353.02/103), National Archives, MMRB.

59. Letters from Maj. Gen. John M. Lentz (then training officer of Army Ground Forces) to the author in response to author's inquiries, 28 September and 30 September 1977; *Landmine and Countermine Warfare, Italy 1943-1944* (Washington, D.C.: DA, Office, Chief of Engineers, 1972), app. E.

60. E.g., see Capt. D.G. Browne, *The Tank in Action* (London: William Blackwood and Sons, 1920), 8-14.

61. Henry A. Shaw, Jr., Bernard C. Nalty, Edwin J. Turnblade, *Central Pacific Drive: History of U.S. Marine Corps Operations in World War II* (Historical Branch, G-3 Division, Headquarters, U.S. Marine Corps, 1966), 215, 503-15; Maj. John N. Rentz, *Marines in the Central Solomons* (Historical Branch, Headquarters, U.S. Marine Corps, 1952), 154-56. Both books have a number of photographs amply illustrating the tactics involved.

62. Report (subject: tank battalions, tank destroyer battalions, and tank companies) by Col. G.B. Devore to the Army Ground Forces Board (AFHQ, NATO), 14 March 1944. USAARMC Library, Fort Knox, Ky. (876 TB 102).

63. Ibid.

64. John Prados, "Cobra: Patton's 1944 Summer Offensive in France," *Strategy and Tactics* No. 65 (November 1977), 4-14; AGF memorandum from General McNair to General Lentz, 10 March 1943.

65. Letter (subject: transmittal of historical report and conclusions) from Lt. Col. George M. Davis (commander of the 760th Tank Battalion) to the commanding general, Fifth Army, 9 February 1944. USAARMC Library, Fort Knox, Ky. (8760 TB 101a).

66. Ibid.

67. Interview with Col. H.M. Brown; *Direct Support*, 11-18; *We Left Home*, 18-22; *History of the 349th Infantry Regiment*, April, 2.

68. Ibid.

69. This and following paragraphs draw on entries for the period from 15 April 1944 through 7 May 1944, *History of the 349th Infantry Regiment*, the *History of the 350th Infantry Regiment*, the *History of the 351st Infantry Regiment*; also, interview with Col. H.M. Brown.

70. Delaney, *Blue Devils*, p. 9, 44.

7. Diadem: The First Three Days

1. Vincent J. Esposito, *The West Point Atlas of American Wars*, 2 vols. (New York: Praeger, 1959), vol. 2, 119-25; George F. Howe, *Northwest Africa: Seizing the Initiative in the West* (Washington, D.C.: Office of the Chief of Military History, DA, 1957), 438-77; Ernest F. Fisher, Jr., *Cassino to the Alps* (Washington, D.C.: Center of Military History, U.S. Army, 1977), 4-6, 19-21; FM 101-10-1, *Staff Officer Field Manual: Organizational, Technical, and Logistical Data* (Headquarters, DA, July 1976), 5-6 through 5-14.

2. Fisher, *Cassino to the Alps*, 3-15, 43, 110-16; Esposito, *Atlas of American Wars*, 99-104;

Wesley Frank Craven and James Cate, eds., *Army Air Forces in World War II*, vol. 3, *Europe, Argument to V-E Day* (Chicago: Univ. of Chicago Press, 1951).

3. Memorandum (subject: future operations in Italy) from Gen. Sir Harold R.L.G. Alexander to Gen. Sir Henry Maitland Wilson, 22 February 1944; operations order No. 1, Headquarters, Allied Armies in Italy, 5 May 1944; both AFHQ documents now on microfilm, National Archives, MMRB.

4. Mark W. Clark, *Calculated Risk* (New York: Harper and Row, 1950), 283-86; Fisher, *Cassino to the Alps*, 103-7.

5. Ibid; see also Fifth Army G-3 planning study dated 26 March 1944, National Archives, MMRB.

6. E.g., see "Lessons Learned in the Italian Campaign," publication of Headquarters, North African Theater of Operations, 13 June 1944, microfilm, USAARMS Library, Fort Knox, Ky.

7. Marcel Vignera, *Rearming the French* (Washington, D.C.: Office of the Chief of Military History, DA, 1957), 72, 117, 178-79; see also "Alphonse Juin," *The Contemporary Review*, December 1944, and "Juin and the French," *Time*, 29 May 1944.

8. Personal letter from Gen. Alphonse Juin to Maj. Gen. John E. Sloan, 15 May 1944, J.E. Sloan Papers.

9. 88th Infantry Division operations overlay and 88th Infantry Division operations order for 11 May 1944; courtesy of Col. Dixie Beggs, formerly G-3 of the 88th Infantry Division.

10. Unless otherwise or more specifically noted, the discussion of the 350th's attack is reconstructed from entries for 11-14 May 1944, *History of the 350th Infantry, 88th Infantry Division* (regimental battle log, National Archives, Suitland, Md.); James C. Fry, *Combat Soldier* (Washington, D.C.: National Press, 1968), 15-38; entries for 11-14 May, *Unit Diary for May* of the 753rd Tank Battalion (independent tank battalion log, USAARMS Library, Fort Knox, Ky.); John E. Wallace, *The Blue Devil "Battle Mountain" Regiment in Italy* (Kensington, Md.: 88th Infantry Division Association, 1977); Chester G. Starr, *From Salerno to the Alps: A History of the Fifth Army, 1943-1945* (Washington, D.C.: Infantry Journal Press, 1948); the *XIV Panzer Corps War Diary; [German] 71st Infantry Division War Diary*; and the *[German] 94th Infantry Division War Diary*, all in the World War II German files, Washington National Records Center (National Archives), MMRB; Fisher, *Cassino to the Alps*, 45-48, 65-66, 71-73; and interviews or letters in response to author's inquiries cited elsewhere in these notes. Information upon which the sources agree is not individually noted; items of controversy or items documented by only one source are noted.

11. Entry for 11-12 May 1944, *History of the 350th Infantry Regiment*; letter from Gen. Alphonse Juin to Maj. General John E. Sloan, 15 May 1944, J.E. Sloan Papers.

12. *The Medal of Honor of the United States Army* (Washington, D.C.: Government Printing Office, 1948), 335.

13. *Unit Diary for May* (753rd Tank Battalion), entries for 11-13 May.

14. Fry, *Combat Soldier*, 31-34.

15. *Unit Diary for May* (753rd Tank Battalion), entries for 12-14 May.

16. Fry, *Combat Soldier*, 34.

17. Unless otherwise or more specifically noted, the discussion of the 351st's attack is reconstructed from entries for 11-14 May, *History of the 351st Infantry Regiment, 88th Infantry Division* (regimental battle log, National Archives, MMRB; *Small Unit Actions*, a collection of interview-based case studies reconstructed for the purpose of instruction, in this case a detailed analysis of the attack Santa Maria Infante, (Washington, D.C.: Historical Division, WD., 1946), 117-73; entries for 11-14 May, *Unit Diary for May* of the 760th Tank Battalion (independent tank battalion log, USAARMS Library, Fort Knox, Ky.); Chester G. Starr, *From Salerno to the Alps*; the *[German] XIV Panzer Corps War Diary*; the *[German] 94th Infantry Division War Diary*, both in the World War II German files, MMRB, Washington National Records Center (National Archives), Washington, D.C.;

Fisher, *Cassino to the Alps,* 42-79; and interviews or letters in response to the author's inquiries cited elsewhere in these notes. Information upon which the sources agree upon is not individually noted; items of controversy or items documented by only one source are noted.

18. Entries for 8-15 May, the *[German] 94th Infantry Division War Diary; Small Unit Actions,* 125.

19. *Small Unit Actions,* 128.

20. Entries for 11-12 May, *Unit Diary for May* (760th Tank Battalion).

21. Ibid.

22. Memorandum (subject: conference of corps and division commanders), 13 May 1944, in II Corps G-3 Journal, National Archives, MMRB.

23. *Small Unit Actions,* 159, 163

24. Entries for 13 May, *Unit Diary for May* (760th Tank Battalion); *Small Unit Actions,* 159.

25. *Small Unit Actions,* p. 163.

26. *Small Unit Actions,* 167.

27. Entries for 13-15 May, *History of the 351st Infantry Regiment.*

28. *Small Unit Actions,* 173; Entries for 11-18 May, the *[German] 71st Infantry Division War Diary* and the *[German] 94th Infantry Division War Diary.*

29. Starr, *From Salerno to the Alps,* 184.

30. Entries for 13-18 May, *History of the 351st Infantry Regiment.*

31. Letter from Mr. William Partin (then an officer of the 88th Quartermaster Company) to the author in response to author's inquiries, 13 December 1977; Starr, *From Salerno to the Alps,* 183.

32. *The Advance on Rome* (restricted-distribution pamphlet prepared by G-3 Section of Headquarters, Fifth Army, shortly after the fall of Rome), 41, J.E. Sloan Papers, author's possession.

33. E.g., read the eyewitness accounts of the fighting in *Small Unit Actions,* 117-73.

34. The infantryman's lack of appreciation for the maintenance implications of armored operations is perennial in all armies. See, for example, DA Pamphlet 20-202 (History Study: German Tank Maintenance in World War Ii), 1954.

35. Noncombat operational readiness rates are now held to be acceptable at 90 percent with modern equipment. The tankers of the 753rd and 760th tank battalions seem to have achieved that statistic if one allows for battle losses under considerably more trying circumstances.

36. Summary for May, *History of the 349th Infantry Regiment;* see also Fry, *Combat Soldier,* 39-59.

37. George R. Thompson, Dixie R. Harris, Pauline M. Oakes, and Dulaney Terrett, *The Signal Corps: The Test* (Washington, D.C.: Office of the Chief of Military History, DA, 1957) 218-41.

38. A particularly vivid illustration of the confusion thus created is contained in Field Marshall Kesselring's intercepted remark, "It is intolerable that a division is engaged in combat for one and a half days without knowing what is going on in its sector." See Fisher, *Cassino to the Alps,* 79.

39. Letter from Dr. Paul C. Richmond (then division surgeon of the 88th Infantry Division) to the author in response to author's inquiries, 3 December 1977; *Small Unit Actions,* 157.

40. See memorandum for chief of staff, U.S. Army (subject: report on Army Ground Forces activities) from Gen. Jacob L. Devers, commander of Army Ground Forces, 10 January 1946, 33-38, J.E. Sloan Papers, author's possession; Fisher, *Cassino to the Alps,* 66; interview with Mr. C.W. Waters (then a rifleman in the 349th Infantry Regiment) Havertown, Pa., 2 July 1977; diary of Brig. Gen. John J. King (then a rifle company commander in the 88th Infantry Division), a copy of which has been provided to the

author courtesy of Brig. Gen. John J. King, 100 Wells Street, Hartford, Conn. 06102; *Small Unit Actions*, 157.

41. Consider the following table of the 350th's and 351st's maneuver companies, remembering that the 349th was not committed at all during the period in question.

	11 May	12 May	13 May
350th			
A Co	Attacking	Reorganizing	Attacking
B Co	Attacking	Attacking	Attacking
C Co	Co in Bn Res	Attacking	Attacking
E Co	Committed	Reorganizing	Support by fire
F Co	Attacking	Attacking	Support by fire
G Co	Attacking	Reorganizing	Support by fire
I Co	Bn in Res	Attacking	Reorganizing
K Co	Bn in Res	Attacking	Attacking
L Co	Bn in Res	Bn in Res	Bn in Res
351st			
A Co	Bn in Res	Bn in Res	Co in Reg Res
B Co	Bn in Res	Bn in Res	Attacking
C Co	Bn in Res	Bn in Res	Attacking
E Co	Attacking	Attacking	Attacking
F Co	Attacking	Defending	Eliminated
G Co	Co in Bn Res	Attacking	Attacking
I Co	Screening	Attacking	Attacking
K Co	Screening	Attacking	Support by fire
L Co	Screening	Co in Bn Res	Attacking

Key: Company (Co) battalion (Bn), regiment (Reg), reserve (Res)

As the table indicates, on 11 May, six of the division's twenty-seven maneuver companies were seriously engaged; on 12 May, nine were seriously engaged, with two of those engaged on 11 May having been relieved; on 13 May, eleven were seriously engaged. Only two companies were in serious contact throughout the full three-day period; one company was eliminated in the course of the battle.

42. Brig. Gen. John J. King Diary.

43. Commendation to artillery officer, II Corps, from Maj. Gen. Geoffrey Keyes, 12 May 1944, J.E. Sloan Papers, author's possession; John P. Delaney, *Blue Devils*, 72-73; summary for the month of May, *History of the 349th Infantry Regiment;* message of General Sloan to the troops of the 88th Infantry Division (subject: impending operations), 9 May 1944, J.E. Sloan Papers, USAHRC, Carlisle Barracks, Pa.; entry for 12 May, the *[German] 94th Division War Diary.*

44. Letter from Capt. Philip Neuschler of the Historical Evaluation and Research Organization, describing quantitative techniques used in Quantified Judgment Model (QJM) analysis of combat records, July 1980 (Captain Neuschler is an associate of Colonel Trevor N. Dupuy in this Defense Department–related body of quantitative historical research); *Small Unit Actions*, 159.

45. Fisher, *Cassino to the Alps*, 120-141; see note 44 above.

46. Author's own experience while tank company commander, then brigade operations officer from 1978 through 1981. Both jobs are utterly dependent upon tactical communications.

47. Trevor N. Dupuy, *Numbers, Prediction, and War* (London: MacDonald and James, 1979), 106.

48. Entry for 13 May 1944, Lt. Gen. Mark W. Clark Diary quoted in Fisher, *Cassino to the Alps*, 65.

49. Delaney, *Blue Devils*, 75.

8. Minturno to Rome: The Pursuit

1. *The Advance on Rome* (restricted-distribution pamphlet prepared by G-3 Section of Headquarters, Fifth Army, shortly after the fall of Rome), para. 2a and pl. I, J.E. Sloan Papers, author's possession.

2. *Kriegtagesbuch des Oberkommando der Wehrmacht (Wehrmacht-führungsstab)*, ed. Helmuth Greiner and Percy Ernst Schramm, (Frankfurt am Main, 1961), 478-81; entry for 1 May in *Zustandsberichte des OB Südwest, 1 June 1944*, (OKW/Organizationabeteilung Kriegtagesbuch) in World War II German files, Washington National Records Center (National Archives), MMRB; Ernest F. Fisher, Jr., *Cassino to the Alps* (Washington, D.C.: Center for Military History, U.S. Army, 1977), 81-100.

3. Unless otherwise or more specifically noted, this chapter's discussion of the 88th's battlefield activities is reconstructed from the entries for 14 May through 7 June of *History of the 349th Infantry Regiment, 88th Infantry Division*, the *History of the 350th Infantry Regiment, 88th Infantry Division*, and the *History of the 351st Infantry Regiment, 88th Infantry Division* (all regimental battle logs, National Archives, Suitland, Md.); *Unit Diary for May* and *Unit Diary for June* of both the 753rd and the 760th tank battalions (independent tank battalion logs, USAARMS Library, Fort Knox, Ky.); John P. Delaney, *The Blue Devils in Italy; A History of the 88th Infantry Division in World War II* (Washington, D.C.: Infantry Journal Press, 1948); James C. Fry, *Combat Soldier* (Washington, D.C.: National Press, 1968); John E. Wallace, *The Blue Devil "Battle Mountain Regiment" in Italy* (Kensington, Md.: 88th Infantry Division Association, 1977); *Small Unit Actions* (Washington, D.C.: Historical Division, War Department, 1946); Chester G. Starr, *From Salerno to the Alps: A History of the Fifth Army, 1943-1945* (Washington, D.C.: Infantry Journal Press, 1948); the *XIV Panzer Corps War Diary*, the *71st Infantry Division War Diary*, and the *94th Infantry Division War Diary*, all in the World War II German files, Washington National Records Center (National Archives) MMRB; Fisher, *Cassino to the Alps*; and interviews or letters in response to author's inquiries cited elsewhere in these notes. Information upon which the sources agree is not individually noted; items of controversy or items documented by only one source are noted.

4. Entries for 14-21 May 1944, in *History of the 349th Infantry Regiment*.

5. Restricted message to II Corps from Maj. Gen. Geoffrey Keyes, 17 May 1944, J.E. Sloan Papers.

6. Letter from Mr. William Partin (then an officer in the 88th Quartermaster Company) to the author in response to author's inquiries, 13 December 1977.

7. The traffic jam is best recreated through two messages surviving in the 88th Infantry Division G-3 Journal: 88th Infantry Division to engineers, 192300 May 1944, and commanding officer, 88th Recon Troop to liaison officer, 200220 May 1944, both MMRB, Washington National Records Center, MMRB. See also Fisher, *Cassino to the Alps*, 91.

8. Entry for 23 May, *History of the 350th Infantry Regiment*; Fry, *Combat Soldier*, 75-89.

9. Fisher, *Cassino to the Alps*, 120-41.

10. Now immortalized in the motion picture *The Devil's Brigade*

11. Entry for May 1944, II Corps G-3 Journal, MMRB, Washington National Records Center, MMRB; Delaney, *Blue Devils*, 84.

12. The material in this and the next paragraph comes mainly from the entries for 20-28 May of the *History of the 350th Infantry Regiment* and Wallace, *"Battle Mountain Regiment,"* 33-49.

13. Summary for May, *History of the 349th Infantry Regiment.*

14. Fisher, *Cassino to the Alps*, 171-72.

15. One picks up, for example, a distinct change in tone, from anxious exhortation to triumphant congratulations, in the body of correspondence from Generals Clark and Keyes to General Sloan during the period 11-28 May, twenty separate documents in the single file marked "Restricted—Commendations to the Officers and Men of the 88th Infantry Division," J.E. Sloan Papers.

16. Fisher, *Cassino to the Alps*, 42-80; Fry, *Combat Soldier*, 99-104; Army Ground Forces letter (subject: training directive effective 1 November 1942) to commanding generals, 19 October 1942, Lieutenant Colonel King Papers, USAARMS Library, Fort Knox, Ky. (320.2).

17. E.g., the seizure of Mount Cirta and the rush through the Dora Extension.

18. Interview with Mr. C.W. Waters (then a rifleman in the 349th Infantry Regiment, Havertown, Pa., 2 July 1977; diary of Brig. Gen. John J. King (then a rifle company commander in the 88th Infantry Division), a copy of which has been provided to the author, courtesy of Brig. Gen. John J. King, 100 Wells Street, Hartford, Conn. 06103; *Small Unit Actions*, 157.

19. See note 3, above; in particular, review the entries for 14-28 May in *History of the 349th Infantry Regiment*, the *History of the 350th Infantry Regiment*, and the *History of the 351st Infantry Regiment*.

20. Entries for May 1944 in *We Left Home* and *Direct Support*, unit histories of the 337th and 338th field artillery battalions, respectively, J.E. Sloan Papers.

21. Letter from William Partin.

22. See, in particular, the summary for May of *History of the 349th Infantry Regiment.*

23. A case in point was the ninety-mule train that finally caught up with the 351st on 19 May after having chased the regiment for three days. 88th Infantry Division G-3 log, message from 351st Infantry, 191945 May 1944. Washington National Records Center (National Archives), MMRB.

24. Entries for 23-25 May, *History of the 350th Infantry Regiment.*

25. Fry, *Combat Soldier*, 59-73; summary for May of *History of the 349th Infantry Regiment.*

26. I.e., during the period 23-25 May 1944.

27. *History of the 350th Infantry Regiment.*

28. In addition to the sources cited in note 3, above, the material in this paragraph and the next is drawn from a letter from Dr. Paul C. Richmond (then division surgeon of the 88th Infantry Division) to the author in response to author's inquiries, 3 December 1977.

29. The paragraphs of communications derive from summary for May of *History of the 349th Infantry Regiment*; Fry, *Combat Soldier*, 75-80.

30. Compare the battlefield narratives for this period (note 3, above) with communications doctrine as now taught, FKG-11-1-4, U.S. Army Armor School, Fort Knox, Ky.

31. See Rudolf Bohmher (then an officer of the 1st German Parachute Division), *Monte Cassino* (London: Cassel, 1964); or Trevor N. Dupuy, *Numbers, Predictions, and War* (London: MacDonald and James, 1979), 106.

32. See note 3, above, and, in particular, the entries for 28 May through 4 June in *History of the 349th Infantry Regiment*, the *History of the 350th Infantry Regiment*, and the *History of the 351st Infantry Regiment.*

33. The big picture sketched in this and the following nine paragraphs can be reconstructed from the sources cited in note 3, above, but that reconstruction has already been done well by at least two authors: Fisher, *Cassino to the Alps*, 203-11; and Dan Kurzman, *The Race for Rome* (Los Angeles: Pinnacle Books, 1977), 469-504.

34. Field Marshall Harold R.L.G. Alexander, "The Allied Armies in Italy from 3 September 1943 to 12 December 1944," *London Gazette*, 6 June 1950.

35. Fisher, *Cassino to the Alps*, 184-202; 36th Infantry Division report of operations for

May and June 1944, in the *Fifth Army History,* Washington National Records Center (National Archives), MMRB.

36. Entry for 5 June, *History of the 351st Infantry Regiment.*

37. See 15, above; see also Delaney, *Blue Devils,* 89-101.

38. Certificate of Capt. Trevor E. Williams, Capt. Frank W. Carmon, 1st Lt. Harry B. Stephens, and 1st Lt. Paul Lehner (all 351st Infantry Regiment), verified by Martin H. Burckes, Lt. Col. adjutant general, 11 June 1944, J.E. Sloan Papers.

39. See, for example, our current doctrine on this subject as represented in *The Study of Leadership* (West Point, New York: Office of Military Psychology and Leadership, USMA, 1970).

40. In particular, survivors of the First Special Service Force—"The Devil's Brigade"— seem to have an active lobby among historians for this honor. The official verdict supports the 88th above other claimants, however. See Starr, *From Salerno to the Alps,* 267.

41. This mood is best captured in Delaney, *Blue Devils,* 89-102.

42. Restricted message (subject: message) from Gen. George C. Marshall to Gen. Mark W. Clark, 7 June 1944, J.E. Sloan Papers; *Biennial Report of the Chief of Staff of the United States Army to the Secretary of War* (1 July 1943 to 30 June 1945), 22; confidential personal letter from Gen. Mark W. Clark to Maj. Gen. John E. Sloan, 5 October 1944, J.E. Sloan Papers; "Something New Has Been Added," *Stars and Stripes,* 3 June 1944; "All Draftee Divisions Chase Nazis 30 Miles," *Washington Post,* 29 May 1944; "88th Division Spearheads Yank Smash in Rome Drive," *Muskogee Daily Phoenix,* 29 May 1944; "The Blue Devils Stumped the Experts," *Saturday Evening Post,* 7 September 1946.

9. Rome to the Alps—and Beyond

1. See War Department memorandum (subject: detailed troop unit basis) from the G-3 to the chief of staff, U.S. Army, 9 January 1942, National Archives, MMRB, 381; *Biennial Report of the Chief of Staff of the United States Army, 1 July 1943 to 30 June 1945, to the Secretary of War,* p. 22, J.E. Sloan Papers.

2. Ernest F. Fisher, Jr., *Cassino to the Alps* (Washington, D.C.: Center of Military History, U.S. Army, 1977), 227-54.

3. Ibid., 237.

4. Delaney, *Blue Devils,* 99-101; letters from Gen. John E. Sloan to Mrs. John E. Sloan, 12 June, 9 August 1944, J.E. Sloan Papers; interview with Col. Horace M. Brown (then Captain Brown, an artillery officer in the 337th FA Battalion and son-in-law to General Sloan), 2 July 1977.

5. 88th Infantry Division, History of Operations, G-3 operational reports with associated memoranda (subject: training in the 88th during reorganization period subsequent to the Minturno Through Rome Drive), 12 June 1944, CARL MN (1029.5), or MMRB, National Archives.

6. Ibid.; for a discussion of "soft spot tactics," see the chapter so entitled in *Infantry in Battle* (Washington, D.C.: Infantry Journal, 1939).

7. Letter from Gen. John E. Sloan to Mrs. John E. Sloan, 26 July 1944, in the J.E. Sloan Papers; interview with Col. Horace M. Brown; entries for 8-12 July in the *History of the 349th Infantry Regiment, 88th Infantry Division,* the *History of the 350th Infantry Regiment, 88th Infantry Division,* and the *History of the 351st Infantry Regiment, 88th Infantry Division,* all regimental battle logs, National Archives, MMRB; entries for 8-12 July in the *14th [German] Army War Diary* in the World War II German holdings, MMRB, National Archives; general orders No. 6 (battle honors), signed by order of the secretary of war (Washington, D.C., 24 January 1945), J.E. Sloan Papers.

8. Delaney, *Blue Devils,* 16, 102; interview with Col. Horace M. Brown.

9. Delaney, *Blue Devils,* 117, 121-24.

10. Helmuth Greiner and Percy Ernst Schramm, eds., *Kriegstagebuch des Oberkom-*

mando der Wehrmacht (Wehrmachtführungsstab) (Frankfurt am Main, 1961), 16-17, 583-84; Chester G. Starr, *From Salerno to the Alps: A History of the Fifth Army, 1943-45* (Washington, D.C.: Infantry Journal Press, 1948), 320-31; entries for 20 September through 2 October 1944, the *History of the 349th Infantry Regiment*, the *History of the 350th Infantry Regiment*, and the *History of the 351st Infantry Regiment*; Fisher, *Cassino to the Alps*, 312-37; general orders no. 10 (battle honors) signed by order of the secretary of war (Washington, D.C., 22 February 1945), J.E. Sloan Papers.

11. General orders no. 53 (battle honors) signed by Order of the Secretary of War (Washington, D.C., 11 June 1946), J.E. Sloan Papers; Delaney, *Blue Devils*, 139-47.

12. Delaney, *Blue Devils*, 147; diary of Brig. Gen. John J. King (then a rifle company commander in the 88th Infantry Division), a copy of which has been furnished to the author by the courtesy of General King; interview with Mr. C.W. Waters (then a rifleman in the 349th Infantry Regiment), Havertown, Pa., 2 July 1977; John D. Forsythe and Chester G. Starr, eds., *Fifth Army History* (Fifth Army Historical Section, 1945), vol. 7, 254-67; "Vedriano—Last Ounce of Effort," in *The Blue Devil* (newsletter of the 88th Infantry Division Assoc., Kensington, Md., April 1981), 2.

13. I am particularly indebted to Col. Dixie Beggs (then G-3 of the 88th Infantry Division) for these insights. Colonel Beggs provided me the use of his collection of wartime papers, which included the training programs and sketches of the training facilities used during this winter interlude.

14. Testimony of Major General Von Schellwitz (commanding general of the German 305th Infantry Division) upon his surrender to the Allies; Delaney, *Blue Devils*, 185-91; Greiner and Schramm, *Fifth Army History* 4 (2): 1400; Fisher, *Cassino to the Alps*, 442, 470-82; entries for April 1944 in the *10th Mountain Division Report of Operations*, National Archives, MMRB.

15. Greiner and Schramm, *Fifth Army History* 4 (2): 1389-1400; entries for 24-27 April 1944, in the *History of the 351st Infantry Regiment*; Delaney, *Blue Devils*, 209-12; entries for 26-29 April 1944, in the *History of the 350th Infantry Regiment*.

16. Entries for 27 April through 2 May 1944 in the *History of the 349th Infantry Regiment*; the *History of the 350th Infantry Regiment*; and the *History of the 351st Infantry Regiment*; interview with Col. Horace M. Brown.

17. Brian Harpur, *The Impossible Victory: A Personal Account of the Battle for the River Po* (New York: Hippocreme, 1980), 171.

18. Here again I am particularly indebted to Col. Dixie Beggs for the operations-related papers he made available to me.

19. See the several Army Ground Forces letters (subject: training directive effective . . .) (320.2) in the Lieutenant Colonel King Papers, USAARMS Library, Fort Knox, Ky.; and the Army Ground Forces letter (subject: training in operations against permanent land fortifications) to commanding generals, 5 January 1943, National Archives, MMRB (353/2).

20. Interestingly enough, Sloan's observations parallel those made in other units in Italy. See the accounts of the 3rd Infantry Division, 34th Infantry Division, and 111th Engineer Combat Battalion preserved in Robert E. Gensler, Senior Analyst, *Landmine and Countermine Warfare, Italy 1943-1944* (Washington, D.C.: Engineer Agency for Resources Inventories, 1972), A. B, and C; see also note 5, above.

21. Harper, *The Impossible Victory*, 171.

22. Starr, *From Salerno to the Alps*, 320-31; Entries for 20 September through 2 October 1944, regimental battle logs; Fisher, *Cassino to the Alps*, 312-17; see diary entries in notes 15-16, above.

23. One gets the impression from Russell F. Weigley's otherwise excellent *Eisenhower's Lieutenants* (Bloomington: Indiana Univ. Press, 1981) 1-31, for example, that the author considers American wheeled vehicle fleets to have been instruments of mobility more than of resupply.

24. See T.O.s 100-1, 200-1, 70-1, 7-12, and 7-17 in *Tables of Organization of Infantry Units* (Washington, D.C.: Infantry Journal, 1941), Infantry School Library, Fort Benning, Ga.

25. Entries for 15-17 April 1945, *History of the 349th Infantry Regiment*, the *History of the 350th Infantry Regiment*, the *History of the 351st Infantry Regiment*; Delaney, *Blue Devils*, 186-203.

26. Interview with Col. Horace M. Brown. Colonel Brown developed a keen sensitivity to the value of spotter airplanes, having once almost been held—erroneously, as it turned out—financially liable for the loss of three of them.

27. Leonard L. Lerwill, *The Personnel Replacement System in the United States Army* (Washington, D.C.: DA, 1954), 330-31, 338-39, 422-23, 434-37; commanders in Italy in effect improvised unit rotation systems, see Starr, *From Salerno to the Alps*, 301-64.

28. Russell F. Weigley, *History of the United States Army* (New York: Macmillan, 1967), 436-40; see also Maurice Matloff, "The 90-Division Gamble" in *Command Decisions*, Kent Robert Greenfield, ed. (Washington, D.C.: Office of the Chief of Military History, 1960), 365-82.

29. Memorandum (subject: report of Army Ground Forces activities) from commanding general, AGF, to chief of staff, U.S. Army, 10 January, 28, J.E. Sloan Papers. Another way to develop this same impression is to review the by-name listing of battle casualties appearing in Delaney, *Blue Devils*, 279-94.

30. *The Army Almanac* (Washington, D.C.: Government Printing Office, 1950), 518-72; Robert R. Palmer, Bell I. Wiley, and William R. Keast, *The Procurement and Training of Ground Combat Troops* (Washington, D.C.: DA Historical Division, 1948)

31. See chap. 2 and Palmer, Wiley, and Keast, *Procurement and Training*, 489-93.

32. See note 30, above; Army Ground Forces letter (subject: equipment for Army Ground Forces) to commanding general, ASF, 6 April 1943, (AGF 401-1), National Archives, MMRB; Marvin A. Kriedberg and Merton G. Henry, *History of Military Mobilization in the United States Army* (DA Pamphlet 20-212, 1955), 674-79; Army Ground Forces memorandum (subject: movement of units from home stations) from Army Ground Forces to War Department OPD, 22 October 1943 (AGF 370.5/939), National Archives, MMRB; see also Bell I. Wiley, "The Preparation of Units for Overseas Movement" in *Procurement and Training*, 561-618.

33. The material in this and the next paragraphs is drawn from *The Army Almanac* and from a perusal of the semiofficial unit histories for each of the divisions (e./g., Delaney) maintained, among other places, in the U.S. Military Academy Department of History Library, West Point, NY.

34. The 92nd, in particular, presents a case study in how not to handle a division; see Fisher, *Cassino to the Alps*, 390-91, 408-10, 420-24.

35. Interestingly, this notion of a warm-up period seems to have stuck even more firmly in the German mind than in our own. I once had the opportunity to talk with the younger General von Senger und Etterlin, son of the famed corps and army commander of the Italian campaign and himself a distinguished soldier. He listened very politely to my several theories concerning the performance of the 88th, then reached back into his own memory to comment that "your 88th" also had an extended and well-managed warm-up period—in his mind, the key to its success.

36. See note 33, above, and to it add a subjective perusal of the appropriate unit-specific entries in the multivolume series *The United States Army in World War II* (Washington, D.C.: Center of Military History, 1947-   ). A full collection of this series is maintained, among other places, in the U.S. Military Academy Department of History Library at West Point, NY.

37. Hugh M. Cole, *The Ardennes: Battle of the Bulge* (Washington, D.C.: Office of the Chief of Military History, 1965), 75-172.

38. See Weigley, *Eisenhower's Lieutenants*, 77-144.

39. For the 88th, see chap. 7. For the 102nd, see Joseph Balkoski, "Operation Grenade," *Strategy and Tactics*, January-February 1981, 1-15. For the 104th, see Weigley, *Eisenhower's Lieutenants*, 414-24.

40. I realize this comment flies in the face of considerable buff-driven adulation of the German army and contests a few studies by scholars with whom I find myself at issue— e.g., Trevor N. Dupuy, *A Genius for War* (Englewood Cliffs, N.J.: Prentice Hall, Inc., 1977) or Weigley, *Eisenhower's Lieutenants*, 727-30. I have made some appropriate qualifications in my text and believe my notes will stand by themselves. See app. 2 for a discussion of Colonel Dupuy's comparison of German and American units.

41. The greater fitness of the American GI was not only the result of the physical rigor of the Army Training Program but also the result of steadily increased German use of older age classes; Percy Ernst Schramm, "The German Wehrmacht in the Last Days of the War," (transl., G. Weber), Manuscript C-020 in the German Military Studies Collection prepared for the historical division of the U.S. army's European command by former officers of the Wehrmacht. Some 213 of 2,500 of these manuscripts have been republished in twenty-four volumes as *World War II German Military Studies* (New York: Garland Pub., 1979). Professor Schramm's study appears in vol. 2. The Germans also seem to have eroded physically during occupation duty; see Lt. Gen. Fritz Bayerlein's discussion in manuscript ETHINT 66, *World War II German Military Studies*, vol. 3.

The Army Training Program provided for extraordinary expenditures of rounds in training. Insofar as small arms were concerned, this largesse was increased by the general consignment of high inventories of steel-cased rounds to training purposes after brass cases were adjudged far more weatherproof and hence, more desirable in real combat; interview with Mr. Will Piznak, small arms consultant to the U.S. Military Academy Military Affairs Club, 29 September 1982. By contrast, the Germans of 1944 and 1945 had far less ammunition to give over to marksmanship, even if comparable training time for recruits had been available; see Schramm. This relative training advantage seems to have manifested itself in those sniper duels recorded in unit histories (see, for example, Delaney, *Blue Devils*, 114) and in comparable small unit exchanges.

Postwar interviews with German commanders indicate a pervasive dissatisfaction with the state of training in 1944-1945. Col. Gen. Alfred Jodl stated "training was deficient everywhere" in manuscript ETHINT 50; Maj. Gen. Rudolf F. von Gersdorff cited the "quantitative and qualitative superiority of the Allied formations," ETHINT 59; Lt. Gen. Walter Staudinger said that of the causes of the failure of the Ardennes offensive," most important was the fact that the Army was not completely trained," ETHINT 52; and Lt. Gen. Fritz Bayerlein simply stated "we had no good infantry divisions [left]," ETHINT 66; all in *World War II German Military Studies*, vol. 3.

On the state of German equipment supplies, see Robert Cecil, CMG, "The Economy, Guns and Butter," in *Hitler's War Machine* (New York: Chartwell Books, 1975), pp. 50-64. For examples of German support inadequacies, see Col. Gen. Alfred Jodl's comments on fuel, ETHINT 51; Lt. Gen. Walter Staudinger's comments on ammunition, ETHINT 62; Gen. Horst Stumpff's comments on transportation and repair parts, ETHINT 61; or Lt. Gen. Fritz Bayerlein's comments on artillery and air support, ETHINT 66; all in *World War II German Military Studies*. A mention of superior American mess and medical support occurs in Cecil, "Economy, Guns and Butter," 96. See also Lt. Gen. Hans Speidel, *We Defended Normandy* (London: Herbert Jenkins, 1951), 167-73; and Gen. Siegfried Westphal, *The German Army in the West* (London: Cassell and Co., 1951), 170-204.

Colonel General Jodl observed that the German divisions in the Ardennes Offensive had not had the opportunity to train as combined arms units and that artillery had not been involved enough in the planning to provide adequate support; ETHINT 50, *World War II German Studies*. Lieutenant General Bayerlein comments on the generally inadequate cooperation among German armor, infantry, and artillery during the battle of

France, and, conversely, compliments the American proficiency in attaining the coopera-
tions of those arms during the same period; ETHINTS 66, 68, and 69, *World War II German
Military Studies*.

42. This was true both in the cases of such major counteroffensives as Avranches (see
Speidel, *We Defended Normandy*, 136-54) or the Ardennes (see Westphal, *German Army in
the West*, 170-97) and in the cases of most local counterattacks in the face of overwhelming
American firepower (see chaps. 7 and 8).

43. Harpur, *The Impossible Victory*.

44. My comment on group surrender is somewhat at variance with E.A. Shils and M.
Janowitz, "Cohesion and Disintegration in the Wehrmacht in World War II," *Public
Opinion Quarterly* 12 (1948). In my defense I point out that the focus of Shils and Janowitz
was more on the social dynamics of primary groups than it was upon the actual statistics
involved. The 1985 Command and General Staff College Battle Analysis (Fort Leavenworth, Kans.) required student officers to analyze six VII Corps battles (1944-1945) in a
detail that sent them through the division daily logs for every division involved. Without
exception, the debriefing officers noted the incidence of German Group and individual
surrenders. My own text describes a number of such surrenders to the 88th, a minor
fraction of the total involved.

On the policy of retaliation, see Charles Whiting, *'44: In Combat from Normany to the
Ardennes* (New York: Stein and Day, 1984), 167-72. On the shooting of deserters, see Don
McCombs and Fred L. Worth, *World War II: Strange and Fascinating Facts* (New York:
Greenwich House, 1983), 546. On terrorist-style disciplinary tactics, see VII Corps
Historical Reports, European Theater of Operations (subjects: November 1944, De-
cember 1944), CARL R11799.

45. Westphal, *German Army in the West*; Speidel, *We Defended Normandy*, 146-155; Maj.
Gen. Rudolf von Gersdorff, ETHINT 59, *World War II German Military Studies*; and Lt.
Gen. Fritz Bayerlein, ETHINT 66, *World War II German Military Studies*. Interestingly,
during their years of air superiority German pilots also found they were more effective
free-lance or interdicting in support of mobile operations than they were as instruments
of close air support. See translations of conversations with Lt. Gen. Heinz Gaedcke and
Brig. Gen. Paul-Werner Hozzel (Columbus, Ohio, Columbus Laboratories Tactical Technology Center, Contract Number DAAK40-78-C-0004, 1978 and 1979).

46. See citations in note 41, above. See also Field Marshall Albert Kesselring, ETHINT
71, *World War II German Military Studies*, and app. 2.

47. My understanding of the actual workings of the German replacement system is a
reconstruction derived from Prof. Dr. Percy Ernst Schramm, Manuscript A-872; Maj.
Gen. Rudolf von Gersdorff, ETHINT 59; Maj. Gen. Friedrich von Mellenthin, ETHINT
65; and Gen. Walter Warlimont, ETHINT 3; all in *World War II German Military Studies*. See
also appropriate passages in Greiner and Schramm, *Kriegtagesbuch des Oberkommando der
Wehrmacht*. A rule of thumb seems to have been that it took six weeks to rebuild an
effective division upon a surviving divisional base. One German unit, the 26th Infantry
Division, was reconstructed from cadre no less than nine times, *Strategy and Tactics* (New
York: Simulations Publications, Inc., 1981), no. 85, 17. The system did not always work as
planned because enemy actions could cut short training periods; see Maj. Herbert
Buechs, ETHINT 36, *World War II German Military Studies*. Sometimes retraining efforts
occurred in the context of unit rotations between more and less active sectors;
see Warlimont, ETHINT 3, and Kesselring, ETHINT 71, *World War II German Military
Studies*.

48. To use Drew Middleton's apt phrase, the Wehrmacht may not have been in its
"high summer" of 1940 or 1941, but it was nevertheless full in the strength of its "Indian
Summer"; Weigley, *Eisenhower's Lieutenants*, 574. See also Dwight D. Eisenhower, *Crusade
in Europe* (Garden City, N.Y.: Doubleday and Co., 1955), 321-65.

49. See Whiting, *'44: In Combat*; see also appropriate entries in Martin Blumenson,

Breakout and Pursuit (Washington, D.C.: Office of the Chief of Military History, 1963). The Germans had additional advantage in that it is considerably easier to integrate partially trained troops into defenses than it is to employ them effectively in offenses; see Army Training and Evaluation Program, 71-2 (Washington, D.C.: DA, 1980).

50. See Weigley, in particular his comparison of the 1st and 104th divisions during the Hürtgen fighting; *Eisenhower's Lieutenants*, 412-31.

51. Starr, *From Salerno to the Alps*, 301-64; T. Dodson Stamps and Vincent J. Esposito, *A Military History of World War II with Atlas* (West Point, N.Y.: U.S. Military Academy, 1953), vol. 2, 187-516, vol. 1, 446-89, 548-614; see also note 45, above.

52. Memorandum (subject: report of Army Ground Forces activities) for the chief of staff, U.S. Army, from the commanding general, AGF, 10 January 1946, J.E. Sloan Papers. Another way to develop the same information is to tabulate the by-name listing of battle casualties preserved in Delaney, *Blue Devils*, 279-94.

53. *The Army Almanac*, 518-27, and app. 1 of this volume.

54. U.S. Congress, 65th Cong., 1st sess. Senate Committee on Military Affairs, *Reorganization of the Army: Hearings Before the Subcommittee on the Committee on Military Affairs on S. 2715*.

55. E.g., see Army Training and Evaluation Program 71-2 (Washington, D.C.: DA, 1980).

56. One thinks, for example, of the changes in tank platoon tactics after the Egyptian SAGGER successes in the 1973 Arab-Israeli War. Compare editions of *The Platoon Leaders Guide* (Harrisburg, PA.: Stackpole) or FM 71-1 *The Tank and Mechanized Infantry Company Team* (Washington, D.C.: DA) before and after the October War.

57. Presentation, "The Army Training System" by Howard G. Crowell, Jr. (DC TNG TRADOC) to the U.S. Army Armor Conference, Fort Knox, Ky., 14 May 1981.

58. See, for example, Martin Reusa, "Maintenance Past and Present," *Army Logistician*, March-April 1980; ST 17-1-1, *U.S. Army Armor Reference Data* (Fort Knox, Ky.: U.S. Army Armor School, 1977); ST 17-161, *Student Guide to Maintenance Management* (Fort Knox, Ky.: U.S. Army Armor School, 1977); Richard L. Routh, "Computing Optimum Repair Parts Inventory Cost," *Army Logistician*, January-February 1981, 16-19; or James M. McGonigle, "AOAP," *Army Logistician*, March-April 1980, 4.

59. James A. Huston, *The Sinews of War: Army Logistics 1775-1953* (Washington, D.C.: Office of the Chief of Military History, 1966), 574-90.

60. Ibid., 656-58.

61. Delaney, *Blue Devils*, 225-77.

62. Interview with Maj. Gen. James C. Smith (principal author of Project Cohort, the Army's most recent initiative to restore small-unit cohesion), Fort Knox, Ky., 14 May 1981; presentation, "Personnel Operations for Tomorrow's Force" by Maj. Gen. Robert M. Elton (Commanding General USA MILPERCEN) to the U.S. Army Armor Conference, Fort Knox, Ky., 13 May 1981; C.M. Virtue, *Company Administration and the Personnel Section* (Harrisburg, Pa.: Military Service Publishing Co., 1957), 237-45; David J. Chester, Neil J. Van Steenberg, and Joyce E. Bruechel, "Effect on Morale of Infantry Team Replacement and Individual Replacement Systems," *Sociometry* 18, December 1955, 587-97; George E. Duberstein, *The Communist Soldier in Vietnam: A Study in Motivation* (Fort Leavenworth, Kans.: Command and General Staff College, 1973).

63. E.g., see John W. Appel, "Prevention of Manpower Loss from Psychiatric Disorders" (undated World War II–vintage study for the chief of the mental hygiene branch) in the J.E. Sloan Papers, USAHRC, Carlisle Barracks, Pa.

64. Interview with Maj. Gen. James C. Smith.

65. Jean R. Moenk, *A History of Large-Scale Manuevers in the United States, 1935-1964* (Fort Monroe, Va.: U.S. Army Continental Army Command, 1969); author's personal experience, having participated in eleven major (multibattalion) field tactical exercises during the period 1971-1981.

66. CAPSTONE presentation to FORSCOM Budget Officer's Conference, Fort McPherson, Ga., 1 April 1981.

Appendix 2. The Mythos of Wehrmacht Superiority

1. The most notable example was Winston Churchill's self-defense in Parliament on 2 July 1942. See David Irving, *The Trail of the Fox* (New York: E.P. Dutton, 1977), 190-91.

2. My favorite example of such nonsense is the German antitank gunner cited in Stuart H. Loory, *Defeated: Inside America's Military Machine* (New York: Random House, 1973), 39.

3. The best single collection of source materials originating with Germans is probably the twenty-four-volume *World War II German Military Studies* (New York: Garland, 1979).

4. S.L.A. Marshall, *Men Against Fire: The Problem of Battle Command in Future War* (Glouchester, Mass.: Peter Smith, 1947); Basil Henry Liddell Hart, *The German Generals Talk* (New York: W. Morrow, 1948); behavioralists often quoted out of context include Eli Ginzberg et. al., *The Ineffective Soldier: Lessons for Management and the Nation* (New York: Columbia Univ. Press, 1959), E.A. Shils and M. Janowitz, "Cohesion and Disintegration in the Wehrmacht in World War II," *Public Opinion Quarterly*, 12 (1948), and S.A. Stouffer et. al., *Studies in Social Psychology in World War II* (Princeton, N.J.: Princeton Univ. Press, 1947-1950).

5. Colonel Trevor N. Dupuy, *Numbers, Prediction, and War* (New York: Bobbs-Merrill, 1979).

6. See, for examples, Martin Van Creveld, *Fighting Power: German and U.S. Army Performance 1939-1945* (Westport, Conn.: Greenwood Press, 1982), and Colonel Trevor N. Dupuy, *A Genius for War: The German Army and General Staff 1807-1945* (Englewood Cliffs, N.J.: Prentice-Hall, 1977); see also Max Hastings, "Their Wehrmacht Was Better than Our Army," *Kansas City Star,* 26 May 1985, ID.

7. *Handbook on German Military Forces* (Washington, D.C.: Government Printing Office, 1945), TM-E 30-451.

8. Classroom instruction in P316, Division Tactics, CGSC 1985; see also Dupuy, *Numbers, Prediction, and War,* 11-12.

9. Robert Walter Samz, *Towards a Science of War Through Some Mathematical Concepts of Macrocombat* (Ann Arbor, Mich.: University Microfilms, 1970), 30-91.

10. I drew the ORSA values in Table A2-2 from the chart of ATLAS curves appearing in James G. Taylor, *Lanchester Models of Warfare* (Arlington, Va.: Operations Research Society of America, 1983), vol. 2, 523. Setting the force ratios at one to one, one can use Fiske's equations to solve for the relative advantages of the defender.

11. *Field Manual 101-31-3* (Nuclear Planning Data), (Washington, D.C.: DA; 1984).

12. Samz, *Towards a Science of War.*

13. Van Creveld, *Fighting Power,* 28-34.

14. Ibid., 42-61, 151-55.

15. John Sloan Brown, *Winning Teams: Mobilization-Related Correlates of Success in American World War II Infantry Divisions* (Fort Leavenworth, Ks.: Combat Studies Institute, forthcoming in 1986), 120-160.

16. E.g., see J. Glenn Gray, *The Warriors: Reflections on Men in Battle* (New York: Harper Colophon, 1970), 131-213.

Bibliographical Essay

There are no general works that study World War II draftee divisions as a genre. John P. Delaney, *The Blue Devils in Italy: A History of the 88th Infantry Division in World War II* (Washington, D.C.: Infantry Journal Press, 1947), is a well-written divisional history that carries the 88th from activation through deactivation, but it does not address larger mobilization issues or provide documentation. Russell F. Weigley, *History of the United States Army* (New York: Macmillan, 1967), gives a useful discussion of the develoopment and experience of draftee divisions in general, albeit without much in the way of detail. General works do exist that cover major subheadings of the material discussed in this study: conscription, mobilization, and the campaign in Italy during World War II.

A study of conscription and the draft should probably start with the well-documented, multivolume *U.S. Selective Service System Special Monographs*. Of these, the most useful for the purposes of the present study was vol. 1, *Backgrounds of Selective Service* (Washington, D.C.: Government Printing Office, 1947), and vol. 2, *The Selective Service Act: Its Legislative History, Amendments, Appropriations, Cognates, and Prior Instruments of Security* (Washington, D.C.: Government Printing Office, 1954). Lt. Col. Leonard L. Lerwill, *The Personnel Replacement System in the United States Army* (DA Pam 20-211) (Washington, D.C.: DA, 1954) narrows his focus concerning this topic to the army in particular.

Issues related to conscription and the draft are woven throughout American history. Contemporary writings that illuminate the issues involved at particular stages in our national development include Jonathan Elliott, ed., *The Debates in the Several Conventions on the Adoption of the Federal Constitution* (Philadelphia: Lippincott, 1888), vol. 3; Henry Cabot Lodge, ed., *The Works of Alexander Hamilton* (New York: G.P. Putnam's Sons, 1885); John C. Fitzpatrick, ed., *The Writings of George Washington from the Original Manuscript Sources* (Washington, D.C.: Government Printing Office, 1944), vol. 26; Richard K. Cralle, ed., *Reports and Public Letters of John C. Calhoun* (New York: D. Appleton and Co., 1864); William T. Sherman, *Personal Memoirs of William T. Sherman* (New York: Webster, 1882); John A. Logan, *The Volunteer Soldier of America* (Chicago: R.J. Peale, 1887); Emory Upton, *Military Policy of the United States* (Washington, D.C.: Government Printing Office, 1912); Leonard Wood, *The Military Obligation of Citizenship* (Princeton, N.J.: Princeton Univ. Press, 1915); John McAuley Palmer, *America in Arms: The Experience of the United States with Military Organiza-*

tion (New Haven, Conn.: Yale Univ. Press, 1941); Harvey S. Ford, *What the Citizen Should Know About the Army* (New York: W.W. Norton, 1942); and Arthur A. Ekirch, Jr., *The Civilian and the Military* (New York: Oxford Univ. Press, 1956). Civil War vintage conscription has received attention from such modern authors as Albert B. Moore, *Conscription and Conflict in the Confederacy* (New York: Macmillan, 1924); and Neil C. Kimmons, "Federal Draft Exemptions, 1863-1865," *Military Affairs* 15 (Spring 1951). The records of Congress provide a detailed discussion of the World War I draft in *Reorganization of the Army: Hearings Before the Subcommittee on the Committee on Military Affairs on S. 2715* (65th Cong., 1st sess., 1917). The World War II draft is most comprehensively discussed in the *U.S. Selective Service System Special Monographs*, cited above. There are at least two engaging discussions of the World War I draft from the draftee's viewpoint: Frazier Hunt, *Blown In by the Draft* (New York: Doubleday, 1918), and Irving Crump, *Conscript 2989* (New York: Dodd, Mead, 1918). S.A. Stouffer, *American Soldier* (Princeton, N.J.: Princeton Univ. Press, 1949), and C.W. Bray, *Psychology and Military Proficiency* (Princeton, N.J.: Princeton Univ. Press, 1948), use more sophisticated techniques to capture the nature of the World War II draftee. Eli Ginzberg, et.al., *The Ineffective Soldier: Lessons for Management and the Nation* (New York: Columbia Univ. Press, 1959) is also very useful for this purpose, albeit more specialized. The draft from the employer's viewpoint is addressed in *Military Service of Employees* (New York: National Industrial Conference, 1940).

The best single-volume historical treatment of mobilization is Marvin A. Kreidberg and Merton G. Henry, *History of Military Mobilization in the United States Army, 1775-1945* (Washington, D.C.: Department of the Army, 1955). James A. Huston, *The Sinews of War: Army Logistics 1775-1953* (Washington, D.C.: Office of the Chief of Military History, 1966), is another valuable survey. One might also read Martin Van Creveld, *Supplying War* (Cambridge: Cambridge Univ. Press, 1977), for a well-written if sweeping survey of military logistics in modern times. The national environment wherein mobilization progressed is the subject of Richard Polenberg, *War and Society: The United States, 1941-1945* (New York, Lippincott, 1972). Briefer treatments, also well done, occur in James L. Abrahamson, *The American Home Front: Revolutionary War, Civil War, World War I and World War II* (Washington, D.C.: Government Printing Office, 1983) and James Titus, ed., *The Home Front and War in the Twentieth Century: The American Experience in Comparative Perspective* (Washington, D.C.: Government Printing Office, 1984).

A number of books describe aspects of American mobilization in World War II. Robert W. Coakley and Richard M. Leighton, *Global Logistics and Strategy: 1940-1945* (Washington, D.C.: Office of the Chief of Military History, 1968), provides a comprehensive logistical survey. Greater detail and more limited focus are provided by Fairchild Byron and Jonathan Grossman, *The Army and Industrial Manpower* (Washington, D.C.: Office of the Chief of Military History, 1960); Ralph Elberton Smith, *The Army and Economic Mobilization* (Washington, D.C.: Office of the Chief of Military History, 1959); Robert R. Palmer, Bell I. Wiley, and William R. Keast, *The Procurement and Training of Ground Combat Troops* (Washington, D.C.: Department of the Army Historical Division, 1948); Maurice Matloff and Edwin M. Snell, *Strategic Planning for*

Coalition Warfare 1941-1942 (Washington, D.C.: Office of the Chief of Military History, 1953); Maurice Matloff, *Strategic Planning for Coalition Warfare 1943-1944* (Washington, D.C.: Office of the Chief of Military History, 1957); Mark S. Watson, *Chief of Staff: Prewar Plans and Preparation* (Washington, D.C.: Department of the Army Historical Division, 1950); *Industrial Mobilization for War* (Washington, D.C.: Civilian Production Administration, 1947); Donald M. Nelson, *Arsenal of Democracy* (New York: Harcourt, Brace, 1946); and Simon Kuznets, *National Product in Wartime* (New York: National Bureau of Economic Research, 1945). Elias Husar, *The Purse and the Sword* (Ithaca, N.Y.: Cornell Univ. Press, 1950), focuses on congressional appropriations. Luther Gulick, *Administrative Reflections from World War II* (Birmingham: Univ. of Alabama Press, 1948), critiques the administrative apparatus responsible for coordinating the various aspects of mobilization. While not discussing mobilization per se, several references provide useful statistical information: George R. Powell, *The U.S. Army in World War II: Statistics* (Washington, D.C.: Department of the Army Historical Division, 1950); J.R. Craf, *Survey of the American Economy, 1940-1946* (New York: McGraw-Hill, 1947); and David Novik and G.A. Steiner, *Wartime Industrial Statistics* (New York: Wiley, 1949). Within the army each of the services has an official World War II history of its own.

These volumes address mobilization responsibilities toward the new divisions insofar as the particular service was concerned: Erna Risch and Chester L. Kieffer, *The Quartermaster Corps: Organization, Supply, and Services* (Washington, D.C.: Office of the Chief of Military History, 1953, 1955); Erna Risch, *Fuels for Global Conflict* (Washington, D.C.: Quartermaster Corps, 1952); Harry C. Thomson, Constance M. Green, and Peter C. Roots, *The Ordnance Department: Planning Munitions for War* (Washington, D.C.: Office of the Chief of Military History, 1955); Harry C. Thomson and Lida Mayo, *The Ordnance Department: Procurement and Supply* (Washington, D.C.: Office of the Chief of Military History, 1960); Chester Wardlow, *Transportation Corps: Responsibilities, Organization, and Operations* (Washington, D.C.: Office of the Chief of Military History, 1951); Chester Wardlow, *Transportation Corps: Movements, Training, and Supply* (Washington, D.C.: Office of the Chief of Military History, 1956); Clarence M. Smith, *Medical Department: Hospitalization and Evacuation, Zone of the Interior* (Washington, D.C.: U.S. Army Medical Service, 1956); Dulany Terrett, *The Signal Corps: The Emergency* (Washington, D.C.: Office of the Chief of Military History, 1956); George R. Thompson, Dixie R. Harris, Pauline Oakes, and Dulaney Terrett, *The Signal Corps: The Test* (Washington, D.C.: Office of the Chief of Military History, 1957); Lenore Fine and Jesse R. Remington, *The Corps of Engineers: Construction in the United States* (Washington, D.C.: Office of the Chief of Military History, 1972); Blanche D. Coll, Jean E. Keith, and Herbert H. Rosenthal, *Corps of Engineers: Troops and Equipment* (Washington, D.C.: Office of the Chief of Military History, 1958). The manner in which these branches and services worked together at higher levels is the subject of Kent R. Greenfield, Robert R. Palmer, and Bell I. Wiley, *The Organization of Ground Combat Troops* (Washington, D.C.: Department of the Army Historical Division, 1947); and of John D. Millett, *The Organization and Role of the Army Service Forces* (Washington, D.C.: Office of the Chief of Military History, 1954).

The campaign in Italy has been the subject of a number of histories; see

Myron J. Smith, Jr., *World War II: The European and Mediterranean Theaters, An Annotated Bibliography* (New York: Garland, 1984) for useful historiography. Before studying the campaign itself, one would be well advised to seek a general understanding of World War II military developments. Vincent J. Esposito, *The West Point Atlas of American Wars* (2 vols.; New York: Praeger, 1959) vol. 2, is excellent for this purpose, and combines concise text with superb graphics. A. Russell Buchanan, *The United States in World War II* (New York: Harper and Row, 1964), is another excellent survey. Henry Steele Commager, *The Pocket History of the Second World War* (New York: Pocket Books, 1945), James L. Stokesbury, *A Short History of World War II* (New York: Morrow, 1980), and Fletcher Pratt's succinct *War for the World* (New Haven, Conn.: Yale Univ. Press, 1950), are also useful, albeit considerably less detailed.

Raymond de Belot, *The Struggle for the Mediterranean, 1939-1945* (Princeton, N.J.: Princeton Univ. Press, 1951) puts the Italian campaign into the context of a narrower geographic focus. W.G.F. Jackson, *The Battle for Italy* (New York: Harper and Row, 1967), and G.A. Shepperd, *The Italian Campaign, 1943-1945* (New York: Praeger, 1968), are both solid histories of the Italian campaign itself. Several other histories of the campaign emphasize the participation of particular nations: Ernest F. Fisher, Jr., *Cassino to the Alps* (Washington, D.C.: Center for Military History, 1977); Eric Linklater, *The Campaign in Italy* (London: His Majesty's Stationery Office, 1951); Marshal Pietro Badoglio, *Italy in the Second World War* (New York: Oxford Univ. Press, 1948); H.A. Jacobsen and J. Rohwer, *Decisive Battles of World War II: The German View* (New York: Putnam, 1965); Dharm Pal, *The Campaign in Italy, 1943-1945* (London: Longmans, 1960); and D.K. Palit, *The Italian Campaign* (Ferozepore, India: English Book Depot, 1956). Lt. Col. Chester G. Starr, *From Salerno to the Alps: A History of the Fifth Army, 1943-1945* (Washington, D.C.: Infantry Journal Press, 1948), and Edmund F. Ball, *Staff Officer with the Fifth Army* (New York: Exposition Press, 1958), both follow the Fifth Army through the campaign in a detailed, yet readable, manner. Several of the senior participants in the Italian campaign have left memoirs: Earl Harold Alexander of Tunis, *The Alexander Memoirs* (New York: McGraw-Hill, 1962); Winston Churchill, *The Second World War: Closing the Ring* (Boston: Houghton Mifflin, 1951); Mark W. Clark, *Calculated Risk* (New York: Harper, 1950); Albert Kesselring, *A Soldier's Story* (New York: Morrow, 1954); Bernard Law Montgomery, *Memoirs: Montgomery of Alamein* (Cleveland: World, 1958); Lucian King Truscott, *Command Missions* (New York: Dutton, 1954); and Gen. Sir Henry Maitland Wilson, *Report by the Supreme Allied Commander Mediterranean to the Combined Chiefs of Staff on the Italian Campaign* (London: His Majesty's Stationery Office, 1946). Martin Blumenson's *Mark Clark* (New York: Congdon and Weed, 1984) is an outstanding biography of the senior commander most important to the 88th Infantry Division.

Operation Diadem was the critical test of the proficiency of the 88th Infantry Division. W.G.F. Jackson, *The Battle for Rome* (London: Batsford, 1969), is a fine history of this important battle, as is Raleigh Trevelyan, *Rome '44: The Battle for the Eternal City* (New York: Viking, 1981). Robert H. Adleman and George Walton, *Rome Fell Today* (Boston: Little, Brown, 1968), and Dan Kurzman, *The Race for Rome* (Los Angeles: Pinnacle Books, 1977), are also useful, if somewhat more journalistic, discussions of Operation Diadem.

Christopher Buckley, *The Road to Rome* (London: Hodder and Stoughton, 1945), is a contemporary account somewhat more narrow in scope. Col. Trevor N. Dupuy, *Numbers, Prediction, and War* (London: MacDonald and James, 1979), brings a massive database and the latest instruments of quantitative analysis to bear upon Diadem and other twentieth-century battles.

The breakout from the Anzio beachhead and the final assaults upon Monte Cassino were crucial to the overall success of Diadem. Histories of these operations offer random discussions of the 88th Infantry Division. The best history of Anzio is Martin Blumenson, *Anzio: The Gamble that Failed* (Philadelphia: Lippincott, 1963). Christopher Hibbert, *Anzio: Bid for Rome* (New York: Ballantine, 1971), Ernest Tidyman, *The Anzio Death Trap* (New York: Belmont, 1968), and W. Vaughn-Thomas, *Anzio* (New York: Holt, 1961), are also useful. Charles Connell, *Monte Cassino: The Historic Battle* (London: Elek, 1963), and Rudolf Bohmler, *Monte Cassino* (London: Cassel, 1964), reconstruct that battle from both the Allied and the Axis points of view.

When one narrows the focus from the larger issues of conscription, mobilization, and the campaign in Italy to the 88th Infantry Division in particular, one encounters a radical reduction in the volume of published material available. Many of the books cited above mention the 88th by name, and most discuss developments that directly affected the division, but only Delaney gives the division consistent attention. For the period before the division's deployment in Italy, one must rely upon special collections, the memories of participants, and archival materials in order to add any dimensions to those developed by Delaney. For the period after the 88th's arrival in Italy, collections, memories, and archival materials may be supplemented with published unit-level accounts, unit combat journals, diaries, and logs.

The collections—other than those in the National Archives—that have proved most useful in this study have been Maj. General John E. Sloan's personal papers (an inheritance from General Sloan, my grandfather); Col. Dixie E. Beggs' personal papers; the Lieutenant Colonel King papers; the United States Army Historical Research Center, Carlisle Barracks, Pa.; The Combined Arms Research Library (CARL) of the Command and General Staff College, Fort Leavenworth, Ks.; the United States Army Armor School Library, Fort Knox, Ky.; and the United States Army Infantry School Library, Fort Benning, Ga. General Sloan's papers include personal correspondence, implementing instructions, and other materials not subject to filing; a selection of official documents subject to filing, and thus available elsewhere; and newspaper and magazine clippings collected by his wife and daughter (my grandmother and mother). Colonel Beggs, the division G-3, maintained a personal file of the operations orders, training publications, and correspondence generated by the division overseas. This material proved particularly useful in reconstructing the fight-train-fight cycle of the 88th in Italy.

The Combined Arms Research Library has complete copies of divisions monthly after-action reports, for the 88th and virtually all other divisions, throughout the war. CARL does have a filing system all its own; I have entered the CARL number in certain notes as appropriate. The Armor School Library has a depository for the battle records, logs, journals, diaries, etc., of armored units in World War II. These proved invaluable in reconstructing the activities of the independent tank and tank destroyer battalions supporting the 88th. The Armor School Library also provided the Lieutenant Colonel King papers, a consolidation of the official documents that directed the new divisions during their activation and training. The Infantry School Library's holdings were helpful insofar as infantry units were concerned; its collection of tables of organization proved particularly useful. The United States Army Historical Research Center has accumulated personal papers from all periods of American military history. It was there that I came across Captain John W. Appel's enlightening study of psychiatric stress in combat in World War II.

Of the documents drawn from the National Archives, a few have been so important to this study as to merit special mention. Insofar as the rest are concerned, the glossary of "Abbreviations and File Numbers" preceding the notes section should be of assistance to those seeking information over and above that already provided by the notes. In the cases of documents that originated within a staff action of the 88th Infantry Division but that also fall under a topic area of the *War Department Decimal File System* (Washington, D.C.: The Adjutant General of the U.S. Army, 1943), I have entered both the staff action of origin and the file number in my notes. Two series of Army Ground Forces letters were particularly important in the activation and training of the new divisions: AGF letters (subject: cadre personnel for new divisions) and AGF letters (subject: training directive effective . . .). These series spanned several years as Army Ground Forces updated and republished original documents. *Preparation for Overseas Movement* (War Department, 1 February 1943, WD 370.5) dominated the operational and logistical activities involved in moving the new divisions overseas. Three wartime publications provided contemporary strategic overviews: *Biennial Report of the Chief of Staff of the United States Army (1 July 1943 to 30 June 1945) to the Secretary of War*; memorandum for the chief of staff, U.S. Army (subject: report of Army Ground Forces activities), from the commanding general, Army Ground Forces, 10 January 1946; and *The Advance on Rome*, a restricted-distribution pamphlet prepared by the G-3 Section of Headquarters, Fifth Army, shortly after the fall of Rome.

The memories of participants have been invaluable in reconstructing the experiences of the 88th Infantry Division. In tapping this source I have been greatly assisted by my father, Col. Horace M. Brown (General Sloan's aide during the formative period of the division, then an officer in the division's artillery) and by Mr. Claude W. "Doc" Waters (then a rifleman in the 88th and now a successful businessman and also editor of the quarterly publication *The Blue Devil*, whose dedication and leadership have meant so much to the 88th Infantry Division Association). These two individuals proved splendid sources in themselves and introduced me to equally knowledgeable and cooperative veterans from several corners of the division's experience: Col. Dixie Beggs, then G-3 of the 88th Infantry Division; Maj. Harvey R. Cook, then special services officer of the 88th Infantry Division; Col. Robert J. Karrer, then inspector general of the 88th Infantry Division; Brig. Gen. John J. King, then a rifle company commander in the 88th Infantry Division; Mr. William N. Partin, then an officer in the 88th's Quartermaster Company; Dr. Paul Richmond, then division surgeon of the 88th Infantry Division; and Col. Peter L. Topic, first an artillery battalion executive officer, then the G-4 of the 88th Infantry Division.

These men graciously wrote detailed responses to my inquiries; several shared diaries, photographs, and written memorabilia as well. Veterans from outside the division also provided useful details: Maj. Gen. John M. Lentz, then the training officer of Army Ground Forces; and Maj. Gen. James C. Smith, a veteran of three wars who has been instrumental in developing COHORT, the Army's current effort to achieve personnel stabilization. Veterans of the 88th regularly contribute articles and photographs to *The Blue Devil;* my notes cite several of these articles. Finally, mention should be made of my own memories of conversations with my Grandfather Sloan, a grand old man with whom I was very close.

A number of published accounts discuss the experiences of the 88th in Italy. Maj. Gen. James C. Fry, *Combat Soldier* (Washington: National Press, 1968), provides a readable narrative of his experience while commanding the 350th Infantry Regiment. *The Blue Devil "Battle Mountain Regiment" in Italy* (Kensington, Md.: 88th Infantry Division Assoc., 1977), is a unit history of the 350th in Italy. The 88th Infantry Division Association has typed and published the regimental battle logs of the division's three infantry regiments: *History of the 349th Infantry Regiment, 88th Infantry Division; History of the 350th Infantry Regiment, 88th Infantry Division;* and *History of the 351st Infantry Regiment, 88th Infantry Division. Small Unit Actions* (Washington, D.C.: Historical Division, War Department, 1946), is a collection of interview-based case studies compiled for the purposes of instruction; it includes a detailed reconstruction of the 351st Infantry Regiment's attack on Santa Maria Infante. Two of the division's artillery battalions produced unit histories: the 337th Field Artillery in *We Left Home* (Milan: S.R. Grafitalia, date unknown) and the 338th Field Artillery in *Direct Support* (J.E. Sloan Papers).

The 88th also figures in the records left by other units such as Paul L. Schultz, *The 85th Infantry Division in World War II* (Washington, D.C.: Infantry Journal Press, 1949). The German experience with the 88th is described in *The [German] XV Panzer Corps War Diary, The [German] 71st Infantry Division War Diary,* and *The [German] 94th Infantry Division War Diary,* all in the World War II German files of the Modern Military Records Division (National Archives). The French units on the 88th's right flank during Diadem are discussed in Marcel Vignera, *Rearming the French* (Washington, D.C.: Office of the Chief of Military History, 1957). Items of direct interest to the 88th figure in a number of special studies: *Landmine and Countermine Warfare, Italy 1943-1944* (Washington, D.C.: Office of the Chief of Engineers, 1972); *Ordnance in the Mediterranean Theater of Operations* (undated World War II pamphlet provided by the U.S. Army Armor School Library); and Charles M. Wiltse, *The Medical Department: Medical Service in the Mediterranean and Minor Theaters* (Washington, D.C.: Office of the Chief of Military History, 1965). Finally, some of the 88th's most honored veterans are treated in *The Medal of Honor of the United States Army* (Washington, D.C.: Government Printing Office, 1948).

This study has been most attentive to the cadre of the 88th Infantry Division, yet I hope it has done some justice to the draftees themselves. There are books that have the front-line soldier himself as an object of study. The most famous of these is probably S.L.R. Marshall, *Men Against Fire: The Problem of Battle Command in Future War* (Glouchester, Mass.: Peter Smith, 1947). John

Ellis, *The Sharp End: The Fighting Men in World War II* (New York: Charles Scribners Sons, 1980) is more recent, and is excellent, as is *Combat World War II*, edited by Don Congdon (New York: Arbor House, 1983). Some of this type of material appears in Studs Terkel, *The Good War: An Oral History of World War II* (New York: Pantheon, 1984), but Terkel's sketches do not focus on combatants per se. A contemporary narrative that described to infantrymen of the time what they were supposed to be trying to do appeared as *Infantry in Battle* (Washington, D.C.: The Infantry Journal, 1939). A more modern analysis is provided by John A. English's excellent *A Perspective on Infantry* (New York: Praeger, 1981).

Col. Trevor N. Dupuy's *Numbers, Prediction, and War* (London: MacDonald and James, 1979) yields valuable insights and does much that is useful. It develops statistics to depict what I believe is an inflated image of the Wehrmacht, however, and a consequent diminishment of the American soldier. See appendix 2. Dupuy's study has assumed a central role in arguments disparaging the performance of American units during World War II. In my mind, the most notable of these occur in Col. Trevor N. Dupuy, *A Genius for War: The German Army and General Staff 1807-1945* (Englewood Cliffs, N.J.: Prentice Hall, 1977); Martin Van Creveld, *Fighting Power: German and U.S. Army Performance 1939-1945* (Westport, Conn.: Greenwood Press, 1982); and Max Hastings, *Overlord: D-Day, June 6, 1944* (New York: Simon and Schuster, 1984). Hastings confronted the issue directly with his inflammatory "Their Wehrmacht Was Better than Our Army," *Kansas City Star,* 26 May 1985, 1D. In the face of this criticism, there has not been much in the way of organized resistance. Even such a sober historian as Russell F. Weigley has expressed his doubts in the excellent *Eisenhower's Lieutenants: The Campaign of France and Germany 1944-1945* (Bloomington: Indian Univ. Press, 1981).

Less inflated estimates of the German soldier appear in Charles Whiting, *'44: In Combat from Normandy to the Ardennes* (New York: Stein and Day, 1984) and Brian Harpur, *The Impossible Victory: A Personal Account of the Battle for the River Po* (New York: Hippocreme, 1980). Charles MacDonald's *A Time for Trumpets: The Untold Story of the Battle of the Bulge* (New York: Morrow, 1984) leaves one feeling proud of the American soldier. Whiting, Harpur, and MacDonald seem good sources; they actually fought the Germans themselves. Unit histories appear from time to time that recount battles from the perspectives of the division level and below. An example is Hugh A. Scott, *The Blue and White Devils: A Personal Memoir and History of the Third Infantry Division in World War II* (Nashville, Tenn.: Battery Press, 1984). It may be that division-level studies offer the ultimate possibility of resolving this issue. In all armies some units are better than others. The best American units of World War II—once seasoned—never met an enemy that outclassed them.

Index